for ~~illegible~~ tariffs ~~illegible~~

STILLING THE
GRUMBLING HIVE

STILLING THE GRUMBLING HIVE

The Response to Social and Economic Problems in
England, 1689–1750

Edited with an Introduction by
LEE DAVISON, TIM HITCHCOCK, TIM KEIRN
AND ROBERT B. SHOEMAKER

ALAN SUTTON · Stroud

ST. MARTIN'S PRESS · New York

Copyright © Tim Keirn, Lee Davison, John Beattie, Nicholas Rogers, Robert B. Shoemaker, Mary E. Fissell, Tim Hitchcock, 1992

First published in the United States of America in 1992

All rights reserved. For information, write:
Scholarly and Reference Division,
St. Martin's Press Inc. · 175 Fifth Avenue
New York · NY 10010

ISBN 0–312–08676–8

Library of Congress Cataloging in Publication Data

Stilling the grumbling hive: the response to social and economic
  problems in England, 1689–1750/edited with an introduction by
  Lee Davison . . . [et al.].
        p.   cm.
  Includes bibliographical references and index.
  ISBN 0–312–08676–8:
  1. England – Social conditions – 17th century. 2. England – Social conditions –
18th century. 3. England – Economic conditions – 17th century. 4. England –
Economic conditions – 18th century. 5. Textile industry – Social aspects – England –
History – 17th century. 6. Textile industry – Social aspects – England – History – 18th
century. 7. Crime prevention – England – History – 17th century. 8. Crime prevention
– England – History – 18th century. 9. England – Moral conditions. I Davison, Lee.
HN398.E5S75   1992
306'.0942'09033–dc20   92–9383
                                   CIP

First published in the United Kingdom in 1992 by
Alan Sutton Publishing Limited · Phoenix Mill · Far Thrupp
Stroud · Gloucestershire

British Library Cataloguing in Publication Data

Stilling the Grumbling Hive: Response to Social and Economic Problems in England,
1689–1750
  I. Davison, Lee
  942.07

  ISBN 0–7509–0144–6

Typeset in 10/11 Goudy.
Typesetting and origination by
Alan Sutton Publishing Limited.
Printed in Great Britain
by The Bath Press Ltd, Avon.

Contents

Contributors

John Beattie
University Professor and Director of the Centre of Criminology at the University of Toronto. He has published *The English Court in the Reign of George I* (Cambridge, 1967) and *Crime and the Courts in England, 1660–1800* (Oxford and Princeton, N.J., 1986) and is now working on crime and the administration of justice in London in the half century after the Revolution of 1688.

Lee Davison
Lecturer in History and Literature at Harvard University. He received both his AM and PhD from Harvard and is presently at work on a book exploring speculation, fraud and financial regulation in eighteenth-century England.

Mary Fissell
Assistant Professor at the Institute of the History of Medicine, Johns Hopkins University. She is the author of *Patients, Power, and the Poor in Eighteenth-Century Bristol* (Cambridge, 1991) and is currently working on early-modern vernacular health texts.

Tim Hitchcock
Lectures in history at the Polytechnic of North London. He was awarded his doctorate by Oxford University in 1985 and has published on the histories of eighteenth-century poor relief, sexuality and religious millenarianism.

Tim Keirn
Lecturer in the history department at California State University, Long Beach. He studied at the University of California at Los Angeles and at the London School of Economics and Political Science. He is the author of articles and reviews in *Historical Research, Parliamentary History, The Journal of British Studies,* and *The Economic History Review*.

Nicholas Rogers
Professor of History at York University, Toronto, and the author of numerous pieces on popular politics in eighteenth-century England. He is also the author of *Whigs and Cities: Popular Politics in the Age of Walpole and Pitt* (Oxford, 1989).

Robert B. Shoemaker
Lecturer at the University of Sheffield. He is the author of *Prosecution and Punishment: Petty Crime and the Law in London and Rural Middlesex, c. 1660–1725* (Cambridge, 1991) and 'The London "mob" in the early eighteenth century', *Journal of British Studies* (1987), and is currently working on a study of female disputants in the eighteenth century.

Abbreviations

BL	British Library
CSPD	*Calender of State Papers Domestic*
GLRO	Greater London Record Office
HCJ	*House of Commons Journals*
HLJ	*House of Lords Journals*
PRO	Public Record Office
SPCK	Society for Promoting Christian Knowledge
SPG	Society for Propagating the Gospel in Foreign Parts
SRM	Societies for the Reformation of Manners

Unless otherwise noted, the place of publication of all printed books is London.

Preface

The idea for this book was conceived in the tea room of the Institute of Historical Research in London. Over cups of tea, and later over beer and whisky in local pubs, first Tim Hitchcock and Tim Keirn, and later Lee Davison and Robert Shoemaker, compared notes on the social and economic problems faced by England after the Glorious Revolution. We began to see patterns in the way such problems were perceived and debated in printed pamphlets and newspapers, and similarities in the sources of initiative for solutions to these problems: the impetus for reform seemed to come from outside the state, from interest groups, local government and voluntary societies. Even when Parliament or the executive provided the machinery for implementing reforms, it quickly became apparent that this was in response to outside initiatives. After many conversations and a few arguments, not only among the four co-editors but also with other contributors, as well as other friends and colleagues, the present volume gradually evolved. Contributors have separately acknowledged individuals to whom they are indebted, but we would here like to thank John Brewer, David Hayton, Joanna Innes, John Styles, Pene Corfield and Bill Weber for their helpful comments and suggestions.

The editorial duties were divided among the four editors, which produced all the difficulties associated with organising anything across two continents and between four cities. Tim Hitchcock and Robert Shoemaker undertook the task of editing all the essays, while Tim Keirn and Lee Davison, with the aid of research provided by their co-editors, were primarily responsible for writing the introductory essay.

August 1991

How Vain is Mortal Happiness!
Had they but known the Bounds of Bliss;
And that Perfection here below
Is more than Gods can well bestow;
The Grumbling Brutes had been content
With Ministers and Government.
But they, at every ill Success,
Like Creatures lost without Redress
Curs'd Politicians, Armies, Fleets;
While every one cry'd *Damn the Cheats*,
And would, tho' conscious of his own,
In others barb'rously bear none.

One, that had got a Princely Store,
By cheating Master, King and Poor,
Dar'd cry aloud, *The Land must sink*
For all its Fraud; And whom d'ye think
The Sermonizing Rascal Chid?
A Glover that sold Lamb for Kid.

Bernard de Mandeville,
'The Grumbling Hive' in *The Fable of*
the Bees: Or Private Vices, Publick
Benefits (6th edn, 1732), pp. 11–12

Introduction

The Reactive State: English Governance and Society, 1689–1750

I
The Early Eighteenth Century in Historical Perspective

This essay, and the volume which it anticipates, is concerned with what might be called the 'long' first half of the eighteenth century, examining some of the developments and changes in English governance and political culture between the Glorious Revolution and the middle of the eighteenth century.[1] Our chronological parameters of 1689 and 1750 are conventional and more or less deliberate. The financial and constitutional settlements engendered by the accession of William III and the impact of sustained war with France brought precipitous change to the relationship between the English state and society.[2] While the year 1750 was unmomentous relative to the consequences of the Glorious Revolution, it serves to focus our attention on the first half of the eighteenth century – a period which has until recently received far less scholarly attention than the latter half of the century.

Indeed, the early eighteenth century has been a relatively ignored field within the English historical landscape. Sandwiched between periods traditionally described in terms of 'revolutionary change', historians have long been attracted to the civil and political strife of the seventeenth century and to the profound industrial and social changes and political reforms of the late eighteenth and early nineteenth centuries. Consequently, there has until recently been relatively little modern research on the first half of the century. Moreover, historical depictions of the character of the early eighteenth-century English state, and the integration of politics and society, have often been drawn based on criteria defined by orthodox historical representations of the antecedent and subsequent periods.[3] In the wake of Namier and Butterfield's assault on Whig interpretations of the eighteenth century, historians have consciously or unconsciously isolated the first half of the century in order to disrupt a linear and teleological progression of events – mainly political, but also economic and social – from the seventeenth to the late eighteenth century. Hence, in contrast to the civil wars, virulent partisan discord and popular political involvement of the seventeenth century, historians have tended to focus on the 'oligarchic' nature of the early eighteenth century, emphasizing the prevalence of political stability and the dominance of a landed ruling class, stressing the evidence of rampant corruption, the weakness of the state, and the absence of broad and open participation in politics and government. Typically, the period has been portrayed as 'the most conservative in modern British history'.[4] While the later eighteenth century has traditionally been depicted as a period of dramatic social change, nascent political radicalism and governmental reform, concurrent with a notion of a dynamic – or at least embryonic – 'industrial revolution', the first half of the century has often served as a static and dissimilar foreground for these momentous events. Studies of early eighteenth-century England have tended to represent the economy in terms of slow or stagnant growth, focusing on a society 'consolidating' rather than 'changing', and portraying social and cultural authority firmly in the grasp of a landed ruling class or an acquiescent bourgeoisie, faithfully emulating the manners and behaviour of the genteel.[5] In sum, the 'long' first half of the eighteenth century has generally been represented as a period of calm situated between two historical storms.

However, more recent scholarship has brought greater attention to the early eighteenth century and is beginning to illuminate its general importance in the changing relationship between the English state and society. New scholarly interest comes in part from the impact of 'revisionism' in early Stuart and late Hanoverian history. Recent studies have argued that these periods were far less stormy, much less revolutionary, and inherently more stable than orthodox interpretations had suggested. For example, revisionism has stressed the consensual nature of early Stuart politics, the prevalence of local harmony, and the strength of popular deference to those in authority. It has depicted Parliament as conservative and reactionary in contrast to the more innovatory approaches of the Crown, as both the legislature and executive contended for dominance within a central government which had little sensitivity to local needs and concerns.[6]

As in the period of the English revolution, scholars studying the 'Industrial Revolution' have toned down considerably the claims made by earlier historians for momentous economic growth, social transformation and political change in the late eighteenth century. The industrial revolution is currently discussed more in 'evolutionary' than 'revolutionary' terms, stressing that it was neither a unitary nor a continuous phenomenon.[7] New emphasis is placed on the economic, social and political continuities rather than on the changes taking place during the eighteenth century. For example, recent work has tended to play down a chronological disjunction between the popular politics and radicalism of the 1790s and that of the earlier part of the century.[8]

To some extent, new-found interest in the early eighteenth century has been stimulated by the recent controversial publications of J.C.D. Clark.[9] Linking the revisionist conclusions of the early seventeenth century with those of the late eighteenth, Clark stresses the importance of monarchy and patriarchy from the seventeenth century through to the end of the Hanoverian age. To Clark, the first half of the eighteenth century is notable for the relationship forged between government and society, dominated by the political interests and cultural persuasion of the monarchy, aristocracy and church.[10] Eighteenth-century England was an 'Ancien Régime' (or 'confessional') state, where politics was defined by issues of religion and dynastic controversy, and governance was firmly controlled by the aristocracy. While drawing attention to the first half of the century, Clark's emphasis on the aristocratic, landed and non-commercial nature of the period is surprisingly similar to an earlier orthodoxy. To some extent, one could argue that he has taken many of the features of the traditional depiction of the early eighteenth century and simply extended them chronologically to encompass and characterize the seventeenth and late eighteenth centuries.[11]

While sharing Clark's enthusiasm for the importance of the first half of the century, we, however, start from the premise that the period should not be characterized as a link, but rather as an essential starting point for important changes in the relationship between the English state and society – changes which reached fruition during the late eighteenth and early nineteenth centuries. While Clark focuses on the crown, church and aristocracy, it is our intention to stress the more dynamic forces working within English society during the decades following the Glorious Revolution, assessing their interaction with government. These forces were essentially commercial, urban and middle class.[12] They were integrally tied to the development of a strong state, which was open to outside influence and participation, and were instrumental in the creation of new forms of governance.

Indeed, our work follows on the heels of recent scholarship that has recognized the importance of the early eighteenth century as a period of profound change in both an evolutionary and revolutionary sense. For example, Paul Langford has done much to reveal the vitality of urban life and culture, stressing the unprecedented contributions of commerce and the middle class to English politics and social formation.[13] Others, notably John Brewer, have shown that the war-torn decades immediately following the Glorious Revolution witnessed a 'financial revolution' and consequently the creation of a strong 'fiscal-military' state that relied heavily on middle-class taxes and commercial success, acquiesced in middle-class participation in government and politics, and indeed sought the endorsement of the urban middle class.[14] Thus, while strong, the

English state in the early eighteenth century was also remarkably 'open' to outside influence as ministers and MPs could not easily ignore the desires of their constituents. The sustained war with France, in league with the constitutional and financial settlements of 1689 and 1690, ensured regular meetings of Parliament and the dominance of legislative as opposed to conciliar forms of central government policy-making.[15] Legislative government and the expiration of press censorship in 1695 engendered a greater public interest in government and politics. The frequency of elections, the vigours of partisan conflict, and the expanding output of a political press extended political discourse to the literate urban classes and politicized them in the process.[16] While partisan conflict and electioneering declined after 1714, urban politics remained vigorous at both a local and national level. The vast majority of parliamentary constituencies were urban ones, and while aristocratic patronage of these boroughs increased over the course of the eighteenth century, the middle class nonetheless continued to play a vital role in the electoral process and constituent-based politics. Indeed, recent research has shown that the political interests of the urban middle class were both national and local, and were independent of the objectives of the landed grandees.[17]

Much of this recent work illuminating the importance of the 'long' first half of the eighteenth century, however, follows a fairly narrow line of inquiry. Linda Colley's study of partisan politics, Clark's analysis of religion and political discourse, and Brewer's work on taxation and the state focus on the traditional elite ranks of English society, examining 'high' religion, political practice and discourse, and analysing the state from the viewpoint of its ability to impose on the livelihoods of its citizens rather than on its ability to respond to their initiatives. Our intention is not to deny the significance or validity of these important studies, but as social historians our purpose is to provide a more compelling social history of politics and governance, illuminating the points of contact established between early eighteenth-century government and those members of society outside the ranks of the traditional landed ruling elite, paying careful attention to the notion that 'real decision-making processes'[18] were not only intricate but made at multiple levels between Westminster and the localities. These points of contact with a dynamic urban middle class were by no means confined to direct or indirect influence on legislation, but were often established at the level of local governing bodies (sometimes newly formed), focusing on national and local domestic economic and social problems as opposed to the religious, dynastic and constitutional controversies that often divided the realm.

The purpose of this collection of case studies then is to reveal the importance of the six decades following the Glorious Revolution as a period of initiation rather than continuation in English history for reasons somewhat different from (but not always antithetical to) those discussed in the current historical literature. The first half of the eighteenth century was an important period of initiative and innovation in governance, with active participation by those outside the traditional confines of the English ruling class, most notably among an increasingly recognizable urban middle class. This participation was facilitated by the rising economic fortunes of this class, whose numbers and social authority were ascendent as the commercial component of the English economy underwent marked expansion during the late seventeenth and early eighteenth century.

In the wake of the ending of press censorship, middle-class interest in governance was also aroused by the energy, vitality and expanding volume of printed political discourse. The extensive production of pamphlets and broadsheets witnessed the development of lower levels of discourse which contrasted both in form and substance with the treatise-based high discourse surrounding state religious and constitutional issues.[19] Much of this low discourse was germane to the Grub Street partisan conflicts between Whigs and Tories, however a significant volume was addressed to the more immediate and mundane issues of, for example, care for the poor, the suppression of vice, and the regulation of trade and industry.[20] These issues were obviously of intense interest to the urban middle class. It is notable that a vigorous printed and public discourse surrounded the social and economic problems faced by contemporaries, informing and debating the pros and cons of contending policies and regulations, as seen in most of the case studies discussed in the chapters below.[21] Clearly, the appearance of such literature addressed to the literate urban classes both reflected new interest in politics and governance and simultaneously whetted the appetite for broader participation in both national and local domestic affairs.

Middle class participation in governance was also a consequence of what we characterize as the 'reactive' nature of the burgeoning English state in the eighteenth century. While the state took an active and leading interest in the affairs of defence, foreign policy, taxation, state religion and the constitution, it was more often than not 'reactive' to the litany of domestic social and economic issues facing the nation, relying on those outside of central government and the legislature for information and initiative. Often, as portrayed in the case studies pertaining to textile and gin legislation below, this took the form of intense lobbying of the legislature – the state's reaction to such prodding coming in the form of statutory economic and social regulation and reform.[22] However, to a significant extent the state's reaction to domestic problems was revealed in an increasing willingness to allow reforming and regulative initiatives and changes to take place within the parameters of local rather than central institutions of government.[23] Of course, the state's relative disinterest in domestic affairs was not new to the eighteenth century. In the Tudor and early Stuart period, domestic issues were generally left to the authority of local magistrates. Yet, with the declining role of the Privy Council in policy-making after the Glorious Revolution, the autonomy of local decision-making increased as JPs acted with even greater independence from central government and as the parish and vestry became increasingly assertive in regulating local affairs.[24]

The purpose of this introduction is three-fold. First, in a general sense, it provides background for the case studies which follow. These case studies illuminate the processes by which economic and social problems were conceived and discussed, and how policies and reforms were constructed outside the traditional realm of high politics and statecraft. All the following essays conform to a more or less uniform framework, examining a particular domestic problem, the debate engendered, and the eventual solution(s) reached. This introduction also seeks to provide a synthesis of current research in the closely related fields of political, economic, and social history in an attempt to provide a more general history of politics and governance in the first half of the eighteenth century. Finally, and perhaps most importantly, this introduction examines the period's significance in terms of the creation and workings of the 'reactive state' within its political, social and economic context.

II
Economy and Society in England, 1689–1750

Studies of the economic history of England during the late seventeenth and early eighteenth centuries are relatively scarce, with most scholarly attention paid to the 'classic' period of the Industrial Revolution – its onset being multifariously dated between 1750 and 1790. Until recently, the first half of the eighteenth century has been characterized in terms of economic deceleration, slow or stagnating population movement, and a depressed agricultural sector manifest in falling grain prices and rents, and rising arrears. Yet, as shall be argued here, this period witnessed remarkable and lasting structural changes as agricultural productivity rose, shedding labour from the countryside and so facilitating rapid urban growth. A growing urban population, juxtaposed with the falling price of bread, expanded domestic consumption of non-necessities which (in conjunction with overseas demand) stimulated manufacturing, commerce and the tertiary sectors of the economy. While these changes were to continue, and for the most part accelerate, in the latter decades of the century, the onset of extensive urbanization and manufacturing and the commercialization of English society clearly pre-date the period of the Industrial Revolution. Such structural changes exacerbated contemporary concerns about a number of social and economic problems, ranging from urban poverty and crime to industrial regulation.

The urban middle classes were the principal beneficiaries of early eighteenth-century economic change, exemplified by their disproportional growth in numbers and prosperity, social authority and political participation between 1689 and 1750. The enhanced social and political status of the middle class manifested itself in a changing domestic regulatory agenda, which responded to their perceived economic and social concerns. First, however, the causes of the growing importance of the middle class must be explained, and a detailed model of this process provides the focus for this section. Demographic and agricultural developments form a necessary starting point for any discussion of the marked urbanization and commercialization which were such important characteristics of early eighteenth-century society.

Demographically, Wrigley and Schofield's evidence confirms the traditional picture of the early eighteenth century as situated firmly between two periods of rapid population growth – that of the sixteenth and early seventeenth centuries and the even more substantial expansion beginning in the last decades of the eighteenth century.[25] English population levels fell slightly during the later seventeenth century and growth was slow and hesitant prior to the mid-eighteenth century. Explanation of these demographic trends is somewhat problematic. Clearly, while expectation of life at birth fluctuated wildly, there is little evidence of general improvement in life expectancy and mortality conditions during this period. Indeed, the second quarter of the eighteenth century alone experienced four severe mortality crisis years (in 1727–30 and 1741–2), the largest number in any sub-period of Wrigley and Schofield's study.[26] High mortality, however, was not 'harvest sensitive' and research has revealed no general correlation between intermittent years of high grain prices and those of heightened death rates. Instead, changes in mortality conditions generally reflected fluctuations in the incidence of epidemic diseases. Although wheat prices were high in 1728, the mortality crisis of the late 1720s was a consequence of the outbreak of a number of diseases in succession, including smallpox, whooping cough and influenza. In contrast, the 1690s, a decade of six deficient harvests, witnessed mortality levels below national averages. Of course, local and regional conditions varied. For example, the rising incidence of typhus mortality in early eighteenth-century London may indicate worsening nutritional conditions below the threshold of subsistence crisis.[27]

Fertility rates rose steadily, if not spectacularly, between 1690 and 1750 as the rates of nuptiality rose, marriage ages began to fall, and the numbers

of illegitimate births swelled (most notably in London).[28] Wrigley and
Schofield have argued that this trend came in response to better living
standards as real incomes appear to have risen from the mid-seventeenth
century, encouraging earlier and more universal marriage. Given that the
positive response of the components of fertility in the 1690s lagged some
thirty years behind the initial rise in real wages, some have not been
altogether convinced by Wrigley and Schofield's 'delayed-response' thesis,
where it is argued that nuptiality decisions were based on the events of the
remembered past as opposed to current economic opportunities. Most
likely, rising fertility was also a manifestation of structural economic
change and proletarianization as expanding numbers of individuals found
themselves working solely for wages (and did so increasingly outside of
agriculture), where an individual's peak earning capacity came earlier in
life.[29]

The moderate rise in population in the first half of the eighteenth
century was not matched by commensurate inflation in the price of grain.
Quite the contrary. In general, domestic agricultural prices plummeted
between 1660 and 1740, although inclement weather did produce
deficient harvests and higher prices from region to region and from year to
year.[30] When juxtaposed with population trends, and accounting for
potential changes in income elasticity, the general fall in agricultural
prices points to significant gains in agricultural output and productivity.[31]
Indeed, further decline in the domestic price of grain was offset by the
expansion of grain exports (stimulated by government subsidy), providing
further evidence of the impressive performance of English agriculture over
the period.[32] Gains in productivity and the introduction of new agricultural techniques varied regionally, making generalization difficult. Yet it is
clear that during the century following 1650 a number of important
innovations became widely diffused, mainly in the more thinly soiled
regions of East Anglia and the downlands of southern England. New crop
rotations and better management of pasturage reduced fallow times,
preserved soil nitrogen levels, and expanded dung supplies, increasing
acreage productivity and allowing for exploitation of the inherent
economic advantages of thin soil in terms of the relatively low labour
requirements involved in ploughing.[33]

The remarkable growth of agricultural productivity and the fall in cereal
prices was perhaps the most important phenomenon of the first half of the
eighteenth century, for its consequences were multiple and far-reaching.
Some forty years ago, H.J. Habakkuk argued that falling agricultural
prices, in conjunction with the burdens of the land tax and the use of strict
settlement, facilitated the rapid concentration of property into fewer and
fewer hands during the half century following the Glorious Revolution.[34]
More recently, historians, having discovered that the English landscape in

1750 was not universally divided into 'great estates' and large tenant farms utilizing wage labour, have argued that Habakkuk overstated the extent of change. The process of property concentration, the expansion in farm size and capitalization, and rural proletarianization are now seen to have been gradual, taking at least another century to complete and with great regional variation. Owner-occupiers and small proprietors survived in significant numbers, especially on the peripheries of production and in pastoral regions where falling grain prices stimulated higher demand for meat and dairy products, increasing the economic viability of some small holdings.[35]

Nonetheless, the general pace of change in landownership during the first half of the eighteenth century was rapid, particularly in the grain-producing regions of southern England and the Midlands. In these regions, falling cereal prices and rents made it imperative for landowners to take greater care in estate management. The need for greater efficiency in the supervision of the tenantry was a principal incentive for the consolidation of estates, the growth of which was often piecemeal but nevertheless concentrated landownership into fewer hands. Given that land values in the early eighteenth century were buoyed by the social enhancements of ownership and falling interest rates, maintaining themselves relative to declining rental rolls, the purchase (and sale) of land under the pretence of efficiency and rationalization availed itself to the large landowner at the expense of the small. Falling rents also increased the need to improve estates to attract wealthier (and more 'liquid') farmers with the capital to implement new agricultural techniques and who were able to protect profit margins in the face of falling prices through cuts in costs.[36] These 'improvements' often took the form of 'engrossing' holdings to reallocate tenancies into larger and better laid out farms, or the promotion of enclosure, or both. Non-parliamentary enclosure was extensive before the mid-eighteenth century, especially in the Midlands where mixed-farming in open fields was being overtaken by enclosed permanent pastoral production as the clayish quality of local soils did not prove readily adaptable to the new crop rotations that were critical for more profitable cereal production in a market characterized by declining prices. Investment in estate improvements such as enclosure was expensive, but it generated higher rental values, enhancing the advantages of larger landowners with greater access to credit.[37]

The period between 1689 and 1750 therefore witnessed an increase in enclosure and farm sizes, and a significant decline in the number of owner-occupiers and small cultivators. Sustained growth in agricultural productivity thus permitted extensive 'shedding' of labour out of direct agricultural production into the broadening industrial and service sectors of the economy. Consequently, it would appear that more than half of all

English men and women were employed outside of agriculture by the mid-eighteenth century. Not all of these dispossessed cultivators or unemployed agricultural labourers moved to urban areas. Many found work in growing rural manufacturing and artisan trades or in local commercial services. Yet according to Wrigley's estimates, the rate of gain in rural non-agricultural employment between 1670 and 1750 (from 26 to 33 per cent of the total workforce) was considerably less than the relative loss in agricultural employment over the same period (from roughly 60 to 46 per cent of the total workforce).[38] It would appear then that most did find their way to rapidly expanding urban areas.

Rising agricultural productivity was thus a root cause of England's phenomenal urban growth during the first half of the eighteenth century, with a proportionately smaller agricultural labour force supporting larger numbers of urban dwellers.[39] Between 1670 and 1750 England's urban population grew from roughly 13 to 21 per cent of the total population – a rate of change equal to, if not greater than, that of the late eighteenth century – and a trend more substantial than the growth of total population over the same period.[40] Given that deaths predominated over births in the larger urban areas (where sanitary conditions were poor and disease transmission was rampant), urban growth was a consequence of substantial migration, especially when one considers that migrants themselves had a higher vulnerability to urban disease. Recent research has revealed that most urban migrants in the late seventeenth and early eighteenth century were drawn to towns by employment opportunities and higher remuneration and were not 'pushed' out of rural hinterlands by subsistence crises as had been the case a century earlier.[41]

As the seat of government of an ever expanding state, the heart of a global commercial and financial network, and the most important English industrial centre, London maintained its position of dominance in the English urban hierarchy during the eighteenth century. London in 1750 probably contained over 600,000 inhabitants – close to ten per cent of the English population. However, the rate of metropolitan growth in the late seventeenth and early eighteenth centuries was much slower than in earlier and subsequent periods.[42] The most dynamic urban growth in the first half of the eighteenth century took place in the larger provincial towns and regional centres, with the urban population outside the metropolis rising from four to twelve per cent of total population between 1670 and 1750. Indeed, it was during this period, as P.J. Corfield has noted, that 'the configuration of modern urban England began to emerge'.[43] Growth was most vigorous in a number of 'new' industrial towns such as Birmingham, Manchester, Leeds and Sheffield, as well as in 'new' port and dockyard towns such as Liverpool and Plymouth. Many older regional centres declined, but those with specialized port functions and industrial hinterlands such as Bristol and Newcastle, or those with a manufacturing base such as Norwich, also experienced significant growth during the first half of the century. In contrast, some smaller country towns experienced decline as transport and communications improvements generally extended the viable market area of larger urban centres at the expense of the small. Many small towns, however, prospered through the specialization of marketing or manufacturing functions within regional trading networks or within configurations of 'satellites' which often surrounded major urban manufacturing centres like Birmingham.[44]

Rapid urbanization then, especially outside the metropolis, was a distinctive feature of English society in the early eighteenth century, and was both a manifestation and reflection of growing agricultural productivity and the expansion of commerce and industry prior to the introduction of steam power and widescale factory production. Falling cereal prices had a positive impact on living standards, expanding levels of disposable income and consumption of non-agricultural goods. Workers released from agriculture into more highly remunerative urban and industrial jobs spent more on manufactured commodities. While price and wage indices are to be used with caution, available evidence reveals that real wages were generally rising between 1690 and 1750. The rise in real wages was caused principally by falling prices, although the secular trend in wage rates was upwards, mainly reflecting the relative scarcity of labour (given the slow growth of population in this period) in expanding industrial, commercial and urban economic settings.[45] The pervasive use of servants in husbandry in agriculture prior to the mid-eighteenth century also seems to point to the relative scarcity of labour as farmers sought to pay workers in kind, the price of which was falling relative to wages. Similarly, manufacturers often attempted to pay workers by 'truck' as opposed to cash to cut burgeoning wage bills.[46]

The rise in agricultural productivity had a significant impact in widening the domestic market for manufactured goods and services through the expansion of levels of real and disposable incomes, and increasing the number of individuals in more remunerative types of work. However, certain factors militate against drawing an overly simplistic relationship between agricultural productivity, a growing home market, and industrial and urban growth. First, and most importantly, even with an increase in real wages the wages of agricultural workers, for example, were still pitifully low, leaving 'little spare for a significant amount of household goods'.[47] Moreover, despite the rapid growth of industrial towns such as Birmingham and Manchester, much (if not most) manufacturing remained rooted in the countryside in the early eighteenth century, exploiting the low wage labour of underemployed agricultural workers. This was especially true of female agricultural workers as they became increasingly marginalized from full-time employment in intensive arable production. Rural industries such as lace and straw-plaiting for hats were rapidly expanding in southern England during the late seventeenth and early eighteenth centuries, relying almost exclusively on cheap female labour.[48] Moreover, wage and price indices tend to pay little regard to female work. While more provincial studies are needed, women migrating to (and working in) the metropolis during the first decades of the eighteenth century had relatively narrow job opportunities. The majority laboured in the lowest paid employment in the service sector, as opposed to higher paid jobs in manufacturing, and much of this work was of a casual nature.[49] Viewed from the vantage point of women's work experience, the expansion in agricultural productivity on consumer demand was marginal.

Moreover, increases in real and disposable incomes were not necessarily spent on manufactured commodites. It is clear that potential savings in the price of bread and higher earnings were often translated into greater levels or changing patterns of food consumption. In general, people in the first half of the eighteenth century ate more expensive wheat as opposed to barley bread, and varied their diet with greater consumption of meat and cheese. As a consequence of rising incomes, tea, coffee, beer and notably gin consumption increased significantly on a per capita basis at the expense of potential purchases of consumer durables.[50] In addition, expansion in the demand for manufactured goods (and many foodstuffs) was diluted by rising levels of indirect taxation, which made significant cuts in the profits of producers and retailers and in the purchasing power of consumers by the mid-eighteenth century.[51]

Despite these qualifications, the expansion of real incomes as a consequence of heightened agricultural productivity did have a positive impact on domestic demand for manufactures and urban services, albeit in the main through the enhanced earnings of the middle class and skilled labour. Indeed, as Patrick O'Brien has pointed out, the early eighteenth century was unique in this respect. After 1740, the intersectoral terms of trade shifted as agricultural prices began their steep late eighteenth-century climb, decreasing the relative importance of the home market in determining English economic growth.[52] Not surprisingly, the expansion of overseas trade and demand takes on added importance in the 'revisionist' discussion of the determinants of economic production during the later decades of the century.[53]

In contrast, the growth of English overseas trade during the first half of the eighteenth century was modest and steady if not spectacular.[54] English commerce was of course global in nature, and underwent significant changes in geographical orientation and emphasis between 1689 and 1750. Imports were dominated by foodstuffs, stimulated by rising home consumption and re-export markets, and raw materials necessary for expanding domestic industries. Imports of finished goods stagnated and fell into relative decline. While most raw materials were shipped from Continental destinations (notably raw silk, yarns and dyestuffs utilized in textile production), foodstuffs such as sugar, tobacco and tea were extra-European in origin. The majority of imported products were bulk cargoes which, in conjunction with the important domestic coasting trade in coal, provided a positive stimulus to England's expansive shipping and shipbuilding industries.[55]

Re-exports of colonial produce and Asian textiles to the Continent increased dramatically, accounting for roughly a third of total exports by the middle of the eighteenth century. Domestic exports were still dominated by woollen manufactures. Unlike many domestic industries, English cloth production was critically reliant on overseas sales.[56] However, while cloth exports rose during the first half of the eighteenth century, the rate of growth slowed and the proportional share of total domestic exports fell from approximately 70 to 45 per cent. The lighter draperies of East Anglia suffered from competing cotton-based fabrics, and manufacturers of the heavier high-quality woollens of the West Country were hurt by French success in the valuable Levant market. By 1750 both regions were in relative decline and failed to meet the domestic challenge of the expanding West Riding worsted and woollen industries, whose cheap durable items found large numbers of Continental buyers. Another significant structural change in manufacturing and overseas trade during the early eighteenth century was the growing importance of the American market to a plethora of nascent industries growing under the protection of tariff barriers and embargoes which were a by-product of English hostilities with France. While unable to compete effectively on the Continent, English silk, paper and especially metal manufacturers were increasingly able to enlarge their sales in the rapidly expanding imperial (and protected) transatlantic markets.[57]

Hence by 1750 foreign trade and overseas demand were of critical importance to the prosperity of woollen cloth and metal manufacture – respectively the most important and fastest growing English industries. The vicissitudes and swings of foreign markets had important repercussions on levels of prosperity and employment in interior urban manufacturing centres such as Leeds or Birmingham and outlying industrial villages and smaller towns, as well as ports such as Exeter or Bristol which serviced the textile and metal trades. However, while impossible to quantify with precision, it would appear that the impact of foreign trade and overseas demand on general English industrial production was secondary to the importance of the home market. Most manufacturers, artisans and cottage workers endeavoured to supply a domestic clientele. Riding the vigour of the home market, and viewed from a macro level, English industrial production appears to have grown significantly between 1700 and 1750. Recent estimates of the industrial sector during this period have nearly doubled its size and output from earlier appraisals, diminishing the industrial achievement of the later eighteenth century in the process.[58]

As many have pointed out, however, aggregate analysis masks the tremendous unevenness and regional variation in industrial growth.[59] Indeed, it is difficult to provide a general characterization of the nature of English manufacturing during the half century or so before the Industrial Revolution. Certain aspects of industrial production such as coal mining and iron production were both expanding and becoming increasingly centralized. The former responded to the growing demand for domestic heating needs in growing urban markets without technical change; the latter grew more slowly in the face of Baltic imports, despite the introduction of 'revolutionary' new technology (notably Abraham Darby's adaptation in 1709 of the blast furnace to coal-based rather than wood-based fuel) the diffusion of which was gradual prior to 1750.[60] Most manufacturing in early eighteenth-century England, however, was on a small scale (as was true well into the nineteenth century) and confined to the workshop or cottage. Most work was done with relatively simple hand tools. While technical change was an on-going process during the early eighteenth century, it was not on the scale of the 'breakthroughs' of the later part of the century. Nonetheless, as recent research has revealed, increases in manufacturing productivity and output were still achieved in traditional hand tool industries through changes in work practice and organization throughout the entire eighteenth century.[61]

Independent artisans were generally dominant in urban manufacture, most notably in the growing number of metal-working shops in Birmingham, Sheffield and surrounding smaller towns and industrial villages.[62] London was the nation's most important manufacturing hub, and unlike provincial manufacturing centres, was anything but a 'one industry' town; literally hundreds of crafts were based in the metropolis. Even in silk production – the most important metropolitan industry – there were at least 7,000 independent masters in 1700.[63] In the countryside, manufacturing continued to proliferate but 'putting-out' or 'domestic systems' of production tended to predominate, especially in textile trades where clothiers employed cottage labour in the spinning and weaving of wool, linen and cotton yarns.[64] Rural manufacturing facilitated urban growth. Emergent industrial towns such as Manchester and Leeds grew prior to the period of factory production as finishing, marketing and service centres for local rural production of cotton and woollen textiles. Indeed, the expansion of rural manufacturing in Lancashire and the West Riding intensified local population densities and industrial 'villages' were rapidly transformed into manufacturing 'towns' during the course of the eighteenth century.

Of course, English commercial and industrial growth was not a continuous process between the Glorious Revolution and the middle of the eighteenth century. Sustained economic prosperity was elusive and downturns were frequent and unpredictable. More predictable were the attendant social problems of rising unemployment and poverty which came with any 'slump'. Downturns were generally a function of poor harvests, financial crises and war. Between 1689 and 1750, England was engaged in three major and expensive wars: the Nine Years War (1689–7); the War of Spanish Succession (1702–13); and the War of Austrian Succession (1739–48). These wars disrupted overseas trade as demand for seamen inflated their wages, and attacks on merchant shipping raised insurance and freight rates. The high cost of war led to higher taxes and diminishing consumption. The burden of remittance to troops abroad put pressure on the balance of payments and, for example, engendered a serious liquidity crisis during the mid-1690s as supplies of silver bullion deteriorated. Of course, some benefitted from wartime government expenditure, most notably those tied to shipbuilding or ordnance production. War also diminished unemployment, although, at the same time local magistrates and overseers of the poor knew that increases in crime and demands for poor relief would follow peace and demobilization.[65]

Indeed, as Brewer has argued, virtually all eighteenth-century financial crises were in themselves a consequence of the state's fiscal difficulties and struggles procuring secure funding of the national debt (even in peacetime), which in turn was the end product of prodigious public expenditure to support war.[66] The impact of a crisis of public credit was always most severe in the metropolis where holders of government debt and stock speculators were most concentrated. However, major crises such as the South Sea Bubble (1720) were well publicized and did psychological damage to private credit outside the metropolis. Given the importance of credit in virtually all aspects of eighteenth-century economic life, the repercussions were serious when even small creditors such as shopkeepers and tavernkeepers panicked and called in debts and reclaimed assets.[67]

In the long run, however, the expansion of real incomes arising from overall gains in agricultural productivity and industrial growth created enhanced levels of consumerism and demand for urban services between 1689 and 1750. Indeed, the so-called 'Consumer Revolution' has become a conspicuous feature of the historiography of eighteenth-century England. Within the historical literature, this 'revolution' is remarkably ambiguous in both structure and chronology.[68] And yet if it is characterized by expanding and diversified consumption, by the social extension of acquisitiveness and materialism, and by the enhanced commercialization of English society, then perhaps it was as characteristic of the first half of the eighteenth century as it was of the second. As noted above, it was only prior to the 1740s that the intersectoral terms of trade between agriculture and industry moved to the benefit of consumption of the latter. Moreover, significant improvements were made in transport even before the 'canal age', through improvements to navigable inland waterways, the growth of shipping capacity in the coasting trade, and, by the 1730s, the extensive creation of turnpikes. Transport improvements lowered freight and information costs, and facilitated inter-regional trade, national marketing, and the dissemination of commercial and fashion news from London to the provinces.[69]

There is plenty of evidence of rising consumerism in the early eighteenth century. For example, the investigations of probate material by Peter Earle and Lorna Weatherill reveal that individuals in both London and the provinces were purchasing a growing volume and greater diversity of consumer and household goods.[70] The bulk of this purchasing power came from middle-class spending, most notably amongst merchants, professionals and shopkeepers, but also amongst the middling ranks of rural society such as farmers and rural craftsmen, whose important role in manufacturing has already been mentioned. The importance of aggregate middle-class purchasing power can not be underestimated. Relative to the landed elite, the middle class was not only vastly greater in number (and growing), but also spent a higher percentage of their earnings on consumer goods. Moreover, as we have seen, economic trends between 1690 and 1750 benefited and inflated the earnings of those involved in trade and industry, or commercial agriculture, while landed incomes were less buoyant as a consequence of declining rents. As for the poor, the aggregate purchasing power of unskilled labour for consumer goods was restricted by the relative paucity of their earnings, but the inventories of even the poorest people who filed wills contain some cheaper household items.[71]

Not surprisingly, urban areas were centres of accentuated consumer demand whose inhabitants were more materially-orientated than their country counterparts; this disparity, at least among the middle classes, diminished only gradually as farmers increasingly visited towns for business and pleasure and became familiar with urban material culture.[72] The heightened materialism and acquisitiveness of urban life reflected the need to reveal wealth and acquire status in communities with a frequent turnover of inhabitants. Given the density of urban populations, individuals allocated more time and attention to their inner living space, avoiding the hustle and bustle of street life.[73] Higher levels of material consumption also reflected greater access to a growing diversity of goods available and displayed in urban areas, the 'newness' and 'discovery' of the commodity stimulating the desire for purchase. The late seventeenth and early eighteenth centuries witnessed a remarkable expansion in retailing and a significant increase in shops and shopkeeping. While fairs, markets and inns were still important for exchange, their significance was in decline relative to shops as rising demand made fixed-location, continuous retailing economically viable in not only the metropolis but in all towns and even some villages. By the mid-eighteenth century, London had roughly one shop per every 30 inhabitants, and even Durham had one shop for every 82 inhabitants. In 1759, England had over 140,000 retail establishments (exclusive of alehouses), and while the wealth of the proprietors of these premises varied greatly, shopkeeping was nonetheless an important occupation, with shopkeepers and tradesmen accounting for the most numerous membership of the middle class, albeit within its bottom ranks.[74]

Cities and towns also witnessed heightened levels of spending on a variety of urban services and entertainments during the early eighteenth century. The bulk of this came from the pockets of the middle class, but the spending of landed wealth in the metropolis and many provincial towns was also prodigious. There was greater demand for the legal, administrative and medical services which were concentrated in urban areas, contributing to the 'rise of the professions' as an important and characteristic English social change during the late seventeenth and early eighteenth centuries.[75] Increases in spending on eating and drinking stimulated greater commercialization in victualling and catering as cities and towns provided particular types of establishments to meet the desires of specific social groups. Taverns, inns and coffee houses proliferated and underwent increasing refinement for members of the middle classes and resident gentry. Victualling houses, alehouses and gin and dram shops expanded in number to meet the demands of the labouring poor.[76]

Finally, middle-class spending, in conjunction with that of the landed elite, led to the increasing commercialization of leisure and entertainment during this period, the provision of commercial entertainment again being concentrated in the metropolis and provincial cities and towns. By 1750, commercial theatre, music and sports had spread beyond the metropolis to a number of provincial towns, catering to growing audiences. The early eighteenth century witnessed the growth of resort and spa towns (such as Bath, Tunbridge Wells and even Shrewsbury) which specialized in the provision of leisure and entertainment facilities for the landed and middle classes. The commercialization of leisure also was a spur to publishing. The first half of the eighteenth century in many ways created a new genre of entertainment-based print culture which included novels, literary journals and a rapidly expanding provincial newspaper press, augmenting that of the metropolis.[77] The commercialization of leisure may have played an important role in creating a fissure between the middle and labouring classes as the former increasingly took part in more refined types of entertainment, although this argument can be stretched too far. Given that literacy in urban areas was relatively high and extended socially beyond the ranks of the middle class, and that the chapbook and 'cheap print' industries were flourishing, it would appear that print culture was not the exclusive preserve of the middle class. Moreover, traditional forms of entertainment such as cock-fighting, animal baiting and prize fighting were also becoming commercialized and attracted audiences from a variety of social backgrounds.[78]

As we have seen, the urban middle class was the principal beneficiary of the economic changes and the expansion of urbanization, commercialization and consumption which characterized the 'long' first half of the eighteenth century. In a significant and somewhat incestuous sort of way, the growth of middle-class income and consumption led to widening and increasing membership within the middle class itself. For example, it is readily apparent that the commercialization of leisure, itself a product of rising middle-class income, created multiple entrepreneurial and proprietal opportunities for a growing number of individuals, from theatre managers and tavern keepers to printers and booksellers. Of course, this ascendant middle class, as we have chosen to define it, was a pluralist bunch.[79] The middle class was divided, and its members did not yet see themselves as a class. Wealth, occupation and residence created significant cultural and cognitive gulfs between, for example, a wealthy London overseas merchant and a Westminster shopkeeper, or between a Norwich clothier and a Chester tavernkeeper. Religion also could prove divisive, as the middle class was split between devotion for Anglicanism and a multiplicity of dissenting congregations. Politics too divided the urban middle class as wealth and religious position created particular and distinctive partisan alliances.[80] Yet for all these divisions and stratifications, the people who made up the middle class did have an important cumulative impact, not only economically, but also politically, for all ranks of the middle class participated in the economic and social reforms discussed below and in the essays that follow.

III
The Sources of Reform and Regulation

The previous section has sought to delineate social, economic and cultural developments which contributed to the growing importance of the middle class, and consequently brought pressure for change and innovation in the

governing of English society. While the commercialization and urbanization of early eighteenth-century society clearly facilitated the growth
and prosperity of the middle class, it was attended by significant economic
and social dislocation. For example, the rapid growth of London and many
provincial towns meant that problems such as poverty, vagrancy and crime
outstripped the ability of traditional methods of addressing them. The
expansion of the press further heightened awareness of these issues,
especially for the middle class, and added to the growing perception that
these problems required attention. Moreover, the growing importance and
assertiveness of the middle class meant that there was a large body of
people who, by virtue of their wealth and experience in local government,
were interested in and equipped to address these problems. Indeed, the
social and economic changes which helped furnish increasing power to the
urban middle classes were accompanied by both the transformation and
growth of existing institutions available to effect the reform and regulation
of society and the economy. We must now turn to these institutions of
governance, for they crucially shaped the response to perceived problems
and the formation and implementation of policy. Vehicles for effecting
policy debate and execution were present at both the central and local
levels, with much of the initiative coming from outside the traditional
confines of the state. Furthermore, it was not simply the presence of such
institutions, but also their accessibility that made them so useful.

At the centre, Parliament was undoubtedly the most meaningful
institution through which policy was determined, and it was an institution
which swiftly became responsive to the needs of the urban middle classes.
The constitutional and political legacy of 1689 combined with the fiscal
exigencies of a government enmeshed in continental warfare to elevate
Parliament's importance, but it soon proved to be a focus for 'government'
in its widest sense, legislating on a plethora of domestic issues. Nevertheless, while MPs could set policy through legislation, others had to
implement their decisions, and Parliament was not always ready or willing
to legislate on social and economic matters. The central state, including
Parliament, had both priorities and limitations which meant local
institutions were often perceived to be far more appropriate vehicles to
address social and economic problems, many of which had national and
societal, rather than simply local implications. Local government authorities such as parish and town officials sought not only to enforce or promote
statutes, but also to erect their own regulatory framework for society. In
addition, extra-governmental institutions – voluntary societies such as the
Society for the Promotion of Christian Knowledge and the Societies for
the Reformation of Manners – could have a great effect, particularly on
local social policy. Whether attempting to address central or local
concerns, many of the increasingly politicized members of the middle

classes worked through a variety of institutions during this period in attempts to create or influence policies directed at the solution of social and economic problems.

At the level of central government, one of the most far-reaching institutional developments was undoubtedly what Brewer has recently described as the growth of the 'fiscal-military' state from the 1690s. The frequent and ever-increasing demands for revenue for the use of the military provoked substantial changes in government, and resulted in a tremendous expansion in administrative machinery.[81] Some significant reorganization had taken place during the 1680s, but administrative expansion greatly increased after the Glorious Revolution, with the most rapid growth occurring under the pressure of war between 1689 and 1714. The wars created a larger and more professional army and naval administration. Moreover, a permanent 'army of civil officers' was established in administrative departments such as the Board of Trade, and also within the fiscal bureaucracy of the Excise and Customs. The number of government employees grew quickly: Geoffrey Holmes estimates that by the 1720s there were 12,000 permanent government employees. By 1760, the contemporary social arithmetician Joseph Massie put the figure at 16,000. Brewer has calculated that the number of full-time employees in the fiscal bureaucracy trebled from about 2500 in 1690 to nearly 7500 at the close of the Seven Years War. Even by the first decade of the eighteenth century, such individuals had become an 'integral part of the middle storeys of English social structure'.[82]

Not only the number of officeholders, but the character of officeholding changed. Administration was marked by an increasing professionalization. Political purges became infrequent by the early decades of the eighteenth century, due in large part to the campaigns to eliminate placemen from Parliament. With less political capital to be gained through appointments, the patronage value of many offices decreased, and so the offices themselves were partly depoliticized. Upper level officials were also sheltered from political storms because their positions required skills which could not easily be replaced, and many of these professionals had long and secure positions in government. As Brewer notes, while no modern bureaucratic state was erected, a compromise was effected between political patronage and administrative efficiency. At the same time, administrative hierarchies developed within government departments, offering opportunities for individuals to rise to high ranking positions. While some aspiring officers came from the ranks of the poorer gentry, the state also created positions through which the urban middle classes could enter government service.[83]

Much of this administrative expansion was engendered by the need to finance the wars between 1689 and 1714. The costs of war were tremendous; revenues, however, fell far short of the money required, and this shortfall spawned a 'financial revolution' – the development of a system of public borrowing and a market in public securities.[84] Much to the dismay of contemporaries, the public debt swelled rapidly, and by the end of the War of Austrian Succession it had risen to nearly £40 million. The absence of war during the 1720s and 1730s led to a small decline in the national debt, but by the close of the Seven Years War in 1763 it had rocketed to £133 million. Although the wars prior to 1715 generated large amounts of unfunded short-term debt, ministries afterwards turned increasingly to long-term funded debts and whenever possible sought to convert the former into the latter. Since the revenue from indirect taxes was the only available means to back loans to the government, effective taxation was critical to the maintenance of government credit.[85] Supply and taxation became the most important functions of central government, dominating discussion within both the executive and legislature. Indeed, during the late seventeenth and early eighteenth century, myriad 'projectors' inundated government officials with unsolicited proposals for taxation and administration, and it was not uncommon for the authors of such projects to have them published.[86] While few received serious consideration, such activity serves as another example of the open and public nature of policy debate.

The character of taxation changed markedly during this period. During the wars between 1689 and 1714 direct taxes on wealth and income (primarily land) made up nearly half the revenues collected, with the remainder divided roughly equally between customs and excise revenues. After the Hanoverian Succession the customs percentage remained fairly steady, but direct taxes and the excise reversed their positions, with the former quickly declining to approximately a quarter of total revenues while the latter increased to about one half.[87] Successive ministries shied away from direct taxation, and the potential for customs revenue was limited by the potential negative economic impact of increasing tariffs as well as widespread smuggling.[88] The excise was all that remained. Since excises were levied on domestic goods and services and also created a great deal of inconvenience for producers, the impact of taxation fell increasingly on the urban middle classes. This shift in the weight of taxation had important consequences for government. As taxes and regulations hit both producers and consumers, their imposition mobilized interest and participation in policy and politics. Those affected by policy decisions made at the centre, whether by the executive or the legislature, did not idly watch them implemented, but rather, through the mechanisms of the open state (as discussed below), sought to change policies which were enacted, influence those under consideration, and propose their own versions of acceptable and beneficial policy. As a result of their footing the bill for British foreign and military policy, the middle class achieved a greater degree of participation in the nation's affairs.

Increasing participation, did not, however, lead to consensus of opinion, and this diversity of views extended to a wide array of domestic non-fiscal problems. Many groups and interests held disparate opinions on the relative importance of any given problem. Every project had proponents and detractors, every proposal solved problems for some, but created them for others. Langford has recently stated that the mid-eighteenth century was characterized by 'the politics of interest', politics which consisted of 'every conceivable kind of interest, ranging from those of small groups of individuals to large classes'.[89] These competing interests used a variety of means to advance their views, but attention was focused on Parliament and legislation, which respectively became the pre-eminent forum for domestic policy discussion and the most readily available vehicle through which to implement policy.

Parliament achieved this status only after the Glorious Revolution. Legislation was a tool of policy earlier in the seventeenth century, but paled in comparison to the activity of the Privy Council, which was by far the most important source of government policy in Tudor and early Stuart England. By the Restoration, the Council, as it became larger and larger, had lost a good deal of its advisory and executive power, and this trend continued through the remainder of the century. Betty Kemp notes that by the end of the seventeenth century, 'instead of taking decisions itself it registered decisions taken by other bodies'.[90] The Privy Council retained some political clout through the end of Anne's reign, but in regard to policy its role was generally restricted to urging the implementation of decisions made elsewhere.

As was mentioned above, the settlements of 1689 and 1690, coupled with the financial exigencies of war, resulted in regular annual parliamentary sessions after 1688. Parliaments prior to the Glorious Revolution did not necessarily meet annually, and as they were subject to sudden prorogation, met for uncertain duration. The wartime revenue and borrowing needs of governments after 1688 often required complex legislation, and increasingly complicated business swiftly led to longer parliamentary sessions, which usually convened during October or November and adjourned sometime between March and May. In short, a legislative calendar quickly emerged. This development had important consequences – no longer hamstrung by uncertainties, legislative activity not only increased but significantly more bills were successfully enacted. In the reign of Charles II the ratio of acts to bills per session was well below 50 per cent, in that of Anne, it hovered close to 75 per cent.[91] The obvious corollary to legislative policy-making was a tremendous growth in statutory regulation. In the 1720s Parliament enacted approximately 50 bills per session, and half of these were private legislation of an inconsequential nature. By the 1760s, this output had increased to nearly 200 predominantly public laws per session. The flood of bills in combination with the unsystematic nature of eighteenth-century legislation could and did create administrative difficulties, and led to continued calls for statute consolidation.[92] Nevertheless, even if there was confusion, by mid-century a large and growing body of statutory laws had come to play an important role in every arena of governance. As perceptions of parliamentary accessibility changed, more and more interests turned to the legislature to address their concerns, and so Parliament became increasingly important to policy formation. Through this mutually reinforcing process, in Langford's words, 'Government was becoming in a real sense a function of the legislature.'[93]

Though its financial needs required regular parliamentary sessions, the impetus for most legislative activity did not come from the central government. Conciliar government had been a relatively closed process, but Parliament was a much more open and accessible institution. Though parliamentary debates were not systematically or fully published until later in the eighteenth century, there was constant reportage and intense public interest in parliamentary activity. Parliament was viewed as a means of redress, an institution to be approached. MPs provided points of contact between those inside and outside government. In stark contrast to the more private discussion that characterised conciliar policy-making, all the mechanisms inherent in legislative decision-making combined to promote the public debate of domestic policy issues. The reactive nature of Parliament meant that much domestic policy was addressed in an ad hoc fashion, as interest or necessity brought an issue before the legislature. Such interests took many forms, and a variety of motivating factors might propel a domestic policy issue into the parliamentary forum.

One motivation can be found in what is the most analysed feature of late seventeenth- and eighteenth-century parliamentary politics – party political division. These divisions were particularly sharp between 1694 and 1715, but even after the advent of the 'Whig supremacy' partisan politics remained important.[94] Though many domestic issues had little to do with party politics and were free from political manoeuvring (and therefore frequently of less importance to politicians), partisan politics engendered increasing political participation and interest, an attraction fostered by the frequent elections prior to the passage of the Septennial Act in 1716.[95] Moreover, political division was not absent from domestic policy debates, and could provide the focus for mobilization of support and opposition to some measures. We can see such divisions in, for example, the promotion of and opposition to the foundation of the Bank of England and the battles over the East India Company. During the 1720s and 1730s, the 'Patriot' opposition took at least rhetorical stands on many domestic issues. Party politics could, therefore, help promote parliamentary consideration of domestic concerns.

But the impetus behind parliamentary activity also came from other quarters. The eighteenth century witnessed the growing importance of constituency politics. Many MPs looked after local interests, and when local grievances were brought to their attention they sought to alleviate them. Colley notes that county MPs were 'expected to instigate and supervise local legislation' and that 'this meant intensive participation in parliamentary committees . . . .'. Langford has recently stated that during the eighteenth century virtual representation worked for the propertied in English society. While the property qualification for MPs did not mandate where such property was to be located, connections of property ownership and residence laid MPs open to the 'legislative demands of friends and neighbours'.[96] Since they were the focus of organized and sometimes powerful commercial interests, MPs from borough constituencies, and especially those from the metropolis, were often very active in responding to the needs of mercantile voters.[97] It was not unusual for MPs to present petitions, draft legislation, and work assiduously for their constituents and others connected to them. Though the eighteenth century political structure was highly unrepresentative, the middle classes nonetheless found representation through responsible MPs.

One of the ways in which MPs and others were alerted to perceived policy needs was organized pressure through parliamentary lobbying by interest groups.[98] Such activity was hardly a post-1688 creation, but the greatly increased importance of Parliament as the key instrument of government quickly resulted in the formation of diverse and increasingly sophisticated lobbies.[99] Such lobbies might organize national petitioning campaigns, employ professional parliamentary agents, and spend considerable amounts of money. A myriad of special interests, most often drawn from the mercantile, manufacturing and financial sectors, sought to influence policy decisions.

Economic interest groups were organized in many ways, but they often took an institutional form. The London livery companies, for example, frequently sought to intervene in parliamentary affairs. Trading entities such as the Bristol Merchant Adventurers and the Levant Company could have highly successful lobbies, and joint-stock companies, most notably the 'monied' companies of the Bank, East India, and South Sea held tremendous parliamentary influence. Municipal corporations, especially where the town was dominated by a single industry, often served as lobbies, and the City of London was a powerful influence on parliamentary affairs. But such corporate bodies were by no means the only manner of organization. More informal groups, most often narrowly organized around a trade or industry, were formed, and these usually focused on a particular issue rather than having a continuous existence. There are also instances of diverse merchants and tradesmen seeking to lobby Parliament on more general concerns.

Interest groups attempted to convince ministers and MPs that their point of view represented the most desirable course of action. Much of this persuasion would have been directed at government officials and MPs perceived to have influence concerning the matter at hand. Such activities were not, however, confined to back-room politicking. Policy debate became increasingly public. While detailed knowledge of parliamentary activity was available to relatively few, the publication of the *Votes and Proceedings* from the 1680s at least furnished those outside Westminster with the bare essentials of parliamentary business. The 1740s saw the publication of the more complete *Journals*. Such news was augmented by reportage in the periodical and newspaper press.[100] Parliament's openness as an institution of government was greatly facilitated by the knowledge those outside the legislature had of its proceedings.

As has been noted above, one of the most significant reasons for the increasingly public nature of policy debate was the use made of the press by those seeking to influence it. One of the widest doors to the open state was found in the printed word. Numerous lobbies, and sometimes individuals, published brief documents designed to state their case. These were often distributed to MPs and government officials. Printed broadsheets gradually became more substantial pamphlets, and most published material was aimed not only at those in government and Parliament, but at a wider public audience. From the 1690s, though much more prevalent by the early decades of the eighteenth century, such issues also appeared more and more frequently in the newspaper and periodical press. The press, as a vehicle to generate sympathetic public opinion, was one of the most powerful means for individuals and interest groups to push the reactive state, and especially Parliament, to address an issue.

While Parliament played an increasingly important role as a forum for policy debate and formulation, local governmental institutions often provided more viable routes for those seeking reform and regulation. Local officials faced a wide range of economic and social policy dilemmas. Among the most important were certainly the relief and employment of the poor, which were topics of constant concern.[101] Contemporaries also worried about the apparently rising tide of crime and vagrancy, problems which were particularly acute in the metropolis and other urban areas.[102] The local governmental structure which had to face these issues consisted of a diverse and often interconnected set of institutions and personnel.[103] Among the most important was the local judicial structure, with justices of the peace at its head. Corporate municipal government also played a role in social and economic policy, although it was parochial administration which was in many cases more significant. We should not, however, create too rigid a boundary between central and local institutions. Justices were appointed at the centre, and those concerned with local government both implemented and actively sought to have statutes passed in Parliament, and further links came through the activities of the assize judges.[104] As has already been emphasized, domestic policy legislation was essentially reactive, and in the case of social policy Parliament often took isolated local experiments and transformed them into national policies which were to be implemented through local institutions.[105] Even if such decisions were taken at Westminster, for most contemporaries local institutions undoubtedly had a more pervasive and immediate impact in the early eighteenth century. As will be discussed below, it was often at local levels, whether through the formation of voluntary societies or other interest groups, that individuals organized in an attempt to effect changes in social and economic policy. In a variety of forms, local institutions, officials and societies played a profound role in the discussion and execution of economic and social policy.

The activity of JPs in social and economic regulation had been gradually expanding for centuries, with justices coming to oversee apprenticeship, poor relief, repair of bridges and highways, alehouse licensing and local rates. The growth in the powers of individual justices to act summarily outside sessions and the disappearance or decline of rival courts further increased their powers during the sixteenth and seventeenth centuries. Anthony Fletcher notes that Stuart England witnessed 'a general quickening of the tempo of local administration that owed . . . much to justices, and little to the [privy] council or the assize judges'.[106] Justices' influence in local governmental affairs increased even more after the Glorious Revolution. Though the politicization of commissions of the peace from the 1680s led to disruption and frequent changes in personnel, the net result was a large increase in the number of justices appointed.[107] Moreover, central government supervision of justices was rare by the accession of George I.[108] Although magisterial activity remained sporadic and generally confined to what were perceived as the most pressing problems, justices came to organize their activities in more sophisticated ways. At quarter sessions procedures were regularized, the powers of the clerk of the peace and chairman of quarter sessions expanded, and county finances rationalized.[109]

The most important change in justices' methods, however, occurred outside quarter sessions, with the increasing responsibilities assumed by groups of local magistrates meeting at petty sessions. Such sessions had been held frequently, though erratically, in the late sixteenth and early seventeenth centuries, stimulated by legislation which encouraged JPs to create subdivisions within each county and which empowered any two justices acting outside quarter sessions to conduct business such as the appointment of overseers of the poor or the licensing of alehouses.[110] Although it is difficult to detect a trend, petty sessions appear to have become both more frequent and regular in some counties in the late seventeenth and early eighteenth centuries.[111] Middlesex JPs found them particularly useful for governing the suburban parishes of the metropolis, where population growth and social problems threatened to overwhelm parish officials.

Petty sessions had no formal institutional basis, and so were an extremely flexible institution. With the increasing autonomy of JPs in the early eighteenth century, these sessions were used to deal with an ever wider set of concerns. Norma Landau has argued that early eighteenth-century petty sessions wielded far more power than those of just a few decades earlier. While seventeenth-century petty sessions confined themselves to issues such as poor relief, vagrancy, bastardy, apprenticeship, alehouse licensing, highways and bridges, rates, appointment of parish officers and the like, eighteenth-century magistrates also used petty sessions more ambitiously in an attempt to address other social problems.[112] A great deal of such activity resulted from increasing statutory regulation, a result of the reactive state discussed above. In Kent, petty sessions supervised the assessment and collection of the land and window taxes, coordinated efforts against a cattle plague, administered turnpikes, and supervised the repair of jails and houses of correction. In Middlesex, groups of justices met privately to coordinate campaigns against gaming and other 'disorderly' houses in the West End. In the 1730s, metropolitan JPs sat outside quarter sessions to enforce legislation against gin.[113] Petty sessions thus provided justices with a potent weapon for reform, a weapon which was even more powerful when justices met in secret and chose their own members.

Another extremely important focus for governance at the local level was the parish.[114] While JPs had supervisory powers over parish affairs, the extent of their direct control was minimal, and except in a few areas administered by particularly active magistrates, parishes were left to their own devices. The English civil parish had been created in the sixteenth century out of the need to regulate both vagrancy and poor relief. Its significance was greatly magnified with the passage of the Elizabethan Poor Law, which demanded the imposition of parish rates. By the 1690s such taxation was nearly universal.[115] Whether run by open or closed vestries, a substantial number of individuals in every parish gained wide experience with social policy questions. Expertise was further disseminated through the filling of the unpaid offices of overseer of the poor and churchwarden, positions which generally circulated amongst ratepayers. The evolution of parish government helped promote interest in voluntary social organizations and activities in many areas of social policy.

With most private charities administered by the parish, and most vestries possessing discretionary use of a reasonable stock of charitable donations, in principle there existed few limits to parish activity and policy initiative. During much of the seventeenth century, however, the small size of most parishes circumscribed the possibilities for action. With the growth of the London suburban parishes, and the emergence of large single-parish manufacturing towns like Leeds and Sheffield, however, some parishes were much freer to pursue their own regulatory initiatives. Moreover, the 1662 Act of Settlement, by explicitly allowing parishes to refuse relief to non-residents, created conditions conducive to experiments in poor-relief policy.[116] From the latter half of the seventeenth century parishes began to undertake administrative innovations in many areas of social policy and community regulation and improvement. Almshouses and workhouses were gradually brought under parish supervision.[117] During the first half of the eighteenth century, parochial administration in the social and economic realms was enhanced through the vehicle of private parliamentary legislation. In almost any area of social policy one chooses to examine – medical care, housing, policing, sewerage or street lighting – the parish became an increasingly important actor.

In urban areas, municipal corporations were significant to local governance. C.G.F. Forster notes that there was a great deal of 'municipal enterprise' in late Stuart England. Sometimes this activity led to clashes with parish officials, as can be seen in disputes at Exeter and Bristol over the collection of rates in support of corporations of the poor. With the power to raise monies through rates vested largely in the parishes, but political power residing in the hands of municipal corporations, discord was likely, and parishes could become obstacles to as well as vehicles for reform and innovation.[118]

After 1689 there was in general a decline in the power and prestige of common councils due to both political and religious conflicts.[119] Corporate government's regulatory and reforming activity grew less significant, though it should be noted that corporate petitions to Parliament were a favoured vehicle to attempt to promote and influence legislation. As has been noted, much of the initiative for reform in towns and cities shifted to parish vestries, but municipal officers, especially mayors and aldermen, remained active, although they often acted in their magisterial capacities. Meeting in borough or corporate sessions, these officials took advantage of the growing powers granted to JPs to rule their towns oligarchically. Separate boards or commissions, which were created by statute with increasing frequency from the early eighteenth century, were empowered to carry out reforms in specific areas such as employment of the poor, paving, lighting, street cleaning and repair, markets and the watch.[120] Members of corporations were regularly instrumental in the creation of such bodies, and often served on them, but the large number of other commissioners usually ensured independence from the corporation. Towns and cities were important sources of social and economic innovation during this period, but reforms were typically implemented not by the ancient corporations, but by magistrates, parish officers, and commissioners, as well as voluntary societies.

Voluntary societies were an important feature of the eighteenth-century middle class political and social landscape, and it was after the Glorious Revolution that the number of clubs and societies began to proliferate, fuelled by the growing prosperity of the middle ranks in towns. Peter Clark has suggested that by the early eighteenth century there may have been over 2000 clubs and societies in London alone.[121] Such institutions also existed in provincial towns. They took many forms, but two of the most significant, due to their widespread impact, were religious organizations – the Societies for the Reformation of Manners, and the Society for the Promotion of Christian Knowledge.[122] It is no accident that they were founded following the Glorious Revolution, for it was only with the passage of the 1689 Toleration Act, which allowed dissenters to have their own preachers and places of worship, that England provided a sufficiently tolerant atmosphere to permit autonomous religious groups to form.[123]

Established in 1690, the Societies for the Reformation of Manners sought to suppress vices such as swearing and cursing, drunkenness, gambling, and immoral sexual behaviour. Although the reformation of manners campaign was inaugurated in London, societies were formed all over the country and 32 had been founded by the late 1690s.[124] The societies worked very much within the established political system, soliciting (and receiving) the support of the King and Queen, Parliament, the Church, and numerous county quarter sessions. During its heyday, the moral reform campaign featured prominently in Parliament, and resulted in some (largely ineffective) legislative activity.[125] Moral reformers sought to work through all levels of government, but it was their tactics on the ground that constituted an innovative approach to social reform. Arguing that parish officers and JPs could not fight the war against vice alone, the societies, made up predominantly of the urban middle classes, encouraged ordinary citizens to act as informers and even to supervise the activities of parish officers. This reliance on informers meant that the reformation of manners campaign was ultimately controlled by its rank and file.[126]

Unsurprisingly, these tactics provoked strong criticism from both ecclesiastical and secular authorities. Justices accustomed to the exercise of considerable flexibility in their enforcement of the law objected strongly to the reformers' efforts to prosecute offenders systematically without regard to the circumstances of individual cases. Moreover, both church and state officials felt threatened by the societies' activities, believing that they sought to undermine the church and discredit the government. Both the presence of dissenters in the campaign and the possibility that those unsympathetic to the government might manipulate the societies were worrisome to many. While William III and several bishops did support the Societies, many churchmen refused to do so. Nevertheless, the societies continued to be active in several parts of the country into the 1720s and 1730s, although their activities bore less and less relationship to the original purposes of the campaign.[127]

Criticism of their innovative methods contributed to their demise, but the Societies for the Reformation of Manners established new methods by which non-governmental interest groups could mobilize pressure for social reform. The SPCK, founded only a few years later in 1698, was due both to its longevity and the scope of its activities, the most important of the early eighteenth-century voluntary societies. An Anglican reaction to the success of dissenting interests, the society's establishment was also an effort to provide an organizational connection for the disparate reforming bodies then in existence. Initially, its aim was to encourage the establishment of charity schools.[128] The society was organized in a system of corresponding and resident members. Correspondents were located throughout the country, and included many parish priests, as well as merchants, manufacturers, enlightened gentry, and even some members of the aristocracy. Residing members lived in the metropolis, and so attended the society's regular meetings. For the most part these were powerful men who held secular positions and included MPs, JPs, members of important London merchant families, and some aristocrats. While the SPCK had an agenda, and was very discriminating in allowing entrance, it welcomed individuals from a broad ideological spectrum. Its organizational structure provided a sophisticated system which facilitated centralized decision-making, but also allowed for the collection of local information. Perhaps mindful of the mistakes of the Societies for the Reformation of Manners, the SPCK successfully sought to maintain a low profile, even while it was becoming increasingly powerful in both national and local government.

While the SPCK described itself as a religious society, its aims went far beyond such a description. The society's activities were shaped by a strong belief that religion served as the cement of an orderly society, and was a means of discouraging all sorts of social deviance, including poverty, indebtedness and criminality. The religious beliefs encouraged by charity schools would also lead to industrial and social discipline. The SPCK pursued a series of projects: it established foreign missions, published moral tracts, attempted to reform debtors' prisons, and was involved in the foundation of both the Georgia colony and the Foundling Hospital. The SPCK acted as a sophisticated parliamentary pressure group, and continually advised the dozen or so MPs among its members on legislation. But it was at the local level, through its widespread influence on education and poor relief, that the Society had its most profound effect. As a result of its vast range of projects, the SPCK was a continually pervasive force in the domestic arena, and it is emblematic of the important contribution made by voluntary societies to early eighteenth-century English governance.

IV
Conclusion

Changes in English society and economy in the late seventeenth and early eighteenth centuries led not only to a growing awareness of social and economic problems, but to a wide range of new initiatives, primarily undertaken by the urban middle classes, to solve them. In seeking to address these problems, reformers and regulators had a vast array of institutional resources at their disposal, both national and local, official and voluntary. What is distinctive about early eighteenth-century governance is how open the state (at all levels) was to the demands of the propertied outside the traditional ranks of the landed governing elite, and how great a role such people played in initiating reform. The early eighteenth-century state was essentially reactive: its involvement in the promotion of economic growth and social welfare took the form of acting on initiatives emanating largely from outside executive government, particularly from interest groups, voluntary societies, and local government. Indeed, this was a distinctive feature of the period. Through its permeability, early eighteenth-century government was beautifully suited to the demands of an increasingly urban and commercial society, and was able to incorporate the demands and requirements of an ever more numerous and prosperous middle class at a multiplicity of levels, ranging from Parliament to parish.

Notes

1   The notion of a 'long' eighteenth century has become almost customary. For examples of such usage, see E.A. Wrigley, 'The growth of population in eighteenth-century England: A conundrum resolved', *Past & Present*, 98 (1983), p. 124; J.C.D. Clark in *English Society, 1688–1832: Ideology, Social Structure and Political Practice during the Ancien Regime* (Cambridge, 1985); 'Introduction' in P. Borsay (ed.), *The Eighteenth Century Town: A Reader in English Urban History, 1688–1820* (1990), pp. 1–38.

2 Of course, especially with the passage of the Act of Union with Scotland (1707), the 'English' state was in fact 'British'. However, the Scottish, Irish, and (to a lesser extent) Welsh perspectives on the state differed radically from the English prospect. Our concern here is solely with the relationship of state and society in England. For Celtic perspectives, see: D. Szechi and D. Hayton, 'John Bull's other kingdoms: The English government of Scotland and Ireland' in C. Jones (ed.), *Britain in the First Age of Party, 1680–1750* (1987), pp. 241–280; B.P. Lenman, 'A client society: Scotland between the '15 and the '45' in J. Black (ed.), *Britain in the Age of Walpole* (1984), pp. 69–94; J.S. Shaw, *The Management of Scottish Society, 1707–1764: Power, Nobles, Lawyers, Edinburgh Agents and English Influence* (Edinburgh, 1983); T.W. Moody and W.E. Vaughn (eds.), *The New History of Ireland: IV, Eighteenth-Century Ireland* (Oxford, 1986); G.H. Jenkins, *The Foundations of Modern Wales, 1642–1780* (Oxford, 1987), esp. chs. 4 and 8.

3 A point rightly argued by J.C.D. Clark in both *English Society*, esp. pp. 27–8, and *Revolution and Rebellion: State and Society in England during the Seventeenth and Eighteenth Centuries* (Cambridge, 1986), ch. 2.

4 J. Cannon, *Parliamentary Reform, 1640–1832* (Cambridge, 1973), p. 24. See also, e.g., J.B. Owen, *The Eighteenth Century, 1714– 1815* (New York, 1974); J.H. Plumb, *The Growth of Political Stability in England, 1675–1725* (1967); B. Williams, *The Whig Supremacy, 1714–1760* (Oxford, 1939).

5 E.g., see J. Cannon, *Aristocratic Century: The Peerage of Eighteenth-Century England* (Cambridge, 1984); A.J. Little, *Deceleration in the Eighteenth-Century British Economy* (1976); W.A. Speck, *Stability and Strife: England, 1714–1760* (1977), esp. ch. 6.

6 For our purposes, it is important to note that the early work of 'post revisionism' argues for greater consideration of local participation in national affairs. See the 'Introduction: after revisionism' in R. Cust and A. Hughes (eds.), *Conflict in Early Stuart England: Studies in Religion and Politics, 1603–1642* (1989), pp. 1–46. The revisionist literature for the period of the 'English Revolution' is extensive. E.g., see M. Kishlansky, *Parliamentary Selection: Social and Political Choice in Early Modern England* (Cambridge, 1986); C. Russell (ed.), *The Origins of the English Civil War* (1973); idem, *The Causes of the English Civil War* (Oxford, 1990); K. Sharpe, *Faction and Parliament: Essays on early Stuart History* (Oxford, 1978).

7 J. Hoppit, 'Counting the industrial revolution', *Economic History Review*, 2nd ser., 43 (1990), esp. p. 174. See also, M. Berg, *The Age of Manufactures: Industry, Innovation and Work in Britain, 1700–1820* (1985); J. V. Beckett and J. E. Heath, 'When was the industrial revolution in the East Midlands?', *Midland History*, 13 (1988), pp. 77–94; D. Cannadine, 'The present and the past in the English industrial revolution', *Past & Present*, 103 (1984), pp. 131–72; N. Crafts, *British Economic Growth during the Industrial Revolution* (Oxford, 1985); P. Hudson (ed.), *Regions and Industries: A Perspective on the Industrial Revolution in Britain* (Cambridge, 1989); E.A. Wrigley, *Continuity, Chance and Change: The Character of the Industrial Revolution in England* (Cambridge, 1988).

8 E.g., see N. Rogers, 'Aristocratic clientage, trade and independency: Popular politics in pre-radical Westminster', *Past & Present*, 61 (1973), pp. 70–86; J. Brewer, *Party Ideology and Popular Politics at the Accession of George III* (Cambridge, 1976); L. Colley, 'Eighteenth-Century radicalism before Wilkes', *Transactions of the Royal Historical Society*, 5th ser., 31 (1981), pp. 1–19; H.T. Dickinson, 'The precursors of political radicalism in Augustan Britain', in C. Jones (ed.), *First Age of Party*, pp. 63–84; M. Harrison, *Crowds and History: Mass Phenomena in English Towns, 1790–1835* (Cambridge, 1988).

9 Notably in *English Society* published in 1985 and in *Reform and Rebellion* which appeared in the following year, see above note 3.

10 '. . . the reigns of the first two Georges stand out as conceptually central to the
viability of the social and political order which prevailed between the Restoration and
the Reform Bill.' Clark, *Revolution and Rebellion*, p. 8. See also his *English Society*, esp.
ch. 2.

11 Indeed, some have argued that Clark's depiction of eighteenth-century England as
aristocratic, religious and pre-industrial is neither new nor accurate. See J. Innes,
'Jonathan Clark, social history and England's "Ancien Régime"', *Past & Present*, 115
(1987), esp. pp. 176–7.

12 We recognize that use of the term 'middle class' as opposed to 'classes', 'ranks' or
'middling sorts' is potentially problematic. Clearly, 'middle class' was not a regular
feature of early eighteenth-century nomenclature. However, we use the term as a
simplified point of historical reference and categorization (interchangeable with
'middle classes'), alluding to a broad (and expanding) spectrum of urban occupational
groups: merchants (inclusive of retailers and shopkeepers), manufacturers (inclusive of
literate and propertied artisans), and professionals (inclusive of the clergy) who were
generally outside the confines of the traditional landed elite. We shall argue that while
this urban middle class was pluralist and culturally heterogeneous, nonetheless its
members had a 'shared' experience in terms of participation in government and
economic and social reform. For the ambiguities surrounding the 'middle class', see P.
Corfield, 'Class by name and number in eighteenth-century Britain', *History*, 72
(1987), pp. 38–61; N. Rogers, 'Paul Langford's "Age of Improvement"', *Past &
Present*, 130 (1991), pp. 201–9; K. Wrightson, 'The social order of early-modern
England: three approaches', in L. Bonfield, R. Smith and K. Wrightson (eds.), *The
World We Have Gained: Histories of Population and Social Structure* (Oxford, 1986), pp.
177–202.

13 P. Langford, *A Polite and Commercial People: England, 1727–1783* (Oxford, 1989).
Regrettably, Langford's most recent work, *Public Life and the Propertied Englishman,
1689–1798* (Oxford, 1991) was not available at this writing. See also, P. Borsay, *The
English Urban Renaissance: Culture and Society in the Provincial Town, 1660–1770*
(Oxford, 1989); P. Corfield, *The Impact of English Towns, 1700–1800* (Oxford, 1982);
P. Earle, *The Making of the English Middle Class: Business, Society and Family Life in
London, 1660–1730* (1989).

14 John Brewer, *Sinews of Power: War, Money and the English State, 1688–1783* (1988); C.
Brooks, 'Taxation, finance and public opinion, 1688–1714' (Cambridge Univ. Ph.D.
thesis, 1971); P.G.M. Dickson, *The Financial Revolution in England: A Study of the
Development of Public Credit, 1688–1756* (1967); D. W. Jones, *War and Economy in the
Age of William III and Marlborough* (Oxford, 1988).

15 For the impact of war-induced expenditure on the constitution, see J. Carter, 'The
Revolution and the constitution' in G.S. Holmes (ed.), *Britain after the Glorious
Revolution, 1689–1714* (1969), pp. 39–58; H.T. Dickinson, 'How glorious was the
"Glorious Revolution" of 1688?', *British Journal of Eighteenth-Century Studies*, 11
(1988), pp. 125–42; H. Horwitz, '1689 (and all that)', *Parliamentary History*, 6 (1987);
A. McInnes, 'When was the English Revolution?', *History*, 67 (1982), pp. 378–88; C.
Roberts, 'The constitutional significance of the financial settlement of 1690', *Historical
Journal*, 20 (1970), pp. 59–76; L. Stone, 'The results of the English revolutions of the
seventeenth century' in J.G.A. Pocock (ed.), *Three British Revolutions: 1641, 1688,
1776* (Princeton, N.J., 1980), esp. p. 65.

16 The historical literature concerning partisan politics and electoral participation in the
reigns of William III and Anne is extensive. See, e.g., G.S. De Krey, *A Fractured
Society: The Politics of London in the First Age of Party, 1688–1715* (Oxford, 1985); D.
Hayton, 'The "Country" interest and the party system, 1689–c.1720', in C. Jones
(ed.), *Party and Management in Parliament 1660–1784* (Leicester, 1984), pp. 37–86;

G.S. Holmes, *British Politics in the Reign of Queen Anne* (1967); H. Horwitz, *Parliament, Policy and Politics in the Reign of William III* (Manchester, 1977); W.A. Speck, *Tory and Whig: The Struggle in the Constituencies, 1701–1715* (1970); idem, 'The electorate in the first age of party', in C. Jones (ed.), *First Age of Party*, pp. 45–62. Though perhaps less virulent, partisan conflict continued during the early Hanoverian period. See L. Colley, *In Defiance of Oligarchy: The Tory Party, 1714–60* (Cambridge, 1982); B. W. Hill, *The Growth of Parliamentary Parties, 1689–1742* (1976).

17 For the role and representativeness of the middle class in the unreformed Parliament, see J. Phillips, 'The structure of electoral politics in unreformed England', *Journal of British Studies*, 19 (1979), pp. 76–100; P. Langford, 'Property and "Virtual Representation" in eighteenth-century England', *Historical Journal*, 31 (1988), pp. 83–115. For urban independence, see N. Rogers, 'The urban oppositon to whig oligarchy, 1720–1760', in M. and J. Jacob (eds.), *The Origins of Anglo-American Radicalism* (1984), pp. 138–42; idem, *Whigs and Cities: Popular Politics in the Age of Walpole and Pitt* (Oxford, 1989); J. Triffit, 'Politics and the urban community: Parliamentary boroughs in the south west of England, 1710–1730', (Oxford Univ D. Phil. thesis, 1985); K. Wilson, 'The rejection of deference: Urban political culture in England, 1715–1785', (Yale Univ. Ph.D. thesis, 1985).

18 Innes, 'Jonathan Clark', p. 171.

19 By 'low' discourse we refer to that '"below" the classical works we associate with canons in literature and philosophy, yet "above" the culture of everyday life'. D. Hollinger, 'The return of the prodigal: The persistence of historical knowing', *American Historical Review*, 94 (1989), p. 617.

20 See below chapters 1, 2, 5 and 7. This is not to say that the issues of poor relief, moral reform and trade were necessarily non-partisan. E.g., see S. Macfarlane, 'Social policy and the poor in the later seventeenth century', in A.L. Beier and R. Finlay (eds.), *The Making of the Metropolis: London, 1500–1700* (1986), pp. 252–77; D. Hayton, 'Moral reform and country politics in the House of Commons', *Past & Present*, 128 (1990), pp. 48–91. For the importance of lower levels of partisan political discourse, see L. Colley and M. Goldie, 'The principles and practice of eighteenth-century party', *Historical Journal*, 22 (1979), pp. 239–46; H.T. Dickinson, *Liberty and Property: Political Ideology in Eighteenth Century Britain* (1977); M. Goldie, 'The Revolution of 1689 and the structure of political argument: An essay and an annotated bibliography of pamphlets on the allegiance controversy', *Bulletin of Research in the Humanities*, 83 (1980).

21 The notable exception being in the case of deliberations surrounding changes in the criminal law.

22 E.g., see below chapters 1, 2 and 3. See also, S. Handley, 'Local legislative initiatives for economic and social development in Lancashire, 1689–1731', *Parliamentary History*, 9 (1990), pp. 14–37; J. Innes, 'Parliament and the shaping of eighteenth-century social policy', *Transactions of the Royal Historical Society*, 5th ser., 45 (1990), pp. 63–92.

23 E.g., see below chapters 4–7.

24 For the decline of the Privy Council and the growing independence of JPs, see, e.g., A. Fletcher, *Reform in the Provinces: The Government of Stuart England* (1986); N. Landau, *The Justices of the Peace: 1679–1760* (Berkeley, 1984), pt. 3; R.B. Shoemaker, *Prosecution and Punishment: Petty Crime and the Law in London and Rural Middlesex c. 1660–1725* (Cambridge, 1991). For the vestry, see, e.g., T. Hitchcock, 'The English workhouse: A study in institutional poor relief in selected counties, 1696–1750' (Oxford Univ. D. Phil. thesis, 1985); P. Slack, *Poverty and Policy in Tudor and Stuart England* (1988); S. and B. Webb, *English Local Government: The Parish and the County* (1906).

25 The following demographic discussion is drawn from E.A. Wrigley and R.S. Schofield, *The Population History of England, 1541– 1871: A Reconstruction* (1981), esp. chs. 7–10; E.A. Wrigley, 'Marriage, fertility and population growth in eighteenth-century England' in R.B. Outhwaite (ed.), *Marriage and Society: Studies in the Social History of Marriage* (1981), pp. 137–85; *idem*, 'Population growth'; R.A. Houston, *The Population History of Britain and Ireland, 1500–1750* (1992).

26 All four years are found amongst the 'top ten' of crisis mortality years between 1541 and 1871. Wrigley and Schofield, *Population*, Table 8.11, p. 333. See also, *ibid.*, Table A3.2. For the importance and prevalence of high mortality in the seventeenth and early eighteenth centuries, see R. Stavins, 'A model of English demographic change, 1573–1873', *Explorations in Economic History*, 25 (1988), pp. 98–116; M.J. Dobson, 'The last hiccup of the old demographic regime', *Continuity and Change*, 4 (1989), pp. 395–428.

27 J. Landers and A. Mouzas, 'Burial seasonality and causes of death in London, 1670–1819', *Population Studies*, 42 (1988), pp. 77– 9. See also, Wrigley and Schofield, *Population*, pp. 341, 663, 669; R.S. Schofield, 'The impact of scarcity and plenty on population change in England, 1541–1871', *Journal of Interdisciplinary History*, 14 (1983), pp. 265–91.

28 The rate of fertility within marriage having been more or less constant. E.A. Wrigley and R. S. Schofield, 'English population history from family reconstitution: Summary results, 1600–1799', *Population Studies*, 37 (1983), pp. 157–84; C. Wilson, 'Natural fertility in pre-industrial England, 1600–1799', *Population Studies*, 38 (1984), pp. 225–240. For illegitimacy, see P. Laslett, 'Long-term trends in bastardy in England' in *Family Life and Illicit Love in Earlier Generations* (Cambridge, 1977), Fig. 3.1; N. Rogers, 'Carnal knowledge: Illegitimacy in eighteenth-century Westminster', *Journal of Social History*, 23 (1989), pp. 355–75; A. Wilson, 'Illegitimacy and its implications in mid-eighteenth-century London: The evidence of the Foundling Hospital', *Continuity and Change*, 4 (1989), pp. 103–64.

29. For alternatives to the Wrigley and Schofield thesis, see D. Levine, *Reproducing Families: The Political Economy of English Population History* (Cambridge, 1987), esp. chs. 2–3; N. Trantner, *Population and Society, 1750–1940* (1985), pp. 100–7; J. Goldstone, 'The demographic revolution in England: A re-examination', *Population Studies*, 40 (1986), pp. 5–33. See also Wrigley and Schofield, *Population*, ch. 10, esp. p. 422; R.S. Schofield, 'Family structure, demographic behaviour, and economic growth', in *idem* and J. Walter (eds.), *Famine, Disease and the Social Order in Early Modern Society* (Cambridge, 1989), pp. 296–304.

30 E.g., the 1690s witnessed a number of bad harvests and relatively high grain prices. W.G. Hoskins, 'Harvest fluctuations and English economic history, 1620–1759', *Agricultural History Review*, 16 (1968), pp. 15–31.

31 R.V. Jackson, 'Growth and deceleration in English agriculture, 1660–1790', *Economic History Review*, 2nd ser., 38 (1985), pp. 333–51. As part of the aforementioned revisionism, agricultural and economic historians have tended to revise estimates of early eighteenth century agricultural productivity and output upwards, and that of the late eighteenth century downwards. In addition to Jackson, see N.F.R. Crafts, *British Economic Growth during the Industrial Revolution* (Oxford, 1985), ch. 2; M. Overton, 'Estimating crop yields from probate inventories: An example from East Anglia, 1585–1735', *Journal of Economic History*, 39 (1979), pp. 363–78; M.E. Turner, 'Agricultural productivity in eighteenth-century England: Further strains of speculation', *Economic History Review*, 2nd ser., 37 (1984), pp. 256–7.

32 In the late seventeenth century, corn bounties were instigated to protect landowners and major producers from the consequences of falling grain prices. Grain exports peaked in the mid-eighteenth century. See A.H. John, 'English agricultural improve-

ment and grain exports, 1660–1765', in D.C. Coleman and A.H. John (eds.), *Trade, Government and Economy in Pre-Industrial England* (1976), pp. 45–67; D. Ormrod, *English Grain Exports and the Structure of Agrarian Capitalism, 1700–1760* (Hull, 1985).

33 For agricultural innovation, amongst an extensive literature, see E.L. Jones, 'Agriculture, 1700–80' in R. Floud and D. McCloskey (eds.), *The Economic History of Britain since 1700* (Cambridge, 1981), vol. I, pp. 66–86; M. Overton, 'The diffusion of agricultural innovation in early modern England: Turnips and clover in Norfolk and Suffok, 1580–1740', *Transactions of the Institute of British Geographers*, new ser., 10 (1985), pp. 205–21; P. Glennie, 'Continuity and change in Hertfordshire agriculture, 1550–1700', pts. I and II, *Agricultural History Review*, 36 (1988), pp. 55–76, 145–61.

34 H.J. Habakkuk, 'English landownership, 1680–1740', *Economic History Review*, 10 (1939–40), pp. 2–17. Strict settlement left the legal ownership of an estate in trust, prohibiting the life tenant from breaking up the estate except under specified conditions or by private Act of Parliament. For a critique of Habakkuk's analysis of strict settlement, see L. Bonfield, 'Marriage settlements and the "Rise of Great Estates": The demographic evidence', *Economic History Review*, 2nd ser., 22 (1979), pp. 483–93; J.V. Beckett, 'The pattern of landownership in England and Wales, 1660–1880', *Economic History Review*, 2nd ser., 37 (1984), pp. 7–11.

35 For the survival of smallholdings and criticisms of Habakkuk, see *ibid.*, pp. 1–22; idem, 'Regional variation and the agricultural depression, 1730–50', *Economic History Review*, 35, 2nd ser. (1982), pp. 35–51; idem, 'The decline of the small landowner in eighteenth-and nineteenth-century England: Some regional considerations', *Agricultural History Review*, 30 (1982), pp. 95–111; M. Reed, 'The peasantry of nineteenth-century England: A neglected class?', *History Workshop*, 18 (1984), pp. 53–76.

36 For land values and estate management, see, amongst an extensive literature, C. Clay, 'Landlords and estate management in England, 1640–1750' in J. Thirsk (ed.), *Chapters from the Agrarian History of England and Wales: Volume 2* (Cambridge, 1990), pp. 289–378; idem, 'The price of freehold land in the later seventeenth and eighteenth centuries', *Economic History Review*, 2nd ser., 27 (1974), pp. 173–89; R.C. Allen, 'The price of freehold land and the interest rate in the seventeenth and eighteenth centuries', *Economic History Review*, 2nd ser., 41 (1988), pp. 33–50; Beckett, 'Pattern of landownership'; idem, 'Estate management in eighteenth-century England: the Lowther-Spedding relationship in Cumberland' in J.A. Chartres and D. Hey (eds.), *English Rural Society, 1500–1800* (Cambridge, 1990), pp. 55–72.

37 For enclosure, see J. Broad, 'Alternate husbandry and permanent pasture in the Midlands, 1650–1800', *Agricultural History Review*, 28 (1980), 77–89; idem, 'The Verneys as enclosing landlords, 1600–1800' in Chartres and Hey (eds.), *English Rural Society*, pp. 27–44; J.R. Wordie, 'The chronology of English enclosure, 1500–1914', *Economic History Review*, 36 (1983), pp. 483–505; M. Reed, 'Enclosure in north Buckinghamshire, 1500–1750', *Agricultural History Review*, 32 (1984), pp. 133–44.

38 The preceding discussion has been based on E.A. Wrigley, 'Urban growth and agricultural change: England and the continent in the early modern period', in R.I. Rotberg and T.K. Rabb (eds.), *Population and Economy* (Cambridge, 1986), pp. 123–68, esp. Table 4. See also, R.C. Allen, 'The growth of labour productivity in early modern English agriculture', *Explorations in Economic History*, 25 (1988), 117–46; P.H. Lindert, 'English occupations, 1670–1811', *Journal of Economic History*, 40 (1980), pp. 701–7.

39 Of course the relationship between enhanced agricultural productivity and urban growth was to some extent symbiotic. Concentrated urban centres of demand (most notably London) provided sufficient stimulus for the commercialization of agriculture and higher levels of efficiency. See E.A. Wrigley, 'A simple model of London's importance in changing English society and economy', *Past & Present*, 37 (1967), pp.

44–70; idem, 'Urban growth'; J.A. Chartres, 'City and towns, farmers and economic change in the eighteenth century,' *Historical Research*, 64 (1991), pp. 138–55; P. Large, 'Urban growth and agricultural change in the West Midlands during the seventeenth and eighteenth centuries', in P. Clark (ed.), *The Transformation of English Provincial Towns* (1984), pp. 169–89.

40 Moreover, this rate of urbanization was much greater than that experienced on the Continent over the same period. Wrigley, 'Urban Growth', Table 4, pp. 152–64.

41 See D. Souden, 'Migrants and the population structure of later seventeenth-century provincial cities and market towns' in Clark (ed.), *Transformation*, pp. 133–68; P. Clark, 'Migration in England during the late seventeenth and early eighteenth centuries', *Past & Present*, 83 (1979), pp. 57–90; M.J. Kitch, 'Capital and kingdom: Migration to later Stuart London' in Beier and Finlay (eds.), *London, 1500–1700*, pp. 224–51; J.L. Landers, 'Mortality and metropolis: The case of London, 1675–1825', *Population Studies*, 41 (1987), pp. 71–6.

42 R. Finlay and B. Shearer, 'Population growth and suburban expansion', in Beier and Finlay (eds.), *London, 1500–1700*, Table 1. See also, B. Dietz, 'Overseas trade and metropolitan growth' and A.L. Beier, 'Engine of manufacture: The trades of London', in the same collection, pp. 115–67; P.J. Corfield, *The Impact of English Towns, 1700–1800* (Oxford, 1982), ch. 5.

43 P.J. Corfield, 'Urban development in England and Wales in the sixteenth and seventeenth centuries', in Coleman and John (eds.), *Trade, Government and Economy*, p. 229. The following discussion of urbanization is based on *idem*, 'English Towns', chs. 1–3; Borsay, *Urban Renaissance*, 'Introduction'; Wrigley, 'Urban growth'.

44 See Large; M.B. Rowlands, 'Continuity and change in an industrialising society: The case of the West Midlands industries', in P. Hudson (ed.), *Regions and Industries*; J.D. Marshall, 'The rise and transformation of the Cumbrian market town, 1660–1900', *Northern History*, 19 (1983), pp. 133–53; M. Noble, 'Growth and development in a regional urban system: The country towns of eastern Yorkshire, 1700–1850', *Urban History Yearbook* (1987), pp. 4–15.

45 L.D. Schwartz, 'The standard of living in the long run: London, 1700–1860', *Economic History Review*, 2nd ser. 38 (1985), pp. 24–41; E.H. Phelps Brown and S.V. Hopkins, 'Seven centuries of the price of consumables, compared with builders' wage-rates', reprinted in E.M. Carus-Wilson (ed.), *Essays in Economic History*, II (1962), pp. 179–96. See also, P. Lindert, 'English population, wages, and prices: 1541–1913', in Rotberg and Rabb (eds.), *Population and Economy*, esp. pp. 50–9; J.A. Chartres, 'Food consumption and internal trade', in Beier and Finlay (eds.), *London, 1500–1700*, pp. 170–76.

46 J. Styles, 'Embezzlement, industry and the law in England, 1500–1800', in M. Berg, *et al.* (eds.), *Manufacture in Town and Country before the Factory* (Cambridge, 1983), pp. 173–202. For servants in husbandry, see A.S. Kussmaul, *Servants in Husbandry in Early Modern England* (Cambridge, 1981); K.D.M. Snell, *Annals of the Labouring Poor: Social Change and Agrarian England, 1660–1900* (Cambridge, 1985), esp. ch. 2.

47 L. Weatherill, 'Consumer behaviour and social status in England, 1660–1750', *Continuity and Change*, 1 (1986), p. 210.

48 G.F.R. Spenceley, 'The origins of the English pillow lace industry', *Agricultural History Review*, 21 (1973), pp. 81–93; E.L. Jones, 'The agricultural origins of industry', *Past & Present*, 40 (1971), pp. 62–3. The marginalization of women's work in agriculture was accelerated by rapid population growth and a surplus pool of labour after 1750. See Snell, *Annals*, chs. 1, 4, and 6; M. Roberts, 'Sickles and scythes: Women's work and men's work at harvest time', *History Workshop*, 13 (1979), pp. 18–9.

49 P. Earle, 'The female labour market in London in the late seventeenth and early eighteenth centuries', *Economic History Review*, 2nd ser., 42 (1989), esp. pp. 338–44.

50 For rising consumption, see Chartres, 'Food Consumption', pp. 174–84; Beckett, 'Agricultural depression', pp. 49–51; K.N. Chaudhuri, *The Trading World of Asia and the East India Company, 1660–1760* (Cambridge, 1978), Tables C.9 and C.19; P. Mathias, *The Brewing Industry in England, 1700–1830* (Cambridge, 1959), Table 36; P. Clark, 'The "Mother gin" controversy in the early eighteenth century', *Transactions of the Royal Historical Society*, 5th ser., 38 (1988), pp. 64–5; and, see below ch. 2.

51 See J.V. Beckett and M. Turner, 'Taxation and economic growth in eighteenth-century England', *Economic History Review*, 2nd ser., 43 (1990), pp. 377–403.

52 P. O'Brien, 'Agriculture and the home market for English industry, 1660–1820', *English Historical Review*, 100 (1985), pp. 773–800. For older views stressing the importance of agriculture and domestic demand throughout the eighteenth century, see W.A. Cole, 'Factors in demand, 1700–80', in Floud and McCloskey, *Economic History*, Vol. I; A.H. John, 'Agricultural productivity and economic growth in England', in E.L. Jones (ed.), *Agriculture and Economic Growth in England, 1650–1815* (1967), pp. 172–93, and the editor's introduction in the same volume.

53 See also, N.F.R. Crafts, 'British economic growth, 1700–1831: A review of the evidence', *Economic History Review*, 2nd ser., 36 (1983), esp. p. 199.

54 The following discussion of overseas trade is drawn from R. Davis, 'English foreign trade, 1700–1774', reprinted in W. Minchinton (ed.), *The Growth of English Overseas Trade in the Seventeenth and Eighteenth Centuries* (1969), pp. 99–119, and the editor's introduction; D.W. Jones, *War and Economy*, Table 10.1.

55 R. Davis, *The Rise of the English Shipping Industry in the Seventeenth and Eighteenth Centuries* (Newton Abbot, 1972); W. Hausman, *Public Policy and the Supply of Coal to London, 1700–1770* (New York, 1981).

56 Perhaps as many as two out of every three English cloths produced were exported in the eighteenth century. G.D. Ramsay, *The English Woollen Industry, 1500–1750* (1982), p. 34. For the English cloth industry, amongst an extensive literature, see H. Heaton, *The Yorkshire Woollen and Worsted Industries* (Oxford, 1965); J. de L. Mann, *The Cloth Industry in the West of England from 1640 to 1880* (Oxford, 1971); E. Kerridge, *Textile Manufactures in Early Modern England* (Manchester, 1985).

57 R. Davis, 'The rise of protection in England, 1689–1786', *Economic History Review*, 2nd ser., 19 (1966), 302–7; J. Price, 'What did merchants do? Reflections on British overseas trade, 1660–1790', *Journal of Economic History*, 49 (1989), pp. 267–84. The growing importance of transatlantic trade (in conjunction with the increase in Anglo-Irish trade) was a major contribution to the growth of the western ports of Liverpool, Bristol, and Whitehaven during the early eighteenth century. Corfield, *Towns*, ch. 3; P.G.E. Clemens, 'The rise of Liverpool, 1665–1750', *Economic History Review*, 2nd ser., 29 (1976), pp. 211–25; W. Minchinton (ed.), *The Trade of Bristol in the Eighteenth Century* (Bristol Record Society, 20, 1957); J.E. Williams, 'Whitehaven in the eighteenth century', *Economic History Review*, 2nd ser., 8 (1956), pp. 393–404.

58 Between 1700 and 1760, Crafts estimates that industrial growth grew at 0.7 per cent per annum. Estimates of industrial growth between 1760–1801 are still significantly higher, despite their revision downwards, but overly reflect the achievements of an 'atypical' sector: mechanized cotton textile production. See Crafts, *Economic Growth*, ch. 2; C.K. Harley, 'British industrialization before 1841: Evidence of slower growth during the industrial revolution', *Journal of Economic History*, 42 (1982), pp. 267–89. For older estimates, see P. Deane and W.A. Cole, *British Economic Growth, 1688–1959: Trends and Structure* (Cambridge, 1969 ed.). Recent revisions to Crafts' figures do not alter those for industrial activity. R.V. Jackson, 'Government expenditure and British economic growth in the eighteenth century: Some problems of measurement', *Economic History Review*, 2nd ser., 43 (1990), pp. 217–35.

59 Hoppit, 'Counting the industrial revolution'; and the excellent introduction in
    Hudson (ed.), Regions and Industries, pp. 6–28.
60 The iron industry provides an example of the disparate regional response to technical
    change. The gradual adoption of coke fuel stimulated the growth of iron production
    near coal deposits (e.g. in the West Midlands, South Yorkshire and South Wales) and
    the slow de-industrialization of charcoal-based areas such as the Kentish Weald. See B.
    Short, 'The de-industrialization process: a case study of the Weald, 1600–1850' in
    Hudson (ed.) Regions and Industries, pp. 156–74; J.R. Harris, The British Iron Industry,
    1700–1850 (1988); C.K. Hyde, Technological Change and the British Iron Industry,
    1700–1870 (Princeton, 1977). For coal, see M.W. Flinn, The History of the British Coal
    Industry, Volume 2: 1700–1830: The Industrial Revolution (Oxford, 1984).
61 Berg, Age of Manufactures; see also C. MacLeod, Inventing the Industrial Revolution: The
    English Patent System, 1660–1800 (Cambridge, 1988), esp. ch.8.
62 See Rowlands, 'Continuity and change'; idem, Masters and Men in the West Midland
    Metalware Trades before the Industrial Revolution (Manchester, 1975); Berg, Age of
    Manufactures.
63 N.K. Rothstein, 'Canterbury and London: The silk industry in the late seventeenth
    century', Textile History, 20 (1989), pp. 33– 47. For metropolitan industry, see Earle,
    Middle Class, ch. 2; Beier, 'Engine of manufacture'. The latter argues that manufac-
    turing was the primary source of metropolitan employment. For the importance of
    commerce, see J. Alexander, 'The economic structure of the City of London at the end
    of the seventeenth century', Urban History Yearbook, (1989), pp. 47– 62.
64 The West Riding provided a dichotomy in this respect. Woollen cloths were produced by
    independent artisans in the countryside; worsted production was conducted on a
    putting-out basis. P. Hudson, 'From manor to mill: The West Riding in transition' in Berg,
    et al. (eds.), Town and Country, pp. 124–44. The following is based on the contributions of
    Walton, Hudson, and Marshall in the important collection, Hudson (ed.), Regions and
    Industries; A.P. Wadsworth and J. de L. Mann, The Cotton Trade and Industrial Lancashire,
    1600–1780 (Manchester, 1965); A. Rogers, 'Industrialisation and the local community', in
    S. Pollard (ed.), Region und Indusrialisierung (Göttingen, 1980), pp. 196–208.
65 The preceding has relied on the excellent discussion in Brewer, Sinews of Power, pp.
    191–2. For the 1690s, see D.W. Jones, 'The economic consequences of William III', in
    J. Black (ed.), Knights Errant and True Englishmen: British Foreign Policy, 1660–1800
    (Edinburgh, 1989), pp. 24–39; idem, 'Sequel to revolution: The economics of
    England's emergence as a Great Power, 1688–1712', in J.I. Israel (ed.), The
    Anglo-Dutch Moment (Cambridge 1991), pp.389–406. For crime, see D. Hay, 'War,
    dearth and theft in the eighteenth century', Past & Present, 95 (1982), pp. 117–60.
66 Brewer, Sinews of Power, pp. 191–2. See also, J. Hoppit, Risk and Failure in English
    Business, 1700–1800 (Cambridge, 1988), ch. 6; T.S. Ashton, Economic Fluctuations in
    England, 1700–1800 (Oxford, 1959), ch. 3.
67 For the importance and pervasiveness of credit, see J. Hoppit, 'The use and abuse of
    credit in eighteenth-century England', in N. McKendrick, et al. (eds.), Business Life
    and Public Policy (Cambridge, 1986), pp. 64–78; J.M. Price, Capital and Credit in British
    Overseas Trade: The View from the Chesapeake, 1700–1776 (Cambridge, Mass., 1980);
    B.A. Holderness, 'Credit in the rural community, 1660–1800', Midland History, 3
    (1978), pp. 94–115.
68 N. McKendrick, 'The consumer revolution of eighteenth-century England' in idem, et
    al., The Birth of a Consumer Society: The Commercialization of Eighteenth-Century
    England (1982), pp. 9–22. For a critique, see B. Fine and E. Leopold, 'Consumerism
    and the Industrial Revolution', Social History, 15 (1990), pp. 151–79.
69 Ironically, transport improvements and industrialization also served to accentuate
    distinctions between regions by making them more specialized. See J. Langton, 'The

industrial revolution and the regional geography of England', *Transactions of the Institute of British Geographers*, 9 (1984), pp. 149–62. For transport improvements see Langford, *Polite and Commercial*, pp. 391–410; T.S. Willan, *River Navigation in England, 1600–1750* (1936); idem, *The English Coasting Trade, 1600–1750* (Manchester, 1967 edn.); J.A. Chartres, *Internal Trade in England, 1500–1700* (1977), ch. 3.

70 The following is based on Earle, *Middle Class*, ch. 10; L. Weatherill, *Consumer Behaviour and Material Culture in Britain, 1660–1760* (1988), esp. chs. 2–4, 8.

71 Of course, few unskilled labourers left inventories and the sample is small. Weatherill, *Consumer Behaviour*, pp. 174–6. Many on low incomes provided a 'second tier' of consumer demand for secondhand goods and clothing. B. Lemire, 'Consumerism in pre-industrial and early industrial England: The trade in second hand clothes', *Journal of British Studies*, 27 (1988), pp. 1–24.

72 Earle and Weatherill part company on the motivations behind consumption. Earle and McKendrick argue that changing patterns of consumption are a function of social emulation, London and discussions of fashion playing an important role in the argument. Weatherill and Campbell argue that material consumption reflects class and gender objectives and regional circumstances. In addition to Earle and Weatherill, see also, N. McKendrick, 'The commercialization of fashion', in *Consumer Society*; C. Campbell, *The Romantic Ethic and the Spirit of Modern Consumerism* (Oxford, 1987), ch. 2.

73 Weatherill, *Consumer Behaviour*, pp. 40–60.

74 See H.C. and L.H. Mui, *Shops and Shopkeeping in Eighteenth-Century England* (1989), ch. 2 and Appendix I; Brewer, *Sinews of Power*, pp. 183–4; I. Mitchell, 'The development of urban retailing, 1700–1815', in P. Clark (ed.), *Transformation*, pp. 259–83.

75 The 'rise of the professions' was also a consequence of the growing fiscal-military state. See, G.S. Holmes, *Augustan England: Professions, State and Society, 1680–1730* (1983); Brewer, *Sinews of Power*, ch. 3.

76 Earle, *Middle Class*, pp. 51–60; P. Clark, *The English Alehouse: A Social History, 1200–1830* (1983); B. Lillywhite, *London Coffee-Houses* (1963); A.M. Everitt, 'The English urban inn, 1560–1760' in idem (ed.), *Perspectives in English Urban History* (1973), pp. 104–18.

77 For the commercialization of leisure and urban culture, see J. H. Plumb, 'The commercialization of leisure' in McKendrick, *Consumer Society*; P. Borsay, 'The English urban renaissance: The development of provincial urban culture, c. 1680–1760', *Social History*, 5 (1977), pp. 581–603; idem, *Urban Renaissance*. See also A. McInnes, 'The emergence of a leisure town: Shrewsbury, 1660–1760', *Past & Present*, 120 (1988), pp. 53–87; Corfield, *Towns*, ch. 4; R.S. Neale, *Bath: A Social History, 1680–1850* (1981).

78 For a critique of the commercialization thesis, see J. Barry, 'Popular culture in seventeenth-century Bristol', in B. Reay (ed.), *Popular Culture in Seventeenth-Century England* (1985), pp. 91–128; idem, 'Provincial town culture, 1640–1780: Urbane or civic?', in A. Wear and J. Pittok-Weston (eds.), *New Directions in Cultural History* (1990). See also Earle, *Middle Class*, pp. 57–60.

79 For our definition, see above, note 12. The following discussion of the divisions and stratifications within the middle class has been informed by Langford, *Polite and Commercial*, pp. 71–6; Rogers, 'Age of improvement'.

80 See, e.g., H. Horwitz, 'Party in a civic context: London from the Exclusion Crisis to the fall of Walpole', in Jones, *First Age of Party*, pp. 173–94; idem, '"The mess of the middle class" revisited: The case of the big bourgeoisie of Augustan England', *Continuity and Change*, 2 (1987), pp. 263–96; De Krey, *Fractured Society*; Rogers, *Whigs and Cities*.

81 For a general discussion of the personnel and professionalization of state office, see Holmes, *Augustan England*, especially chs. 8–9. For civil administration in the fiscal-military state, see Brewer, *Sinews of Power*, ch. 3. For the effect of war on the economy, see Jones, *War and Economy*. See also the introduction in H. Roseveare, *The Treasury, 1660–1870* (1973). For the army, see J. Childs, *The British Army of William III* (Manchester, 1987); T. Hayter, *The Army and the Crowd in Mid-Georgian England* (Totowa, N.J., 1978).

82 Holmes, *Augustan England*, pp. 239, 255. For specific estimates on the size of various departments, see Brewer, *Sinews of Power*, pp. 66–9. See also J.H. Plumb, *The Growth of Political Stability*, esp. ch. 4.

83 See Brewer, *Sinews of Power*, ch. 3. Brewer notes that this opportunity was open to only a small proportion of the middle and lower classes, *ibid.*, p. 217. See also Holmes, *Augustan England*, pp. 244–5.

84 Dickson, *The Financial Revolution*, provides a detailed examination of this process. See also J. Hoppit, 'Financial crises in eighteenth-century England', *Economic History Review*, 2nd ser., 39 (1986), pp. 38–59; *idem*, 'Attitudes to credit in Britain, 1680–1790', *Historical Journal*, 33, (1990), pp. 305–23; S.R. Cope, 'The Stock Exchange revisited: A new look at the market in securities in London in the eighteenth century', *Economica*, 45 (1978), pp. 1–21. For parliamentary regulation of the financial revolution, see L. Davison, 'Public policy in an age of economic expansion: The search for commercial accountability in England, 1690–1750', (Harvard Univ. Ph.D. thesis, 1990), chs. 1–5.

85 See Brewer, *Sinews of Power*, esp. chs. 4 and 7. See also P. O'Brien, 'The political economy of British taxation, 1660–1815', *Economic History Review*, 2nd ser., 41 (1988), pp. 1–32; J.V. Beckett, 'Land tax or excise: the levying of taxation in seventeenth- and eighteenth-century England', *English Historical Review*, (1985), pp. 285–308. On the land tax, see M. Turner and D. Mills (eds.), *Land and Property: The English Land Tax 1692–1832* (New York, 1986). On customs tariffs, see R. Davis, 'Rise of protection'.

86 See Brooks, 'Taxation, finance and public opinion'; Brewer, *Sinews of Power*, p. 82.

87 The following discussion of the burden of direct taxation and the excise is based on Beckett, 'Land tax'; O'Brien, 'British taxation'; Brewer, *Sinews of Power*, pp. 211–17.

88 On smuggling, see P. Monod, 'Dangerous merchandise: smuggling, jacobitism, and commercial culture in Southeast England, 1690–1760', *Journal of British Studies*, 30 (1991), pp. 150–82; R.C. Nash, 'The English and Scottish tobacco trades in the seventeenth and eighteenth centuries: Legal and illegal trades', *Economic History Review*, 2nd ser., 35 (1982), pp. 354–72; H.C. and L.H. Mui, 'Trends in eighteenth-century smuggling reconsidered', *Economic History Review*, 2nd ser., 28 (1975), pp. 28–43; W.A. Cole, 'The arithmetic of eighteenth-century smuggling: A rejoinder', *Economic History Review*, 2nd ser., 28 (1975), pp. 44–9; C. Winslow, 'Sussex smugglers' in D. Hay, *et al.*, *Albion's Fatal Tree: Crime and Society in Eighteenth-Century England* (1975), pp. 119–66.

89 Langford, *Polite and Commercial*, p. 722. For lobbying and the role of interests, see below chapters 1–3.

90 B. Kemp, *King and Commons*, (1957); pp. 116–19. See also, J.P. Kenyon, *The Stuart Constitution: 1603–1688* (Cambridge, 1966), ch. 12; J. Carter, 'Law, courts and constitution', in J.R. Jones (ed.), *The Restored Monarchy, 1660–1688* (1979), pp. 71–93.

91 These calculations are based on the data presented in J. Innes and J. Styles, 'The "Bloody Code" in context: eighteenth century criminal legislation reconsidered' (unpublished paper, 1984), graphs 1 and 2. Our thanks to the authors for allowing us to draw on some of their tentative conclusions. The 1690s appear to be a transitional decade for legislative enactment, as it was not until after 1700 that the success rate consistently topped 50 per cent.

92 D. Lieberman, *The Province of Legislation Determined* (Cambridge, 1989), especially ch. 9. See also Langford, *Polite and Commercial*, p. 709; Brewer, *Sinews of Power*, p. 231; Innes, 'Social Policy'.
93 Langford, *Polite and Commercial*, p. 706.
94 For party politics, see the reference above, note 16.
95 See Speck, 'The electorate'; *idem, Whig and Tory*; G.S. Holmes, 'The electorate and the national will in the first age of party', reprinted in *idem, Politics, Religion and Society in England, 1679–1742* (1986), pp. 1–34.
96 Langford, 'Virtual Representation'. See also, Colley, *In Defiance of Oligarchy*, p. 128.
97 Two examples can be found in Sir John Barnard and Edward Clarke. See Brewer, *Sinews of Power*, p. 233; L. Davison and T. Keirn, 'John Locke, Edward Clarke and the 1696 Guineas legislation', *Parliamentary History*, 7 (1988), pp. 228–40; and below, ch. 2. For a discussion of other MPs working for constituents, see J.V. Beckett, 'A back-bench M.P. in the eighteenth century: Sir James Lowther of Whitehaven', *Parliamentary History*, 1 (1982), pp. 79–97; C. Brooks, 'Interest, patronage and professionalism: John, 1st Baron Ashburnham, Hastings and the revenue service', *Southern History*, 9 (1987), pp. 51–70. See also T.K. Moore and H. Horwitz, 'Who runs the House? Aspects of parliamentary organization in the late seventeenth century', *Journal of Modern History*, 43 (1971), pp. 205–27.
98 We are grateful to John Styles for providing us with a copy of his unpublished paper, 'Interest groups, lobbying and Parliament in eighteenth-century England' (1986) from which much material is drawn. See also Brewer, *Sinews of Power*, ch. 8, and below chapters 1 and 2.
99 For lobbying efforts a century earlier, see I. Archer, 'The London lobbies in the late sixteenth century', *Historical Journal*, 31 (1988), pp. 17–44; D.M. Dean, 'Public or private? London, leather and legislation in Elizabethan England', *Historical Journal*, 31 (1988), pp. 525–48. See also *Parliamentary History*, 8, pt. 2 (1989), a special issue focusing on interest groups and legislation in Elizabethan parliaments.
100 Brewer, *Sinews of Power*, p. 227; S. Lambert, 'Printing for the House of Commons in the eighteenth century', *Library*, 23 (1968), pp. 25–46; M. Harris, *London Newspapers in the Age of Walpole* (1987); J. Black (ed.), *Politics and the Press in Hanoverian England* (Lewiston, N.Y., 1989); G.A. Cranfield, *The Development of the Provincial Newspaper: 1700–60* (Oxford, 1962); G.C. Gibbs, 'Government and the English press: 1695 to the middle of the eighteenth century' in A.C. Duke and C.A. Tamse (eds.), *Too Mighty to Be Free: Censorship and the Press in Britain and the Netherlands* (Zutphen, 1987), pp. 87–106.
101 On poor relief generally, see P. Slack, *Poverty and Policy*; S. and B. Webb, *English Poor Law History: Part I, The Old Poor Law* (1927). For Corporations of the Poor, see Macfarlane, 'Social policy'; and below ch. 7. For workhouses, see Hitchcock, 'English workhouse'; and below ch. 6. On houses of correction, see J. Innes, 'Prisons for the poor: English bridewells, 1555–1800', in F. Snyder and D. Hay (eds.), *Labour, Law and Crime: A Historical Perspective* (1987), pp. 42–122.
102 On vagrancy, though for an earlier period, see A.L. Beier, *Masterless Men: The Vagrancy Problem in England, 1560–1640* (1985). On settlement procedures, see N. Landau, 'The laws of settlement and the surveillance of immigration in eighteenth-century Kent', *Continuity and Change*, 3 (1988) pp. 391–420; *idem*, 'The regulation of immigration, economic structures and definitions of the poor in eighteenth-century England', *Historical Journal*, 33 (1990), pp. 541–72. The number of works on crime is voluminous. The literature is surveyed in J. Innes and J. Styles, 'The crime wave: Recent writing on crime and criminal justice in eighteenth-century England', *Journal of British Studies*, 25 (1986), pp. 380–435. The most wide-ranging recent work is J.M. Beattie, *Crime and the Courts in England* (Oxford, 1986). For concern about petty crime see R.B. Shoemaker, *Prosecution and Punishment*. See also below chapters 3 and 4.

103 On local government see Webb, *Local Government*. More recent studies include
     Fletcher, *Reform in the Provinces*; G.C.F. Forster, 'Government in provincial England
     under the later Stuarts', *Transactions of the Royal Historical Society*, 5th ser., 33 (1983),
     pp. 29–48; L.K.J. Glassey, 'Local government', in Jones, *First Age of Party*, pp.
     151–72; J.M. Rosenheim, 'County governance and elite withdrawal in Norfolk,
     1660–1720', in A.L. Beier, *et al.* (eds.), *The First Modern Society* (Cambridge, 1989),
     pp. 95–126. On JPs, see N. Landau, *The Justices of the Peace, 1679–1760*; L.K.J.
     Glassey, *Politics and the Appointment of Justices of the Peace* (Oxford, 1985).

104 Innes, 'Social Policy', p. 67.

105 Workhouses provide a good example, see below, ch. 7.

106 Fletcher, *Reform in the Provinces*, p. 116. See also E. Moir, *The Justice of the Peace*
     (Harmondsworth, 1969), pp. 15–42; Landau, *Justices*, pp. 6–7.

107 Landau, *Justices*, p. 26; Glassey, 'Local Government', p. 160.

108 Fletcher, *Reform in the Provinces*, p. 359; Landau, *Justices*, pp. 7–8, 39. For a contrary
     view, see Glassey, 'Local Government', pp. 170–1.

109 E.G. Dowdell, *A Hundred Years of Quarter Sessions* (Cambridge, 1932), pp. 190–2;
     Forster, 'Government in provincial England', p. 37–8; Landau, *Justices*, p. 37.

110 F.A. Youngs Jr., 'Towards petty sessions: Tudor JPs and divisions of counties' in D.J.
     Guth and J.W. McKenna (eds.) *Tudor Rule and Revolution* (Cambridge, 1982), pp.
     201–16; Landau, *Justices*, pp. 27–8, 213; Fletcher, *Reform in the Provinces*, pp. 122–35.

111 Landau, *Justices*, pp. 213–14, and sources cited therein; Glassey, 'Local government',
     pp. 161–2.

112 Fletcher, *Reform in the Provinces*, pp. 124–31; R.B. Shoemaker, 'Crime, courts and
     community: The prosecution of misdemeanors in Middlesex County, 1663–1723',
     (Stanford Univ. Ph.D. thesis, 1986), pp. 54–7; Landau, *Justices*, pp. 214–15.

113 Landau, *Justices*, pp. 219–20, 252–3; Shoemaker, *Prosecution and Punishment*, sect.
     9.2; and, see below ch. 2.

114 For the creation of the civil parish, one of the oldest works and still one of the best is
     E.M. Leonard, *The Early History of English Poor Relief* (Cambridge, 1900). See also the
     works of S. and B. Webb cited above, note 24. More recent relevant studies include P.
     Slack, *The Impact of Plague in Tudor and Stuart England* (1985); idem, *Poverty and
     Policy*; J. Pound, *Poverty and Vagrancy in Tudor England* (1971). See also J. Barry, 'The
     parish in civic life: Bristol and its churches, 1640–1750' in S.J. Wright (ed.), *Parish,
     Church and People: Local Studies in Lay Religion 1350–1750* (1988), pp. 152–78.

115 Slack, *Poverty and Policy*, p. 170.

116 Snell notes examinations under the settlement laws were intended to investigate those
     applying for or in imminent need of poor relief. Snell, *Annals*, pp. 17–19. Landau has
     recently argued that the settlement laws were a means to regulate immigration.
     Landau, 'The laws of settlement' and *idem*, 'The regulation of immigration'. See also
     Finlay and Shearer, 'Population growth', pp. 37–59.

117 See Hitchcock, 'English workhouse'.

118 See Macfarlane, 'Social policy', and below ch. 6. See also Forster, 'Government in
     provincial England', p. 39.

119 Political squabbling within a municipal corporation is best documented for London.
     See Horwitz, 'Civic context', pp. 173–94; De Krey, *Fractured Society*, chs. 5–6; I.G.
     Doolittle, 'Walpole's City Elections Act', *English Historical Review*, 97 (1983), pp.
     504–29; N. Rogers, 'The City Elections Act (1725) reconsidered', *English Historical
     Review*, 100 (1985), pp. 604–17.

120 As Borsay has recently noted, research on the role of town authorities in civic
     improvement is surprisingly thin. See the 'introduction' to Borsay, *Eighteenth-Century
     Town*, pp. 22–5. On urban improvement, reprinted in the same volume, see E.L. Jones
     and M.E. Falkus, 'Urban improvement and the English economy in the seventeenth

and eighteenth centuries', pp. 116–58. For some discussion of municipal government, see Corfield, *English Towns*, ch. 9.

121 P. Clark, *Sociability and Urbanity: Clubs and Societies in the Eighteenth-Century City* (Leicester, 1986), pp. 5–7.

122 For the reformation of manners movement, see G.V. Portus, *Caritas Anglicana* (1912); D.W.R. Bahlmann, *The Moral Revolution of 1688* (New Haven, 1957); A.G. Craig, 'The movement for the reformation of manners, 1688–1715', (Edinburgh Univ. Ph.D. thesis, 1980); W. Speck and T. Curtis, 'Societies for the Reformation of Manners', *Literature and History*, 3 (1976), pp. 45–62. For a discussion of the revival of the movement in the latter part of the century, see J. Innes, 'Politics and morals: The reformation of manners movement in later eighteenth-century England', in E. Hellmuth (ed.), *The Transformation of Political Culture: England and Germany in the Late Eighteenth Century* (Oxford, 1990). See also below ch. 5. For the SPCK, see below ch. 7, and L.W. Cowie, *Henry Newman: An American in London* (1959).

123 See O.P. Grell, *et al.* (eds.), *From Persecution to Toleration: the Glorious Revolution and Religion in England* (Oxford, 1991); J. Spurr, 'The Church of England, comprehension and the Toleration Act of 1689', *English Historical Review*, 104 (1989), pp. 927–46; M.R. Watts, *The Dissenters* (Oxford, 1978), ch. 4; G.V. Bennett, 'Conflict in the Church', in Holmes (ed.), *Britain after the Glorious Revolution*, pp. 155–75.

124 Religious societies existed before the Glorious Revolution, but met privately. Some religious societies had been established in London around 1678, but these societies had little effect outside their membership. The relationship between these societies and those formed a decade later is unclear, but they did have active members in common. Craig, pp. 85–93.

125 See Hayton, 'Moral reform'.

126 See below, ch. 5.

127 See below, ch. 5, and Shoemaker, *Prosecution and Punishment*, ch. 9. See also T. Isaacs, 'The Anglican hierarchy and the reformation of manners, 1688–1738', *Journal of Ecclesiastical History*, 33 (1982), pp. 391–411; Bahlmann, *Moral Revolution*, pp. 86–99.

128 On charity schools, see M.G. Jones, *The Charity School Movement, A Study in Eighteenth Century Puritanism in Action* (Cambridge, 1938); J. Simon, 'Was there a charity school movement', in B. Simon (ed.), *Education in Leicestershire: A Regional Study* (Leicester, 1968); R. Unwin, *Charity Schools and the Defence of Anglicanism: James Talbot, Rector of Spufforth 1700–08*, Borthwick Papers, 65 (1984).

Part One: Industry

1

Parliament, Legislation and the Regulation of English Textile Industries, 1689–1714

Tim Keirn
California State University, Long Beach

England's own Productions is the Foundation of all its Wealth, Navigation and Merchandize; and the due Improvement thereof, especially in the Wooll, is what ought to be principally regarded and promoted; and the Packs in the Honourable House of Lords bespeak no less.[1]

The Nine Years War (1689–97) and the War of Spanish Succession (1702–13) dominated the last 25 years of Stuart rule as the waging of war made unprecedented demands on finance, manpower and resources, and significantly affected English politics, society and the economy.[2] Prolonged war with France brought particular problems to labourers, manufacturers and merchants employed in English textile industries. Disruptions brought to overseas markets by attacks on merchant shipping, movements of large numbers of troops, and international monetary instability brought volatility and depression to the export performance of English textiles, especially to that of woollen fabrics, the most important export item. Contemporaries decried the situation whereby the high wartime costs of cloth encouraged foreign entrepreneurs to exploit 'such Inconveniences to promote their own Woollen Manufacturers at Home,' diminishing the extent of overseas markets.[3] Imports of raw and semi-finished factors of production were also imperilled by wartime uncertainties in overseas markets, most notably in the case of supplies of dyestuffs and raw silk and thread. Moreover, stiff increases in domestic levels of taxation, and periodic bad harvests and shortages of silver currency damaged levels of disposable income and diminished demand for textile products in the home market.[4] While important for woollen textile producers, the home market was vital to the prosperity of the fledgling silk-, cotton- and flax-based industries, where growing English consumption of non-woollen textiles during the later decades of the seventeenth century was being increasingly met by domestic production.[5]

Thus, the age of William III and Anne was a period of economic crisis for most of those involved in English textile production. Increasingly, textile merchants and manufacturers turned to Parliament for solutions to their commercial distress. The following case study will examine the parliamentary regulation of the textile trades and industries during the late seventeenth and early eighteenth centuries, paying close attention to the type of legislation initiated, the process of legislating, and the economic ideas informing parliamentary decision making on commercial policy issues.

The process of commercial policy making in Parliament was extremely fragmentary and usually instigated by private interest groups without government direction (except, notably, in revenue matters). Indeed, as we shall see, textile bills were instigated by an extensive variety of sectional interests. In this sense, the state's involvement in economic affairs was 'reactive'; that is, it took little interest in directing economic affairs and acted only when spurred by the initiatives of interested groups and individuals from London and the provinces. The reactive nature of the state, in conjunction with the rise of Parliament as the key policy-making body within government, allowed for relatively open access and broad participation in the formulation of economic measures at the end of the seventeenth century. As a consequence, economic legislation in general, and textile legislation in particular, was rarely consistent or systematically integrated with other statutes, and was threatened by repeal or revision with any change in the partisan or sectional composition of the Commons.[6]

Broadly speaking, decision making in respect to the regulation of the economy in the seventeenth century was transformed from a conciliar process of policy formulation to a parliamentary one. Economic policy in Tudor and early Stuart times mainly derived from the small and relatively private confines of the Privy Council; the economy was regulated more by edict and proclamation than by statute. Yet as the influence of the Privy Council began to wane in the late seventeenth century, its role as a policy maker was taken over by Parliament, a move which was much enhanced by the certainty and regularity of legislative meetings after the Glorious Revolution.[7]

As a consequence of the constitutional and financial settlements of the Glorious Revolution and the growing costs of government during the long continental wars of William III and Anne, Parliament met every year after 1689. Furthermore, sessions were of longer duration as the concept of a fixed parliamentary session became institutionalized in the 1690s, with the legislature convening in the late autumn and adjourning (usually) in the late spring. This schedule suited the needs of William III who prorogued

Parliament to lead troops in the fields of Ireland and Flanders in the summer months. Moreover, troops could not be put in the field without funds, and it was this necessity and the priority of extensive programmes of fiscal legislation which also contributed to the length and regularity of the parliamentary session.[8] Sessions were not ended until all major supply bills had been concluded. As a result, by the beginning of the eighteenth century, the termination of each session became increasingly predictable to MPs who could assess their own legislative strategies – say to initiate a new bill or to forestall one in progress – on the basis of the perceived progress of revenue legislation.

The onset of annual sessions of Parliament of a longer duration and an anticipated termination date had two important ramifications. First, it expanded the ability of Parliament to legislate, which was in turn reflected in the growing number of bills initiated and acts passed in each session. Beginning in the 1690s, there was a considerable increase in the workload of the legislature on a year to year basis when compared with the output of the Cavalier Parliament.[9] Secondly, increasing sophistication in legislative management by Crown and sectorial interests alike, in conjunction with the extended duration of parliamentary sessions, led to a marked increase in the success rate of legislation (manifest in a ratio of acts-to-bills per session) from the 1690s into the middle of the eighteenth century. In the reign of Charles II the ratio was well below 50 per cent, in that of Anne it hovered close to 75 per cent.[10]

These general legislative trends were also paralleled in parliamentary consideration of textile bills. In the period 1689 to 1714, the number of pieces of legislation concerned directly with textile industries increased dramatically. Between 1660 and 1685, Parliament considered 67 textile bills, a workload which nearly doubled (concurrent with general legislative trends) to 122 bills during the period 1689–1714.[11] Again in line with general trends, only 27 per cent of these bills passed in the former period compared with a success rate of 66 per cent during the reign of Queen Anne. The 1690s were again transitional as 82 textile bills were considered, only 40 per cent reaching the statute book. The heightened volume of legislation pertaining to English textile industries during the reign of William III clearly reflects both the crisis economic conditions of the 1690s relative to the greater economic stability experienced during the reign of Anne, and the experimental nature of the decade in regards to legislation, which witnessed growth in both the numbers and types of bills submitted.[12]

Legislative regulation of the economy of England in the late seventeenth and early eighteenth centuries generally reflected four overlapping objectives: to promote domestic tranquillity; to procure revenue to meet the growing expenditure requirements of the state; to support domestic industry and manufacturing to maintain high employment levels; and finally, to protect and enhance the volume of the nation's overseas trade. As the most important manufacturing sector in the early modern English economy, textile production, especially that of woollen cloth, encompassed all of these regulatory intentions, in one way or another. The situation was confused, however, by the fact that there was no homogeneous English textile interest, but rather a plethora of often competing sectional interests, divided by regional specialization, product differentiation, occupational divisibility, and highly competitive overseas and domestic markets. There was often little cooperation (and indeed much antagonism) to be found between woollen, linen, lace and silk producers over policy objectives. Indeed, even within the woollen textile sector, the West Country serge manufacturers did not necessarily see eye-to-eye with the bay clothiers of East Anglia or the broadcloth producers of Yorkshire. Added to this was the traditional conflict of interest between the manufacturer, his source of raw material, the seller of his produce, and his labour force. These conflicts were reflected in the differing legislative agendas of landowners, clothiers, merchants, and weavers.

From this complex amalgam of motives, objectives and interests came a large number of parliamentary bills and statutes which were directly concerned with the regulation of textile manufacture. Historians in the past, such as Ashley, Lipson and Cherry, have characterized the period 1689 to 1714 as one where economic legislation increasingly moved towards a position of free trade and laissez faire. More recently, Ekelund and Tollison have argued that the 'Rise of Parliament' in the late seventeenth century was counterbalanced by the 'decline of mercantilism', seeing the period as one of 'significant deregulation of the economy'.[13] On the other hand, scholars such as Davis, Cooper, Harte, and Appleby have characterized the period as one of economic protectionism and more virulent 'mercantilism'.[14]

From the general analysis of textile legislation, it would appear that none of these positions is entirely satisfactory. As noted, the volume of parliamentary regulation of English textile manufacturing increased quite significantly in the late seventeenth and early eighteenth centuries as measured by the number of bills initiated and statutes enacted. Yet, many of these new statutes acted as vehicles for deregulation. For example, statutes were passed liberalizing the export of broadcloth by first breaking the monopoly of the Hamburg Company in 1689, followed later by that of the Russia Company in 1699.[15] Moreover, in 1700, the ancient aulnage duty on cloth was finally removed in agreement with the contemporary view that: 'It hath been thought of Intelligent Persons that the Woollen Manufactures (and all other native products) should be exported free . . .

from all Impost and charge . . . the recompense may be made by Impost upon some forren commodity.'[16] Indeed, throughout the 1690s, clothiers and weavers lobbied MPs, organized petitioning campaigns, and argued in the press 'to lessen the aulnage burden to support the cloth trade'. Seven previous legislative attempts to either abolish the aulnage or 'make it payable to the custom house', instead of to the private collectors of the patentee (the Duchess of Richmond), met with effective opposition, especially in the House of Lords where one bill was defeated and another died in committee.[17] The actual abolition of the aulnage in 1700 without obstruction in the Lords may reflect that the initiative was tacked on to a money bill. In addition to the aulnage, the bill removed all remaining export duties on cloth and on grain as well, much to the benefit of the personal estates of landed MPs and peers.[18]

Beginning in the 1690s, statutes were also enacted which freed restrictions on the supply of some raw and semi-finished materials. In 1690, the Levant Company, working in tandem with the London silkthrowers and West Country clothiers with interests in the Turkey trade, managed to obtain a statute limiting the import of silk thread into England to Italian sources (and only by sea), permitting only the import of raw silk from Turkey, Persia and Asia. The Levant Company argued that imports of raw silk made up 75 per cent of their imports, a trade which was threatened by the import of silk thread, negatively affecting the company's ability to sell English cloth in Turkey. The Silkthrowers complained that the import of silk thread threatened the livelihoods of 200,000 workers and their families.[19] However, in 1694, the London merchants trading to Italy, in coalition with the London and Canterbury silk weavers, and the Royal Lustring Company, obtained a statute exempting the Italian trade in silk thread from the Navigation Acts, allowing this trade to proceed overland and through Holland to avoid the wartime disruptions to trade in the Mediterranean. Parliament failed to acknowledge the objections of the Levant Company (who feared that such an exemption would facilitate the illicit trading of Levant goods via the Netherlands), but fell sway in committee to arguments stressing the importance of the domestic silk industry to the balance of trade, the damage done to silk manufacture by shortages of high quality thread, and the superiority of numbers of weavers and their families when compared to the silkthrowers.[20] Two similar statutes were enacted in 1702 permitting the import of Italian and Neapolitan silk thread from any port, excluding those at war with England.[21] Cloth manufacturers and dyers also sought exemptions from the Navigation Acts to increase supplies and to lower the wartime costs of essential raw materials. In 1708, the importation of cochineal was permitted in Spanish vessels without payment of alien duty against the objections of English merchants in the Spanish trade.[22]

Yet on close examination, it would appear that most textile bills in this period sought to expand the regulatory apparatus applicable to textile manufacturing. Most of this legislation was of a local and particular nature. Nevertheless, most legislation affecting English textiles had the objective of either enhancing the export performance of a particular textile product, or protecting that product from imports. Export performance, and its perceived positive correlation with the balance of trade, and correspondingly the level of employment, was clearly a priority of most pieces of legislation concerned with woollen textiles, and was restated repeatedly in petitions, pamphlets, and in preambles to bills and statutes.[23]

For example, virtually all commentators condemned the illicit export of English and Irish wool to overseas competitors (wool exports having been prohibited since the early seventeenth century) as a major contribution to the ill fortunes of the domestic woollen industry. It was a contemporary maxim that England's wool was 'a Treasure greater than Spain's Mines' and that 'keeping our Wool from being exported into Forein Parts, is allowed by all Woollen Manufacturers to be the only means to frustrate the French, or any other Nation to rival us in our Woollen Goods'.[24] Between 1689 and 1714, there was virtually no vocal opposition to prohibiting the export of wool, despite its potentially detrimental impact on wool prices and landed rents. While there was no unitary 'landed interest' amongst parliamentary lobbyists, nonetheless advocates for the strict suppression of wool exports were careful to make clear correlations between the prosperity of trade and industry and that of land and agriculture.[25]

Parliament struggled with the challenge of prohibiting (and enforcing) the export of raw wool in numerous sessions, considering fourteen bills to this effect in the 1690s and on three occasions during the reign of Anne. Bills were enacted attempting to strengthen prohibitions on the export of English wool and fullers earth by a number of devices, including increasing and establishing regular naval surveillance of shipping movements along the Kentish and Sussex coasts, registering coastwise trafficking of wool, and implementing more efficient monitoring of overland movements of wool in coastal areas (e.g., prohibiting the transport of wool after dark). In 1689, a body of wool commissioners was established to oversee the enforcement of the ban on wool exports.[26]

Indeed, MPs and government officials were swamped with vast numbers of 'projects' submitted by clothiers, wool factors, customs officers and professional 'projectors'.[27] Many of these projects addressed contemporary dissatisfaction with the wool commissioners, who lacked the salaries and resources to regulate the 'Corruption of Officers' and the 'Avarice of Traders'.[28] Projected bills sought to expand the authority of the wool commissioners to all maritime towns and to increase salaries to all officers; others sought to reinstate capital punishment (recently repealed in the case of wool exporting) for 'Owlers' ought to be 'hung like a Thief, a Traitor and a Murderer'.[29] It would appear some of these projects were drafted into actual pieces of legislation. The Taunton MP Edward Clarke received numerous 'Heads of Proposals' for legislation to restrict 'owling', and drafted a bill (which apparently failed) to punish wool smugglers with transportation to the colonies. Clarke also had a hand in drafting the 1696 statute which restricted Irish wool imports to designated English ports.[30]

In addition to the pernicious practice of wool exporting, contemporaries also felt that export performance suffered from the declining reputation of English textile quality in overseas markets. The Gloucestershire clothier and pamphleteer John Blanch remarked in 1694 that:

> If one cloth in ten be made of false materials, it will very much disparage the other nine. The complaint of one man abused with English Cloth, will make a greater noise against us [in foreign markets] than several that are well used will retrieve.[31]

Complaints were widespread regarding the use of poor quality materials, the straining and stretching of cloth, and the use of unskilled and unapprenticed labour. Many saw this as the end result of a lack of regulation in production. As one anonymous pamphleteer noted:

> The whole of this [problem] being sufficiently confirmed by those many good statutes formerly made to guard it against all Inconveniences; but as the worthy Makers of those good Laws are now asleep, so are their Laws too, and every Man's Rule is freely become his own choice; nay the greatest trial of skill of late Years has been, who could make the Worst Cloth, which I think doth justly call for the Inspection of this present Parliament.[32]

Consequently, a large number of pieces of legislation loosely entitled 'bills for regulating the woollen manufacture' were submitted in this period. Much of this new statutory regulation was initiated simply to replace (or reinforce) that which was once (or was still) provided by municipal corporations or industrial companies whose control over the quality of manufacture, and the enforcement of apprenticeship, was declining in the late seventeenth century. The poor success rate of this type of legislation perhaps reflects the legislator's recognition of the difficulties involved in establishing an effective regulatory machinery regarding the quality of output.

In 1709, an act to be enforced by the fullers imposed a standard size on Yorkshire broadcloth to protect against straining.[33] In 1712, in response to the complaints of the drapers of Gloucestershire and Somerset, a similar piece of legislation concerning medley cloth was enacted into law. Soon many drapers complained that the provisions of the 1712 Act were easily avoided for 'these Mill-men are not at all qualified for so great a Trust, because of their constant Dependence upon the Clothiers for their Employment.' In 1714, a bill to transfer enforcement from local fullers to the factors at Blackwell Hall was initiated by the drapers but was opposed by the clothiers and failed to pass into law.[34] The West Country clothiers' hostility to the factors was vented in legislation against the privileges of Blackwell Hall and its control of the London cloth market. However, an act in 1697 did nothing to rescind the factors' control over the level of quality of cloth exchanged in the metropolis, but did seek to restrict 'private' dealings by the factors after public market hours. In 1699, the clothiers solicited Parliament 'to get the Act enlarged to the greater damage of Blackwell Hall' by curtailing the factors' ability to sell cloth in exchange for credit which often forced clothiers to purchase Spanish wool at disadvantageous prices from the factors on the basis of their credit and lack of ready cash. This bill was not enacted and the legislative conflict between the West Country clothiers and the Blackwell Hall factors continued into the 1720s and 1730s.[35] Again, such regulatory initiatives remained a matter of local option and circumstance. For example, Parliament rejected a call for reinforcement of apprenticeship laws to protect quality in the western serge industry in 1702, yet upheld it for the bay weavers of Colchester in 1715.[36] Legislative solutions to the problem of quality were also imposed on linen production. In response to the 'divers Abuses and Deceits . . . with respect to the Lengths Breadths and unequal sorting of Yarn which tends to the great debasing and under-valuing of Linen Cloth both at Home and in Foreign Parts', the size and quality of Scottish linen was regulated by Parliament in 1712 and 1714.[37]

While much of the legislation pertaining to cloth production dealt specifically with means to promote overseas trade, Parliament also attempted to encourage the consumption of woollen cloth in the home market directly, much to the chagrin of those engaged in non-woollen textile trades. Although most sumptuary laws in England had disappeared in the early seventeenth century, as late as 1666 it was enacted that all were to be buried in a sheet of wool, rather than linen, on penalty of £5 paid by the survivors of the deceased.[38] Legislative attempts to coerce the living into woollen cloth were less successful. A bill in 1689 for 'enjoining the wearing of woollens six months a year' elicited a riotous response from the London silk weavers.[39] Representatives of the London Company of Weavers petitioned the Commons to have their counsel heard. However, the Commons, 'to shew their bravour', refused the petition and passed the bill. When the bill went to the Lords, the 'House was besett with soe numerous and mutinous a rabble, that this day, for their security, they were by their order guarded with 2 companies of the trayne bands.' Members of the Lords attempted to calm the crowd of weavers (numbering by one estimate between 10,000 and 15,000) 'but their eloquence prevalyed very little, the rabble frequently interrupting them with their clamorous shouts'.[40] The weavers were eventually dispersed when convinced that a proviso would be added to the bill, in sympathy with their own petition, seeking to prohibit the wearing of all foreign silk fabrics. The bill was defeated 'unanimously' on its second reading, apparently pressured by the rumour that weavers were fermenting into 'New Tumuls'.[41] In 1709, an anti-sumptuary bill to limit the 'unhappy Custom of frequent and tedious Publick Mournings for Foreign Princes', while stimulating some support in the press from those involved in the silk and lace industries, evoked little interest elsewhere and was defeated in the Commons.[42]

Statutory attempts to control consumption to benefit domestic textile industries, did so principally by restricting or prohibiting foreign imports through protective tariffs or outright prohibitions. Perhaps most notable was the case of Irish cloth. The Irish woollen industry – already bound by the Navigation Acts – was further restricted in 1699 when legislation was enacted prohibiting the import of Irish cloth into English markets in an attempt to protect the home market for West Country serge manufacturers, and to make it easier to restrict illicit exports of Irish cloth to European and North American markets.[43] Between 1685 and 1710, a number of bills were enacted protecting English horn button manufacturers by prohibiting the import of foreign buttons, and in 1699 and 1710 acts were passed at the urging of the Levant Company, suppressing the manufacture of English cloth buttons to encourage the domestic manufacture of buttons with raw silk and mohair.[44]

In the 1690s, the rural producers of lighter woollen fabrics and the silk weavers of London, Norwich and Canterbury mounted a legislative campaign to prohibit the consumption of Asian silk and coloured calicos. In 1697, consideration of such legislation led to another occupation of the lobby of Parliament by the London weavers (this time in support of legislation), and extensive rioting directed against their legislative opponents: the East India Company and the linen drapers.[45] The 1697 bill failed when the Lords and Commons could not agree on a Lords' proviso which sought to extend a proposed ban on Asian textiles to all foreign silks, many MPs then finding the 'mobs bill' too draconian.[46] An Act, narrower in scope, passed in 1700, prohibited the wearing of silk and calico fabrics manufactured and dyed in Persia, China or India, but permitted the import of semi-finished calicos (for dyeing in England) and finished textiles for re-export. The weavers coordinated their legislative strategy with a fiscal measure emanating from the Committee of Ways and Means that implemented a 15 per cent increase in import duties for Asian textiles (dyed and undyed). In a paper presented to Robert Harley, the weavers noted: 'They do not ask for a prohibition of the whole, least they should too much lessen the funds upon which moneys are lent, and because the Imposition may ad what the prohibition takes away.'[47]

It was the general extension of the tariff barrier on the import of finished linens and silks in this period, not alone the embargoes on French trade during wartime, which helped channel home consumption to domestically-produced textiles. For example, the Royal Lustring Company's charter was confirmed by Parliament in 1697, accompanied by a number of statutes implementing restrictive duties on various types of foreign silks (1698), and an outright prohibition on French alamodes (including even those imported from Holland) in 1708.[48] Tariff barriers on imported finished silk of all origins increased throughout the late seventeenth and early eighteenth centuries. Notably, the negotiated commercial clauses of the Treaty of Utrecht, proposing to lower tariff barriers and liberalize trade between Britain and France, were defeated in Parliament in 1713. As a consequence the tariff barrier against French textile imports remained high even in peacetime.[49]

Tariffs on imported linen textiles also increased in this period, including those from Scotland, affording greater protection to English and Irish linen producers.[50] Domestic production of linen was also given direct legislative support in 1692 by providing tithe exemptions for fields sown with flax and hemp.[51] In 1696, the struggling English sailcloth industry gained an exemption from export duties and gained further encouragement in 1713 from legislation which both established a bounty for English sailcloth exports and raised the import duty on Dutch sailcloth. Moreover, the 1696 Act also encouraged the Irish linen industry by removing all English import duties on Irish linen, a promotion which gained greater urgency after the aforesaid Irish cloth exports were prohibited in 1699.[52] In 1705, Irish linen was exempted from the Navigation Acts, which also banned all Scottish linen imports into Ireland. This legislation permitted direct exports of Irish linen to the American colonies, despite the opposition of Scottish and Lancashire linen manufacturers.[53]

The corpus of textile bills and acts to which I have been referring were public as opposed to private pieces of legislation. As noted, they were largely of local origin with little government involvement. The exception to the rule was in the case of tariffs, where the executive had a powerful influence on commercial policy. Customs legislation was usually initiated by direct representation from the Treasury through resolutions in the

Commons Committee on Ways and Means. Passage of the bills emanating from the committee were then 'managed' by the chairman or a government placeman. In an influential article, Davis argued that the 'Rise of Protection' offered through tariffs to English manufacturers in this period was a manifestation of the fiscal necessities of the state: to finance war in the reigns of William III and Anne, and later to lower the land tax and reduce the principal of the national debt under Walpole. According to Davis, this financial imperative overrode any economic-cum-commercial considerations to protect industry, promote exports and to expand employment, over the objections of importing merchants who, as Thomas Tryon noted, sought 'Customs and Imports be made easie for . . . Merchants are . . . the Engines of the Whole Nation, and if encouraged, have an innate power to set all hands at work.'[54]

On closer inspection of the legislative process, it clearly would be foolish to deny the importance of the fiscal priorities of the state in this matter. Indeed, the state's need for revenue and the silk weavers' demand for protection were by no means mutually exclusive. Yet, Parliament did not simply rubber stamp increases in tariff levels without due consideration of their economic and political ramifications.[55] Legislators, as well as lobbyists and government ministers, recognized that the raising of effective tariffs in the name of 'protection' had firm limits. Exorbitantly high rates of duty on imports served the same purpose as an outright prohibition in terms of marginal revenue, lessening trade and instigating smuggling, by which 'the fair Trader must be ruined, our Woollen and other Manufacturers greatly lessen'd in their Consumption, and [also] the Customs, which were given towards payment of the National Debt'.[56] Moreover, taxes on exports were in direct violation of contemporary maxims about facilitating economic expansion and employment through the maintenance of a positive balance of trade.[57] In general, duties on exports during the period were either left alone, reduced or as noted in the case of 'finished' cloth in 1700, abolished.

Given that few had the stomach for the monumental task of wholesale revision of the Book of Rates (last revised in 1660), especially in wartime, the extension of tariffs in the period of 1689 to 1714 was a jumbled and unsystematic affair. The Treasury, and the Committee of Ways and Means, assessed tariffs on a statute by statute, commodity by commodity basis which both reflected and encouraged sectional disputes. Consequently, the formation of customs policy was remarkably open to outside influence. Lobbying in Parliament and in the press by interested parties for and against customs legislation could be vociferous. To a significant extent, Parliament served to adjudicate between the fiscal pleadings of Crown ministers and the desire for tariff protection or free trade among various sectional interest groups.

This can be seen in a number of examples. The ramifications of the repeal of all cloth export duties in 1700 engendered a number of commercial and fiscal problems which initiated pressures for and against further fiscal legislation (or deregulation) between competing factions in the woollen cloth industry. In the spring of 1707, customs officers began to prohibit the export of undyed broadcloth in the belief that an older unrepealed prohibition of 14 & 15 Henry VIII c.3 came into force with the recent expiration of the aulnage patent. The clothiers of Gloucestershire and Wiltshire petitioned Parliament for legislation allowing for the free export of white broadcloth. This was opposed by the dyers and some of the merchants of London who claimed that the export of cloth 'undressed' was a loss of 10 to 15 per cent 'value' on the balance of trade. Out of the committee investigating the validity of the clothiers' claims came two pieces of legislation providing both a compromise between the aggrieved parties and revenue for the state. One act repealed all prohibitions on the export of undressed broadcloth; the other placed a duty of 5 shillings on each broadcloth exported.[58] The former act also cleared up some of the confusion arising out of the expiration of the 1689 Act which had broken the monopoly of the Hamburg Company, the ambiguity of which caused much conflict between merchants in and out of the company trading to Germany.[59]

The expiration of cloth export duties in 1700 had also repealed, reinforcing an earlier statute of 1673, any additional alien duties levied above and beyond those found in the Book of Rates. This raised the xenophobic rancour of merchants seeking additional alien duties on cloth exports to put English merchants 'on an equal foot'. Given the hostility of clothiers to any further 'burden' on exports, legislation to such effect was not passed.[60] On the other hand, Parliament rejected the calls of manufacturers against the interests of the merchants for the removal of various drawbacks on the re-export of dyestuffs, as was the case, for example, in the defeat of the logwood bill, initiated in response to the petitions of the clothiers of the West Country and East Anglia, in 1704.[61]

Moreover, attempts to tamper with the various differentials in linen duties were the occasion for much wrangling between interested parties. In 1706, merchants involved in the Dutch trade failed in a legislative attempt to overturn a favourable rate of duty on German linens in the Book of Rates which discriminated against Dutch and Flemish products. Yet, as Lord Shrewsbury noted privately, Parliament recognized the 'gross mistake' of the discrepancy in the level of duty between German and Dutch linen, yet was 'tender to change the security' of those who lent money to the Crown on customs advanced, and moreover 'we have too many in this nation who cry out, though unjustly, that the Dutch trade with the French and grow rich by this war, this hinders many from consenting to the expedient proposed'. Thus, public credit and political expediency figured highly in Parliament's decision to uphold a discriminating level of tax against Dutch linen.[62]

Partisan politics could, on occasion, also determine the outcome of textile legislation. As noted, between 1689 and 1701, the monopoly of the Hamburg Company was opposed in a number of pieces of legislation, revolving around attempts to have its monopoly reconfirmed. While this was essentially a free trade versus monopoly debate carried out in the press and before Parliament, nonetheless it does not appear to have been a simple contest pitting merchant against manufacturer. The company's charter was supported by the London mercantile community and by the clothiers of the West Riding and East Anglia (who were apparently well served by the company), fearing that without the company's monopoly 'it is to give our woollen trade to foreigners'.[63] The opposition to the company was well organized and centred among West Country clothiers (apparently not well served by the company) and merchants in the western outports. Numerous pamphlets were published and a large number of petitions was circulated in the West Country and submitted to Parliament. Opposition to the company was led by the West Country MPs Sir Walter Yonge and Edward Clarke, the former arguing from a traditional anti-monopoly position that: 'the more hands our cloth is carried out by the better, it raiseth your wool and is for the benefit of the country'.[64] It is notable that fairly clear party divisions were drawn on this issue. Analysis of all known tellers, speakers and committee chairmen reveals that of 25 MPs supporting the company, 22 were Tories; and of 19 MPs opposing the company, 18 were Whigs. Despite exhaustive lobbying by the company – petitions were drawn up and circulated in the West Riding; pamphlets published; and MPs and peers were entertained by the company in London – efforts to retain its charter were unsuccessful.[65]

However, the partisan nature of the Hamburg issue was atypical of most legislation affecting English textiles, reflecting the obvious political and ideological connotations of the free trade versus monopoly theme and involving, in this instance, an institutional combatant.[66] Most textile legislation did not directly involve corporate or formalized interests, but instead revolved around the concerns of local and more informally organized merchants, manufacturers and artisans. As such, most parliamentary contests over textile issues revolved around conflicting constituent interests, not partisan struggle. The local constituent orientation of textile legislation is exemplified in the analysis of the MPs nominated to serve on over 50 second reading or investigative committees in the Commons between 1689 and 1714. What appears is a clearly identifiable group of 25–30 'cloth MPs' nominated to virtually all pertinent committees. To a man, they represent cloth-producing constituencies in the

West Country, East Anglia, Lancashire and the West Riding. There is no political preference amongst them, including Whigs such as Clarke, Yonge and Sir John Guise (the 'Clothiers' Patron), and Tories such as Thomas Blofield and Sir Robert Davers.[67]

While a significant number of these 'cloth MPs' confined their parliamentary activity only to local constituency matters, nonetheless many, such as Yonge and Clarke, appear to have been active on all types of legislation.[68] And yet in Clarke's papers in the Somerset Record Office, there is clear evidence of his concern for the matters of his Taunton textile-producing constituents. Clarke maintained a steady correspondence with the clothiers and weavers of Taunton: speaking for them at committee stage; submitting legislation and petitions; drafting bills, clauses, and provisos on a number of textile issues, including legislation pertaining to wool exports, Blackwell Hall, Irish woollens, and the Hamburg Company. Clarke kept abreast of all textile legislation of concern to his constituents, obtaining large numbers of pamphlets pertaining to both sides of textile debates, keeping himself informed of the current state of the argument, say between the Hamburg merchants and the clothiers.[69] Clarke was not afraid of disagreeing with his constituents. For example in 1700, the weavers of Taunton wrote to Clarke complaining of 'the multitude of young women' who engaged in weaving without apprenticeship 'because they can gett a little more by weaving then by goeing to service, and because they can have more Liberty than in Service att Housewifry'. Yet, Clarke rejected their desire for a special Act of Parliament enforcing apprenticeship in the Taunton trade, noting that it would cost a 'greate security of money and yet will not stop the mischeife being prevented'. However, Clarke did offer to give them his 'utmost assistance' if the other MP for Taunton (Sir Francis Warre) was of 'a different opinion'. This appears to have been the case, for in 1702 Clarke submitted a petition for the Taunton weavers, at the request of the mayor, for the reinforcement of apprenticeship. As noted, the forthcoming piece of legislation failed.[70]

Few MPs left papers as extensive as Clarke's, however most of these 'cloth MPs' were equally active in the legislative process. They gave manufacturers relatively easy access to the legislature and economic-policy making. While Clarke drafted legislation along lines and proposals drawn up by his constituents, others actually had the interested parties themselves see to the initial drafting of the bill. For example, Cyril Arthington (MP for Aldborough), who appears to have guided the Yorkshire Broadcloth Bill through Parliament in 1709, noted that the bill had been drawn up by clothiers with the assistance of a solicitor. Once submitted they had to make a few alterations to meet the objections of 'a very few Interested or Ignorant Merchants' and then the bill breezed through committee and the floor of the House. While this was an issue which encountered very little parliamentary opposition, nevertheless the cost of getting the legislation passed into law was not insignificant, costing well over £100 to pay for the fees of parliamentary clerks, solicitors and other Yorkshire MPs, and what appears to be a substantial amount of cash for Arthington's 'dinner Money'.[71]

The cost of legislating was of course high. Sometimes opposing interests sought to reach an accommodation outside of Parliament to avoid the hassle and expense of legislation. For example, the West Country clothiers sought meetings with the Blackwell Hall factors. Only the rejection of this overture by the latter led to legislation.[72] The enormity of fees paid to parliamentary clerks and doormen, in addition to the need to procure legal counsel, made up a significant proportion of the cost of legislating. Sympathetic MPs had to be found to deliver petitions, initiate bills, to chair and attend committees and organize support within Parliament, and witnesses and evidence had to be garnered for investigative and second reading committees. MPs and witnesses had to be attended to, transported and entertained; the cost in time and money rising with any opposition or delay to the legislation.[73] Lobbying activities included coordinating petitioning campaigns across different communities and regions to guard against the taunts from opposition groups of being allied to a 'private interest', it being a given that all merchants and manufacturers sought local legislation under the rubric of promoting a greater public good, the viability of the claim being enhanced by strength in numbers.[74] Under the same pretence many disparate groups often met to coordinate petitioning and pamphleting campaigns for and against particular legislative measures. For example, the Levant Company met with both the London silk weavers and silkthrowers to assist one another in the calico legislation, sharing strategies for arguments in print, organizing petitions, and coordinating testimony before parliamentary committees.[75] As we have seen, the silk weavers had their own successful if unorthodox means of lobbying Parliament. Surrounding Parliament and occupying its lobbies, the weavers threatened MPs and blocked the way of those opposing the calico bill, allowing only 'those that were for it to pass and repass at pleasure.' Their actions may have been orchestrated by MPs in support of the calico bill. Two principal promoters of the bill, Henry Hobart and Thomas Blofield, were accused of 'stirring them up' and of putting words in 'their mouths to say they [the weavers] were bought and sold like sheep'.[76]

If a bill did meet opposition, the cost of legislating could increase exponentially as lobbying activities were stepped-up in response. Indeed, a high percentage of textile legislative initiatives were unsuccessful and were repeatedly initiated in Parliament over a number of sessions. Yet, repeated failure is not always a manifestation of contention and on some occasions reflects a mere lack of legislative interest. Some textile bills of local concern were routinely tabled or delayed when the legislative calendar became too crowded with revenue bills. And yet other bills, of equally local interest, were clearly occasions for parliamentary scrutiny and debate. For example, a seemingly quite trivial proposal to prohibit the import of foreign wool carding tools in 1711 led to a parliamentary struggle between a plethora of interests (clothiers, wool carders, card manufacturers, leather and metal manufacturers, and importers) and an extensive pamphleteering campaign.[77]

In conclusion, one of the most important ramifications of the late seventeenth century transformation of policy formulation from a conciliar to a parliamentary process was that policy making increasingly became a public exercise. This was a vital component of the reactive nature of the English state after 1688. As we have seen, merchants and manufacturers, although not directly represented in Parliament in great numbers, had relatively open access to commercial policy making through legislation. In seeking to influence the making of policy in the legislature, as opposed to that of the executive, arguments and initiatives had to be made public through the vehicle of the press in a bid to mobilize opinion 'out of doors'. Hence, beginning in the 1690s, there was a dramatic proliferation in the volume of published economic literature, most of it appearing in the shortened form of the broadsheet and pamphlet (and to a lesser extent the newspaper), for ease of dissemination and wider diffusion of ideas. Virtually all economic literature in the late seventeenth and early eighteenth centuries addressed itself to parliamentary considerations and was generally polemical in stance. Consequently, the shift from conciliar to legislative forms of policy making, and ultimately that from a closed to an open character of the state, had a profound impact on economic print culture, witnessing a transition from a treatise-based to a pamphlet-based medium.[78]

Thus, textile legislation between 1689 and 1714 generated a large volume of economic literature in advocacy and opposition to legislative initiatives.[79] The publication of broadsheets and pamphlets by interested parties served two purposes. One, it was vital to generate public opinion in support of a particular measure (although this in itself was no guarantee of success), by distributing pamphlets in coffee-houses and taverns, and attaching broadsheets to walls and pillars in markets and exchanges. To facilitate allegiance to a wider public, all textile interests claimed to represent and protect the standing economic shibboleths of the age: land and woollen cloth. And two, the press was also instrumental in making one's case known 'within doors'. Pamphlets were distributed directly to MPs, and the doormen in the lobby 'kept every sort of the Papers that are delivered'.[80] There is ready evidence of policy makers having read or possessed pamphlets. Many such as Clarke studied them closely, making notes and annotations on their margins. Others used them as convenient scratch paper on which to note current proceedings and alternative points of view in the House.

The content of this broadsheet literature provides evidence of the economic ideas involved in the construction of public opinion and of those notions informing the decisions of legislators. Conclusions are of course impressionistic. Given the volume of the literature, it is impossible to assess the popularity of an idea put forward, or to what extent it convinced, with statistical precision. However, a number of general points can be made about contemporary economic discussion. The first point is that economic discourse in these textile debates was quasi-economic in that, for the most part, debate in the press (and in Parliament) was not structured around disagreement over principals of economic theory or analysis. Instead, most of the discourse was concerned with differences of opinion on the ramifications of particular policy decisions and, as such, debate revolved around questions of observation, quantification and history. Much disagreement revolved around the question of locating the proper framework of observation for assessing who should win and who should lose as a result of a particular policy initiative. For example, as we have seen, much of the debate revolving about legislation pertaining to the Italian silk trade focused on weighing the comparative damage done to weavers and throwers in the silk industry by imports of Italian silk thread, versus the numbers of individuals actually involved in the respective trades. Moreover, proof of argument was increasingly presented in quantitative guise in the early modern period. Clearly numbers were convincing despite the fact that, for the most part, the figures presented in published debates were usually unsubstantiated. Legislation concerning the prohibition of wool exports and calico imports was especially dominated by printed numerical schemes, proving their point by weight of numbers, without recourse to arithmetic sophistication or statistical precision.[81] Finally, the language and rhetoric of economics in the late seventeenth and early eighteenth centuries was permeated by a sense of history. History, like numbers, was convincing and the proof of most economic puddings was more often than not expressed in terms of the past; for example, apprenticeship or the monopoly of the Hamburg Company should be enforced because of its success in previous generations. Moreover, history, like numbers, was also presented in an unsubstantiated form, resembling more of a mythical conception of past trade and commerce than a true historical one.[82]

The second point is that despite occasional references to the importance of domestic commerce and consumption in the works of the more 'liberal' economic writers of the day, virtually all of the broadsheet and pamphlet literature concerned with textiles continued to view foreign trade as the sole means to creating wealth.[83] In this sense, the theoretical and analytical framework of economic thinking in this period was dominated by the logic of a balance of trade, viewing the nation's commerce as an amalgam of bilateral trades within an economic world where wealth was fixed. Virtually all legislative decisions concerning textiles were assessed as to their effect on the balance of trade.[84] For example, prohibitions on Flemish lace imports were removed in 1699, despite vocal opposition of Devon and Buckinghamshire lace producers, on the basis that Flemish retaliatory prohibitions on English cloth served to negate the Anglo-Flemish balance of trade. This bilateral conception of trade was tied to an almost dialectical construct which juxtaposed self-interest to the public good. In this sense, lace manufacturers who sought a prohibition on Flemish imports, despite its impact on the balance of trade, were depicted punitively as pursuing their own private interest at the expense of the public.[85]

Hence advocacy of such diverse issues as a free trade in cloth and Flemish lace, prohibiting the export of wool, and maintaining the quality in textile production were all justified by reference to a manipulation of the trade balance which correspondingly was seen to attract wealth, expand employment and inflate landed incomes. This was true even in the arguments of linen drapers and the East India Company in support of calico imports. In his longer tract, *Considerations upon the East India Trade* (1701), Henry Martin advocated the free consumption of imported calicos, stressing the overall positive stimulus of domestic consumption (even of imports) to employment and wealth creation. Yet Martin noted that his tract was 'contrary to receiv'd Opinions'. Indeed, the broadsheet defence of calicos was made on more traditional grounds, arguing that calico imports ultimately promoted the export of woollen cloth from returns in India or re-exports of calicos to Europe, or stressing that people shall import cheap silks from elsewhere, 'enriching our Neighbours'.[86]

In closing, consumption was still conceived from the vantage point of the zero sum game. The stock of wealth was perceived to be fixed. This was well integrated with the xenophobic nature and national orientation of economic rhetoric which clearly depicted English gain in wealth as a consequence of another nation's loss. Domestic consumption was treated ambivalently at best, that is it did not contribute to the creation of wealth, and, at worst, was portrayed as a destroyer of wealth (and employment) once created. Bombarded with pamphlets, broadsheets, petitions, and proposals and drafts of bills from a multiplicity of textile interests, MPs legislated from the vantage point of 'receiv'd Opinion'. Consequently, there was a general congruance forged between the contemporary formulation of economic ideas and processes, and legislation which sought to protect and promote textile exports and employment, weighing the relative strength of contribution to such an objective from competing interest groups. In this sense, economic ideology and regulation were linked through the medium of the open and public process of legislating, a distinctive feature of the reactive nature of the English state at the turn of the eighteenth century.

Notes

1 *Reasons Humbly Offered to the Consideration of the Lords Spiritual and Temporal, on Behalf of the Bill to Restrain the Wearing of East-India and Persia Wrought Silks* (1700?). The following is a much revised version of a paper read to the design history seminar at the Victoria and Albert Museum in the autumn of 1987.

2 See J. Brewer, *The Sinews of Power: War, Money and the English State, 1688–1783* (New York, 1989); P.G.M. Dickson, *The Financial Revolution in England: A Study in the Development of Public Credit, 1688–1756* (1967); D.W. Jones, *War and Economy in the Age of William III and Marlborough* (Oxford, 1988).

3 *Reasons Humbly Offered to the Honourable House, against the Bill for Supporting the Merchants Adventurers of England in Their Trade to Germany, Commonly Called the Hamborough Company* (1694?).

4 W.G. Hoskins, 'Harvest fluctuations and English economic history, 1620–1759', *Agricultural History Review*, 16 (1968); Jones, *War and Economy*, ch. 1.; idem, 'The economic consequences of William III', in J. Black (ed.), *Knights Errant and True Englishmen: British Foreign Policy, 1660–1800* (Edinburgh, 1989).

5 This was especially true of the English silk industry. See P. Earle, *The Making of the English Middle Class: Business, Society and Family Life in London, 1660–1730* (Berkeley, Ca., 1989), pp. 19–21; E. Kerridge, *Textile Manufactures in Early Modern England* (Manchester, 1985), esp. ch. 9.

6 For similar lack of coordination and confusion in the statutes of the criminal law, see D. Lieberman, *The Province of Legislation Determined: Legal Theory in Eighteenth-Century Britain* (Cambridge, 1989), chs. 9 and 10.

7 C.G.A. Clay, *Economic Expansion and Social Change: England, 1500–1700* (Cambridge, 1984), II, pp. 203–6; M.R. Julian, 'English economic legislation, 1660–1714' (Univ. of London M.Phil. thesis, 1979), ch. 1; B.E. Supple, *Commercial Crisis and Change in England, 1600–1642* (Cambridge, 1959), ch. 10; P. O'Brien, T. Griffiths and P. Hunt, 'Political components of the Industrial Revolution: Parliament and the English cotton textile industry, 1660–1774', *Economic History Review* 2nd ser., 44 (1991). For a similar transformation in social policy, see J. Innes, 'Parliament and the shaping of eighteenth-century English social policy', *Transactions of the Royal Historical Society*, 5th ser., 40 (1990).

8 For discussions of the growth and regularity of parliamentary sessions, see J. Innes and J. Styles, 'The crime wave: Recent writing on crime and criminal justice in eighteenth-century England', *Journal of British Studies*, 25 (1986), pt. 6; S. Handley, 'Local legislative initiatives for economic and social development in Lancashire, 1689–1731', *Parliamentary History*, 9 (1990), 16–17.

9 These calculations are based on the figures presented in: J. Innes and J. Styles, 'The "Bloody Code" in context: Eighteenth century criminal legislation reconsidered' (unpublished paper, 1984), graphs 1 and 2. My thanks to the authors for allowing me to draw on some of the tentative conclusions of this report on work in progress.

10 The 1690s appear to be a decade in transition in this respect. The success rate of legislation did not consistently rise over 50 per cent until after 1700. *Ibid.*, Graph 2.

11 The following data is based on the reworking of Julian, Table III and pt. III, in conjunction with reference to the *House of Commons Journal* (hereafter *HCJ*) and the *House of Lords Journal* (hereafter *HLJ*). By 'textile bill' I refer to any piece of legislation addressed to the regulation (or deregulation) of raw materials, labour, production, or trafficking pertinent to the trade, manufacture and consumption of woollen, silk, lace, cotton or linen fabrics in England. Many of these bills were local initiatives, but all were public as opposed to private pieces of legislation. For private and local legislation, see S. Lambert, *Bills and Acts: Legislative Procedure in Eighteenth-Century England* (Cambridge, 1971); Handley, 'Local legislative initiatives'.

12 In the early 1690s, legislators were not yet inculcated with a sense of the length of the session and a large percentage of bills died in committee. Even revenue bills, which were one of the few types of legislation usually sponsored by members for the government, did not always succeed. However, in the reign of Anne, they rarely failed as relations between Parliament and the Treasury were better coordinated. See C. Brooks, 'Taxation, finance and public opinion, 1688–1714', (Cambridge Univ. Ph.D. thesis, 1971), ch. 5.

13 R.B. Ekelund and R.D. Tollison, *Mercantilism as a Rent-Seeking Society: Economic Regulation in Historical Perspective* (College Station, Texas, 1981), pp. 65–73. See also W.J. Ashley, 'The tory origins of free trade policy', in *Surveys Historic and Economic* (1900); G.L. Cherry, 'The development of the English free-trade movement in Parliament, 1689–1702', *Journal of Modern History*, 25 (1953); E. Lipson, *The Economic History of England* (1931 edn.), II, p. 264.

14 J.O. Appleby, *Economic Thought and Ideology in Seventeenth-Century England* (Princeton, 1978), ch. 9; J.P. Cooper, 'Economic regulation and the cloth industry in seventeenth-century England', *Transactions of the Royal Historical Society*, 5th ser., 20 (1970); R. Davis, 'The Rise of protection in England, 1689–1786', *Economic History Review*, 2nd ser., 19 (1966); N.B. Harte, 'The rise of protection and the English linen trade, 1690–1790', in N.B. Harte and K.G. Ponting (eds.), *Textile History and Economic History* (Manchester, 1973).

15 1 Wm and Mary c.32; 10 Wm III c.6. For the Russia Company, see J.M. Price, 'The tobacco adventure to Russia', *Transactions of the American Philosophical Society*, new ser., 51 (1961).

16 BL Loan 29/141/bundle 4, Sir Edward Harley to Robert Harley, 27 Nov. 1691.

17 BL Add. MS 51,335/f.28, Samuel ? to Charles Fox (MP for Cricklade), 15 Oct. 1690.

18 See Northamptonshire Record Office, Maunsell (Thorpe Malsor) Papers, 561/12, Newsletter, 9 March 1700; *HCJ*, 13, p. 186; 11 Wm III c.20. The Act did provide for the continued collection of the aulnage until the expiration of the patent in 1707.

19 See 2 Wm and Mary c.9; *HCJ*, 10, pp. 359, 385, 393–5; *Reasons for Passing the Turkey Companies Bill, to Discourage the great Importations of Thrown Silk* (1692?). The bill was in fact drafted by members of the Levant Company. PRO, SP 105/145/174; 105/155/139–40.

20 See 5 Wm and Mary c.3; *HCJ*, 11, pp. 9, 25, 31; *House of Lords MSS*, new ser., 1, pp. 321–23; *Considerations Humbly Offered by the Weavers for the Bringing Fine Italian Silks over Land* (1694?).

21 1 Anne c. 21 and 22. An attempt in 1693 to secure the import of Italian silk thread on any foreign vessel was rejected in committee. H. Horwitz (ed.), *The Parliamentary Diary of Narcissus Luttrell, 1691–1693* (1972), p. 432.

22 6 Anne c. 60; *Reasons Humbly Offer'd to the Honourable House of Commons, for Passing the Bill for a Free Importation of Cochineal for a Limited Time* (1708?); *Reasons Humbly Offer'd for the Importation of Cochineal from Spain in Spanish or Neutral Ships during the Present War* (1708?).

23 'The True way for Increasing the Riches of the Nation in General, and the Artizan in Particular, is to Imploy them in Commodities Exported, not consumed in the Kingdom'. Sir Francis Brewster, *Essays on Trade and Navigation* (1695), p. 55.

24 Quoted from Joseph Coles, *England to Be Wall'd with Gold and to Have Silver as Plentiful as Stones in the Street* (1700), p. 5; Richard Carter and Peter Ellers, *A Scheme for Preventing the Exportation of Wool* (1713).

25 'Our Wool being Exported, Our Trade is Exported also . . . which will tend much to the unpeopling of our Nation, and consequently to the great abatements of the Rent of Lands, which will greatly tend to the loss and prejudice of the Revenues of the Nobility and Gentry of this Nation.' *Reasons against the Exportation of English and Irish Wool* (1696). For the absence of a landed interest, see J. Styles, 'Interest groups, lobbying and Parliament in eighteenth century England' (unpublished paper, 1986).

26 See 1 Wm and Mary c. 32; 4 and 5 Wm and Mary c. 24; 7 and 8 Wm III c. 28; 9 Wm III c. 40.

27 E.g., see BL Loan 29/35/bundle 24, Mr. Brayne to Harley, 20 April 1702; PRO CO 389/14, 15 July 1696. For 'projecting', see Brooks, 'Taxation, finance and public opinion', ch. 7.

28 *Observator*, n. 58, 7–11 Nov. 1702.

29 Joseph Coles, *England to be Wall'd*, p. 5.

30 Somerset Record Office, Sanford MS, DD/SF 2755, 2922 and 4107A(10).

31 John Blanch, *The Interest of England Considered in an Essay upon Wooll, Our Woollen-Manufactures and the Improvement of Trade* (1694), p. 22.

32 *Reasons for the Decay of the Clothing-Trade* (1691), p. 2.

33 7 Anne c. 13; *HCJ*, 16, pp. 76, 132.

34 Seven petitions from various groups of West Country clothiers were heard against the bill. See *HCJ*, 17, pp. 558, 639; *Reasons Humbly Propos'd to the Drapers by the Clothiers* (1714); *The Draper's Bill* (1714).

35 Quoted from the Blackwell Hall Committee Minute Book held at the Guildhall Library, MS. 12,851, 6 Feb. 1699. See also 8 & 9 Wm III c. 9; *House of Lords MSS*, new ser., 3, pp. 366–67; *Reasons for Restraining the Factors of Blackwell-Hall, from Dealing in Spanish and English Wooll* (1698?); *The Gentleman's Magazine*, 9 (1738), 89.

36 While the petition of the Taunton weavers for vigilance in the maintenance of apprenticeship did not lead to a statute, nevertheless, the parliamentary committee investigating the validity of the weavers' claims did resolve for a bill (later enacted) prohibiting both the embezzlement of materials by weavers and the payment in provisions instead of coin by clothiers. See 1 Anne 2, c. 22; *HCJ*, 14, pp. 31, 67. A petition by West Midlands JPs of 'tumultuous riots' by textile and metal labourers saw the Act renewed and made perpetual in 1711. *Ibid.*, 16, p. 519; 9 Anne c. 32; J. Styles, 'Embezzlement, industry and the law in England, 1500–1800', in M. Berg *et al.* (eds.), *Manufacture in Town and Country before the Factory* (Cambridge, 1983).

37 Preamble to 10 Anne c. 23. See also 13 Anne c. 23.

38 See N.B. Harte, 'State control of dress and social change in pre-industrial England', in D.C. Coleman and A.H. John (eds.), *Trade, Government and Economy in Pre-Industrial England* (1976).

39 *HLJ*, 14, p. 311. While no copy of the bill survives, it was described as legislating that 'no body, men nor women, shall come to Court in any thing but Wollen, except for linings, and all women under such a quallity, to weare hats.' Sir Charles Lyttleton to Lord Hatton, 8 Aug. 1689, in E.M. Thompson (ed.), *Correspondence of the Family of Hatton* (Camden Society, new ser., 12, 1878).

40 Charles Hatton to Lord Hatton, 15 August 1689, *ibid.*, p. 138. Colonel John Birch (MP), the chief promoter of the bill, fled into the country, 'for had he come to Parliament, I verily beleeve he had been torn to pieces.' *ibid.* Another observed the

22   STILLING THE GRUMBLING HIVE

weavers shouting that 'they would not be whipped with a Birchen Rod.' Dr. Williams' Library, Morrice 31.Q Entering Book, vol. 2, f.596.

41 BL Loan 29/140, Edward to Robert Harley, 17 Aug. 1689. See also *The Weavers of London do Humbly Offer to the Serious Consideration of both Houses of Parliament, That this Kingdom will Sustain great Evils and Damage by Enjoyning the Wearing of Woollen Manufacture* (1689).

42 See *The Case and Representation of the Merchants, Manufacturers, and other Traders, in Respect to Foreign Mournings* (1709?); *The Case of Multitudes of Tradesmen and Manufacturers in Respect to Publick Mournings* (1709); *The Review* (facsimile edn., 1938), 6, pp. 45–7.

43 H.F. Kearney, 'The political background to English mercantilism, 1695–1700', *Economic History Review*, 2nd ser., 11 (1958–9); P. Kelly, 'The Irish Woollen Export Prohibition Act of 1699: Kearney re-visited', *Irish Economic and Social History*, 7 (1980).

44 The Levant Company argued that the import of raw silk and mohair for buttons stimulated English exports of cloth to Turkey, bringing greater benefit to land and trade than if the wool had been employed domestically in the production of buttons. *To the Reasons Already Offer'd by the Levant-Company, for the Bill now Depending in the Honourable House of Commons, for Regulating Buttons and Button-Holes* (1710?). See also 4 Wm and Mary c.10; 10 Wm III c.2; 8 Anne c.11.

45 Houses belonging to prominent members of the East India Company and shops of the calico drapers were vandalized. Richard Lapthorne to Richard Coffin, in R.J. Kerr and I.C. Duncan (eds.), *The Portledge Papers* (1928), pp. 249–50. The weavers were incited by the drapers' 'ill Language, calling the women whores, and pulling out their East-India Silks and Callicoes, and shewing of it to them, as they passed along.' HCJ, 11, p. 683. A crowd surrounding the East India House was disbursed when Sir Owen Buckingham paid 40 shillings to 'the Rabble'. India Office Library, B41, Old East India Company Minutes, 22 Jan. 1697. For a general account, see O'Brien *et al.*, 'Political Components'.

46 In fact, the proviso was added by opponents of the bill who sought (and succeeded) to scuttle the bill by adding a clause 'which they say will be the occasion of flinging it out.' HMC, *Lord Kenyon MSS.*, Thomas Wilson to Roger Kenyon, 20 Feb. 1697, p. 415. See also Bodleian Library, Carte MS. 130, Robert Price to the Duke of Beaufort, 23 Feb. 1697.

47 BL Loan 29/286, 'Reasons and Proposals of the Weavers' in Robert Harley's papers, dated 11 Dec. 1699. Given that neither the bill for prohibition or imposition was read before February, it would appear that the weavers had some early knowledge of the session's fiscal legislative agenda.

48 8 & 9 Wm III c.30; 9 Wm III c. 30; 6 Anne c.3.

49 See D.C. Coleman, 'Politics and economics in the age of Anne: The case of the Anglo-French trade treaty of 1713', in Coleman and John, *Trade, Government and Economy*.

50 9 Wm III c.45; and see, Harte, 'Protection'.

51 3 Wm and Mary c.3. The Act was subsequently renewed throughout the period.

52 7 & 8 Wm III c. 39; 12 Anne c.12.

53 3 & 4 Anne c.7; HCJ, 14, pp. 498, 515.

54 Thomas Tryon, *Some General Considerations Offered Relating to Our Present Trade* (1698), p. 18. See also Davis, 'Rise of protection'.

55 For example, the attempt in 1708 of the Treasury to gain a further duty on woollen yarns imported from Ireland was rigorously opposed by the clothiers at all legislative stages until it was eventually defeated. See HCJ, 15, pp. 594, 625–26; BL Add. MS 21,133 fos. 81–2.

56 'A Letter from a Merchant to a Member of Parliament about the Clandestine Running of Goods', BL Add. MS 61,358, fos. 150–60.

57 Although one MP confided privately that a duty on cloth exports should be revived to 'cause a True Balance of Trade (which is very needful for thy Kingdom) so when the Commons finds it needful to knew the balance of trade it will be more exact than it is today.' BL Loan 29/285, Sir Robert Davers to Robert Harley, 9 Feb. 1711.

58 6 Anne c.43; 6 Anne c.44; *HCJ*, 15, pp. 457–60.

59 See *Reasons Humbly Offered for Supporting the Company of Merchant Adventurers of England, In Their Trade to Germany* (169?).

60 *A Proposal for Raising Six Thousand Pound per Annum, without Charge of Collecting* (1714?).

61 Giving 'more regard to the Revenue than our Manufactures.' BL Add. MS 34,521, John Cary to Lord Somers, f. 69. It was a habitual complaint of clothiers and dyers that the drawback allowed on indigo and logwood served only to profit the importing merchant foreign competitors. See *HCJ*, 14, p. 276; *Reasons against Charging Trade with Annuities* (1707), p. 5.

62 HMC, *Buccleuch MS*, II, pp. 717–18.

63 Speech of MP John Sanford, *Luttrell Diary*, p. 428.

64 *Ibid.*, p. 427. See also Somerset Record Office, Sanford MS DD/SF 4511, fos. 2, 4 and 7.

65 Even after repeated legislative failure in the 1690s, the company was still angling in 1707 and 1710 for Robert Harley to submit another bill in their favour, without success. See BL Loan 29/285, H. Hughes to Harley, 28 Oct. 1710; 29/286, William Gore to Harley, 10 Dec. 1707.

66 Legislative assaults on the monopolies of other chartered trading companies during the 1690s were also characterized by partisan conflict. See T. Keirn, 'Commercial Monopoly and the Debates on the African Trade', in J. Brewer and S. Staves (eds.), *Conceptions of Property* (forthcoming); H. Horwitz, 'The East India Trade, The Politicians and the Constitution: 1689–1702', *Journal of British Studies*, 17 (1978); Price, 'Tobacco Adventure'.

67 For reference to Guise, see Somerset Record Office, Sanford MS, DD/SF 4511, Robert Yate to Sir John Guise, 27 Jan. 1694.

68 For a topology of constituent-based politics and MPs, see T.K. Moore and H. Horwitz, 'Who runs the house? Aspects of parliamentary organization in the later seventeenth century', *Journal of Modern History*, 43 (1971); Innes, 'Parliament'.

69 Observations based on extensive perusal of the voluminous personal papers of Edward Clarke in the Sanford collection. See also L. Davison, and T. Keirn, 'John Locke, Edward Clarke and the 1696 Guineas legislation', *Parliamentary History*, 7 (1988).

70 Somerset Record Office, Sandford MS, DD/SF 1100, 19 Oct. 1700 to 19 Nov. 1700, unpaginated.

71 BL Stowe MS, 748/79, Arthington to William Neville, 17 March 1709.

72 Guildhall Library MS 12,851, Blackwell Hall Committee Minute Books, fos. 14–24. See also Handley, 'Local legislative initiatives', pp. 22–23.

73 For example, the Exeter Weavers Company spent close to £56 attending the committee considering duties on Irish yarn in 1708. Devon Record Office, DRO 58/7/10/2. For the cost of carriage fees, transporting MPs and peers to support the Hamburg Company bill, see Guildhall Library MS 11,892, Eastland Company, Treasurer's Account Book. For the failure of the Hamburg Company to adequately entertain 'friends and great men', see BL Add. MS 37,663, Rycaut to Gore, 18 April 1693. For more information on fees and the costs of lobbying, see Brewer, *Sinews of Power*, pp. 236–39.

74 For example, in campaigns against the Hamburg Company or the Irish cloth industry, the wording of large numbers of parliamentary petitions sent from various groups of West Country clothiers is remarkably similar.

75 This despite the fact that (as noted) the Levant merchants and weavers were at cross purposes over Italian silk legislation. See PRO, SP 105/156, fos. 7–12.

76 See Northamptonshire Record Office, Montagu (Boughton) MS, Vernon-Shrewsbury Letterbooks, 21 Jan. 1697; HMC, *Le Fleming MSS*, William Fleming MP to Sir Daniel Fleming, 21 Jan. 1697, p. 346.

77 See *HCJ*, 16, pp. 471, 512–13, 520. See *A Dialogue between Dick Brazenface the Card-Maker, and Tim. Meanwell the Clothier* (1711).

78 For an example of the closed, private and treatise-based nature of economic policy making in the Restoration period, see T. Keirn and F. Melton, 'Thomas Manley and the rate of interest debate, 1667–1673', *Journal of British Studies*, 29 (1990).

79 To provide some notion of volume, the calico legislation during the 1690s stimulated the publication of at least 70 titles (the vast majority being pamphlets and broadsheets) discovered in searches in the British, Goldsmiths', and Kress Libraries and in various manuscript collections of government officials and MPs.

80 Cumbria Record Office, Lonsdale MS, LW2/D34, James Lowther to Sir John Lowther, 13 Dec. 1698.

81 See *Considerations about the Transportation of Wool* (1697?) revealing that two million pounds value per annum was lost to England over a period of twenty years. See T.S., *The Profit and Loss of the East-India Trade, Stated, and Humbly Offer'd to the Consideration of Parliament* (1700), for an 'impartial' and unsubstantiated numerical account of the £1,716,000 lost per annum in England due to the import of calicos.

82 A significant number of tracts hark nostalgically to the Elizabethan 'Golden Age' of English trade. See, e.g., *The Languishing State of Our Woollen Manufacture* (1695?); J. Blanch, *The Interest of England Considered* (1693).

83 Most noted are the treatises of Nicholas Barbon, Bernard de Mandeville, Henry Martin, and Roger North. See Appleby, *Economic Thought and Ideology*, ch. 7; T. Cowen, 'Nicholas Barbon and the origins of economic liberalism', *Research in the History of Economic Thought*, 4 (1987).

84 See Coleman, 'Mercantilism'; *idem*, 'Queen Anne'.

85 For example, Sir Richard Cocks (MP, Gloucestershire) felt that Sir Walter Yonge had obtained a statute making the lace prohibition more effectual (1698) 'to serve some little inconsiderable member of the craft . . . to create himself a private interest.' Bodleian Library MS, Eng.Hist.b.209 f. 90. See also D.W. Hayton, 'Sir Richard Cocks: The political anatomy of a country whig', *Albion*, 20 (1988).

86 *Eleven Queries Humbly Tener'd, Relating to the Bill for Prohibiting the Wearing of East-India Silks, and Printed and Dyed Calicos* (?1697). Martin quoted in C. MacLeod, 'Henry Martin and the authorship of "Considerations upon the East India Trade"', *Bulletin of the Institute of Historical Research*, 56 (1983).

2

Experiments in the Social Regulation of Industry: Gin Legislation, 1729–1751

Lee Davison
Harvard University

Almost every affliction of eighteenth-century society was laid at the door of what Dorothy George called 'the orgy of spirit-drinking'. Concern was most intense between the late 1720s and early 1750s, a period which saw seven statutes designed to regulate the consumption and production of spirits in an unparalleled attempt to place an important product of home industry out of the reach of most of its market. This essay will examine the forces at work in the adoption of this legislation and the problems associated with its implementation. Concern outside central administration, particularly among the members of voluntary societies and local government, focused attention on the subject, prompting increasing debate in the press and encouraging the passage of new statutes. Attempted solutions created new problems, and so led to a continuing debate over the necessity and effectiveness of the remedies adopted. Economic and 'moralist' interest groups, using both the vehicles of public debate and parliamentary pressure, contributed to the process of policy formation. With revenue involved, the central government had a clear stake in the outcome of the debate. This study of attempts to curb gin consumption will therefore shed light on the influence of lobbies and interest groups, perceptions of the role of state intervention and taxation, the role of the press, and ideas about law enforcement during the eighteenth century.

The demonic status attained by gin in the 1720s is surprising in light of the almost unremitting parliamentary promotion of the distilling industry for the preceding thirty years. The most important element of this policy was the removal of the monopoly of the Distillers Company, which allowed virtually anyone to enter the trade.[1] Short-term restrictions in response to grain shortages only briefly interrupted this trend of de-regulation. Historians have argued that from the late 1720s, an increasing furore over the perceived dangers to society of gin consumption by the poor resulted in a dramatic reversal of state policy, with restrictive statutes replacing earlier encouraging laws.

Until very recently, Dorothy George's discussion of the issue has been the only authoritative assessment of the measures used to cure the 'gin epidemic'. She divided the chronology of gin regulation into two periods. The first included the laws of 1729 and 1736–8, which George believed to have failed because of widespread evasion and opposition from the mob. The second encompassed the acts of 1743 and 1751, which she felt represented the beginning of a realistic policy of regulation due to the linkage of the retail trade in spirits to the public house.

Recent work by Peter Clark has added to our understanding of both the spirit trade and the forces behind the 1736 law. He argues that both the shape and social structure of the spirit trade have been misunderstood and that gin was sold in more respectable premises and by more respectable people than has previously been thought. The inability to trace adequately the poorer end of the trade, however, makes Clark's case less convincing. He is undoubtedly correct in contending that opponents of gin carried on a 'sensationalist' propaganda campaign, and that contemporary assertions that gin was responsible for high mortality and crime rates were simply wrong.[2] While this is worth noting, Clark's approach takes too little account of the importance of public perceptions. The claims of competing interests during the eighteenth century were frequently exaggerated, but were just as frequently believed. While Clark considerably sharpens our picture of individuals behind the regulation, his view of the 1736 law does not depart significantly from that of George – this was a draconian statute which failed because of widespread popular resentment.[3]

This view suffers from an insufficient investigation of why certain methods were chosen above others, and of the willingness and ability of officials to enforce them. This study will suggest that all the regulation prior to 1751 was ineffectual because the traditional dictates of economic and fiscal policy always carried more weight than even the most pressing social policy objectives. As we will see, the one period of stringent enforcement was in response not to drunkenness, but to disorder. Concentrating on the decade following 1733, a period which saw what both historians and contemporaries have characterized as the harshest measures, this essay will examine the public debate over the need to regulate liquor consumption, the passage and content of bills, and reactions to the laws and their enforcement. The complex amalgam of interests and motivations of proponents, opponents and the government will be analysed, as will the way in which they combined to set parameters for policy. Regulation of spirits was a story not of failure to reform, but of contemporary limits on possible action. Social and moral reformers had the power to create a general and vociferous debate on issues which held out the expectation of concerted effort by central and local government, but their zealousness gave them aspirations beyond the boundaries of achievable policy.

Excessive drinking had been condemned from time immemorial by the clergy as a vice inimical to both morality and salvation. Drunkenness was seen both as a symptom and a cause of moral decay and public disorder, and while alehouses grew to be more respectable by 1700, drunkenness remained a subject of public concern. The Societies for the Reformation of Manners paid it some attention, believing it needed to be eradicated for the good both of the individual and the public. Yet these reformers concentrated on prosecuting offences such as 'lewd and disorderly' conduct and sabbath-breaking; little organized moralist opposition existed to government moves to encourage the production of spirits. Until well into the reign of George I, the industry and the ever increasing revenue it generated continued to hold a charmed place in the eyes of government.[4]

Contemporaries believed much of the gin trade was carried out in alleys and cellars, and by street hawkers, accompanied by the cry of 'Bung your eye!' The idea that small tradesmen dealt in spirits is borne out by the returns on gin-sellers from a survey of Westminster carried out in 1725. Chandlers were the ubiquitous purveyors of low-quality spirits: 65 per cent of sellers were identified as chandlers, while only 12 per cent were named as keepers of dram or gin-shops, and just 5.5 per cent as distillers.[5] Returns detailing the licensing status of retailers revealed that almost 80 per cent did not possess a licence.[6] Peter Clark has suggested that chandlers were not necessarily poor, but relative prosperity did not automatically mean respectability, and in any case, the perception of 'inferior' sellers acquired a life of its own in the minds of contemporaries.[7]

As spirit production increased and retailers multiplied, metropolitan JPs became concerned, setting up a committee of the Middlesex bench in 1725. They investigated the numbers of retailers, which led to the constables' returns noted above, and found more than 6000 places within the Bills of Mortality selling strong waters, a total described as 'far beyond all proportion to the reall wants of the inhabitants'. The justices voiced particular worry over the poor's penchant for such liquors, and were not alone in predicting disastrous consequences from the excessive use of spirits by the poor. In the same year the College of Physicians petitioned the Commons, noting that the 'fatal effects' of gin drinking had rendered many people prone to disease, indigence, and to becoming a burden on the nation.[8] Contemporaries believed idleness, poverty, immorality and crime were on the increase, and while gin had not yet achieved pride of place as the primary cause of evil in society, its causal role had clearly been identified.[9]

In the second half of the 1720s, with production of domestic spirits rising steadily, discussion over the use of liquors began to appear in the press. The justices ordered their committee report printed in the *Daily Courant*, and pamphlets dealing with the issue began to appear. General attacks on drunkenness saw strong waters as the chief offender.[10] Not surprisingly, Daniel Defoe wrote on both sides of the argument: he composed a defence of the distillers in 1726, arguing that home industry and exports were to be encouraged, and that the distilling industry should be protected against foreign competition. He dismissed assertions that the health of drinkers was at risk. Only the excesses of the populace created a problem, and the duty to prevent such improper use rested with magistrates, not distillers.[11] Just one year later Defoe had changed his mind, at least regarding some distillers, arguing along with magistrates that the lower end of the trade consisted of 'sinners against the people'.[12]

Against the background of efforts by magistrates and a general tide of opinion against spirits, a presentment of the Middlesex grand jury in 1729 provided the immediate impetus for a parliamentary initiative. Shops selling gin were identified as public nuisances which inured people to debauchery and led them to a life of penury and crime.[13] The 1729 bill, a revenue measure, was prepared by members of the government, and appears to have had full ministerial backing. There was little debate over the measure, and its passage through the Commons took just three weeks. The bill was designed to make distilled compound spirits more expensive by laying a duty of 5 shillings per gallon on all such liquors.[14] Other important provisions included annual £20 licences for spirit retailers and the prohibition of street hawking under a £10 penalty. The Distillers Company opposed the bill and spent considerable money lobbying against it. The Company also arranged for the publication of tracts to aid their cause. Although it gave up the attempt to prevent passage after the bill went through the Commons, the Company swiftly began a campaign to have it repealed, and appointed a committee to this end in 1731.[15]

Reaction to the law was not particularly vociferous. The duty was substantial, but had been aimed only at retailers and the lower end of the distilling trade. The most important members of the industry, the malt distillers, were not a direct target. This emphasis would remain a keystone of policy during the height of the 'gin craze'. Production could only be cut by a sustained effective enforcement of both duties and licensing across the entire trade, a task which went unaccomplished prior to 1751. Contemporaries branded the 1729 law a failure, providing Walpole's reason for advocating its repeal in 1733. Retailers and compounders had found ways to sell and produce spirits, derisively named 'Parliament Brandy', which did not fall within the scope of the legislation.[16] Licensing was minimal.[17] There was an initial drop in production – 1730 witnessed a 20 per cent decrease from the 1728 figures – but by 1733 all the ground lost had been reclaimed and pre-Act levels of production were surpassed by 1734.[18]

The law was repealed not simply because it had failed, but as a result of another parliamentary resolution to encourage the production and export of domestic spirits. Not only were restrictions removed, drawbacks were given for export and further duties added to imports. Repeal was not unopposed, but the fact that there was no groundswell of opinion against it is reflected in its swift passage through the Commons. The Distillers lobbied hard for repeal during the session, spending over £100.[19] It was money well spent, for the industry was again free of the shackles of regulation. To this point, in 1734, regulatory law had been more an anomaly than a policy.

Production and consumption soared immediately, galvanizing a coalition of reformers to press for new regulation. Perhaps the greatest asset the new campaign possessed was its parliamentary champion, the Master of the Rolls and independent Whig, Sir Joseph Jekyll. When Jekyll took up a cause, he pursued it with zeal, and he was strongly identified with the crusade against gin.[20] Gathered around Jekyll were members of what one might call the general 'moralist' lobby, people connected with the SPCK, the SPG, the Georgia Society, and the now fading Societies for the Reformation of Manners. Many were associated with several of these organizations. MPs such as James Oglethorpe and Erasmus Phillips were involved in the attack on gin, as were several churchmen. Thomas Wilson, a cleric and member of the SPCK, played an important role both in the public debate and in preliminary efforts outside Parliament, while the Bishop of London, Edmund Gibson, showed keen interest in the issue. Stephen Hales, a trustee of the Georgia Society and a noted physician, both advised Wilson and contributed an influential pamphlet to the debate. Metropolitan magistrates such as Nathaniel Blackerby, Thomas Lane and Sir John Gonson continued to voice their concerns, and were directly connected with these groups.[21]

All of these individuals contributed directly or indirectly to a public debate which was extensive and vigorous, taking the shape of broadsides, pamphlets and articles in the periodical press. In contrast to the 1729 Act, that of 1736 precipitated the publication of numerous substantial works and near constant coverage in the London newspapers. As was common during the eighteenth century, active exchanges took place between authors, each citing and attempting to refute the arguments of their opponents.

The 1736 bill (to be discussed below) was fundamentally different from most economic legislation, which was designed to raise revenue, protect domestic industry, or influence the relative position of competing economic interests. Here a coalition of outside pressure groups was attempting to restrain an economic interest purely for the public benefit. Most eighteenth-century social policy was seen as harmonious with economic well-being, but in this case social and economic policy clashed.

One strategy used in the pamphlet debate to overcome this apparent conflict was to concentrate on the effect the consumption of spirits had on the human body and public health. Increasing concern had prompted further development of themes discussed in the 1720s and earlier. During the period between 1733 and the 1736 Act, the 'pernicious' effects of spirits on public health were enumerated repeatedly in an effort to lay the groundwork for strict regulation. Proponents hoped to show that not only was excessive drinking of these liquors harmful, even moderate use was unhealthy. The first sortie against the effects of spirits on health came in the form of Dr. Stephen Hales's *A Friendly Admonition to the Drinkers of Brandy, and other Distilled Spirituous Liquors*. First published in 1733, it went through several editions, and formed the basis of argument for several other works. For the time, Hales's work was fairly clinical, and he took care to note whenever findings had been proved by experimentation. He stated that spirits directly contributed to diseases of the liver as well as the destruction of the circulatory and digestive systems, and that they were poison to human bodies.[22] While many died immediately, Hales claimed that most were gradually swept away by the damage done by gin.

Thomas Wilson, drawing on both Hales's pamphlet and conversations with him, spent a good deal of time on questions of public health in his own works. He repeated many of Hales's claims, but also tried to place the problems in the larger context of danger to the social and political order. He felt the consequences of gin consumption extended into the realms of social and economic policy, even to Britain's place in the world. Wilson decried the oft-criticized practice of mothers giving gin to children to keep them quiet, but in his view the results of pregnant women drinking liquor were far more disturbing. Unborn children were adversely affected, and nursing mothers and wet-nurses would also pass on a measure of this 'poison'. The children of these mothers would either be killed, or, if they survived, would do so only to live a miserable life, a burden to the state. Wilson took a slightly less empirical route to the conclusion that these children would also, through some unexplained process, tend to become excessive drinkers themselves.[23]

Contemporary economic wisdom held that anything which tended to decrease the population would lead to a decline in the strength of Britain's commerce and her ability to play a powerful role on the world stage. Zealous opponents of gin claimed thousands of deaths from the liquor annually, and while defenders of the distilleries could claim relatively insignificant numbers of deaths ascribed directly to excessive drinking (no more than two to three per week within the Bills of Mortality even in the period of most acute scrutiny), the claim of indirect death through disease and increased child mortality did not fall on deaf ears. Arguments from the standpoint of public health were among the most telling, as they were difficult to answer, forcing defenders of the distilleries to gloss over them with simple assertions about the wholesome qualities of their products.

While advocates of restraint or prohibition argued that concerns over public health, order and morality all tipped the scales on the side of regulation, they also exerted a great deal of effort arguing their point from a purely economic stance. Jekyll, in correcting a draft of Wilson's work, asked 'that its Moral Reflections might be kept to the last and not intermixt in the Body of the Treatise'.[24] He clearly felt neither Parliament nor the public needed to be convinced of moral decay, but it was indispensable to prove that regulation would not lead to economic decline.

The symbiotic relationship between the distillers and the landed interest had been held up as the former's principal asset since the 1690s. Hales had warned Wilson that regulation would lead to 'great clamour' from the country gentlemen. He asked Wilson to prove that farmers lost more due to gin-drinking's effects on grain consumption than the distillers could claim to add through the purchase of grain. Wilson followed Hales's instructions. After first estimating there were about 400,000 gin-drinkers in metropolitan London, he proceeded to calculate how much less food gin-drinkers consumed due to loss of appetite and re-allocation of income to buy liquor. He arrived at an annual loss of more than £1,000,000 from a decrease in both food consumption and efficiency of labour. He claimed that for every pound the distillers laid out for grain, spirits took away three from demand for the produce of farmers.[25] Equally mathematical responses came from defenders of the distillers as the bulwark of the landed interest. One writer asserted that Wilson underestimated the industry's demand for grain, which he claimed injected an immediate £400,000 annually into the land. Regulation, he predicted, would result in plummeting grain prices.[26] Another contended that the distilleries supported 200,000 acres, and so furnished the livelihoods of 10,000 families and provided work for many ancillary trades.[27]

While the well-being of the landed interest was utilized as a justification by each side, other more specific interest groups were both used and spoke for themselves in the debate. The 1729 law had not been directed at the plantations, but the 1736 bill was all-encompassing; domestic spirits drawn from molasses and imported rum would be under the same regulation as gin. Proponents of the law declared that rum was as unwholesome as geneva, and that colonial interests had to be subordinate to those of England.[28] The sugar trade predicted economic and political disaster for Britain. The colonies were lauded as a support to navigation and trade, a market for home manufactures and an important source of customs revenue. One author believed distillers provided over 5 per cent of the market for molasses, and the combination of that loss and new duties would finish the plantations.[29] The sugar lobby asserted that 20 per cent of their production consisted of molasses used for rum; oversupply and price falls would follow.[30] The enactment of the bill would mean a sugar monopoly for the French.

The London distillers clearly stood to bear the brunt of the dislocation caused by regulatory proposals. The Distillers Company again waged an active campaign against the bill. In July 1735, before the bill was even introduced, the Company began an exercise in damage limitation, instructing its standing committee on parliamentary matters to prepare proposals to lay before the Treasury or Parliament attesting to the distillers' willingness to address complaints levelled at retailers.[31] These efforts, at least on the surface, failed to win sympathy. The Company's position was simple: the bill would lead to the utter destruction of the trade. The distillers contested the necessity of prohibition, an outcome they believed inevitable should the bill pass. They were willing to admit that if the evil generated by excessive drinking 'was so epidemical, that the Publick is endanger'd by it' and no other remedy was available, it would be just for the legislature to destroy a trade for the public good.[32] The distillers made such statements from necessity rather than conviction, and they were simply an attempt, albeit an unconvincing one, to take the moral high ground from their opponents.

Such a position continued to elude them. If the relative merits of the economic assertions were debatable, where the distillers lost out most convincingly was over questions of public health, public morals and public order. These had been assiduously linked with such economic issues as employment, population, and productivity, but involved a fundamentally different set of ideas. Wilson tried his best to put them into numbers, but they went beyond quantification. As abstract notions of the public good, they were irreproachable reasons for regulation. All the distillers could do was vainly attempt to discredit the allegations made against their product.

To say the least, difficulties would have beset any attempt to argue that spirits tended to increase public morality, and the best the defenders of the distilleries could do was contend that spirits were no worse than any other tipple. There was, however, a belief that gin especially was different, that it engendered a drunkenness that was not only more noxious to health, but one which corrupted the mind, body and soul more than any other liquor. In part, this was a result of the perceptions of the environment in which it was consumed; the gin-cellar tempted men to vice more than the respectable public house. During the 1743 debate on repealing the 1736 law, other alcoholic beverages were said to produce 'the old English sort of drunkenness, which proceeded from hospitality and good-fellowship', while gin led to an intoxication which 'admits of no mirth, no conversa-tion: the company grow mad before they well know what they are about, and the more they drink, the more ripe they grow for any wickedness'.[33] Drinking gin, according to contemporary comment, gave people false courage, leading them to enter into unlawful enterprises and to revenge old wrongs, which in turn resulted in breaches of the peace, the disturbance of neighbourhoods, and litigious and expensive prosecutions. After drinkers spent all their money on gin, they needed to finance their addiction, and so committed 'desperate Attacks, High-way and Street Robberies, attended sometimes by the most cruel unheard of Murthers'.[34] Gin had taken its place as the great destroyer of society.

Renewed expressions of magisterial concern around London had an important effect on debate. The reformers in Parliament were directly connected to those sitting at quarter sessions; Oglethorpe asked Wilson to take a letter to Thomas Lane, a Westminster JP, enquiring about the powers of enforcement available to justices, and Lane agreed to discuss the problem with Jekyll. Grand jury presentments concerning gin were made in the City, Middlesex and Tower Hamlets in 1735–6, and the Middlesex JPs issued a report at their January sessions. This report, which concentrated on crime and the inability of existing laws to deal adequately with the situation, opened the debate on the bill in the Commons. Though containing nothing novel, it came at just the right time to capture a mood among certain sections of government and society, a climate recognized by supporters in Parliament who felt it was absolutely necessary to use 'the present conjuncture' to end the abuse.[35] Their efforts would end in one of the most sweeping pieces of social legislation passed during the first half of the century.

A bill would have been introduced independent of magisterial actions, for Sir Joseph Jekyll was determined on one. In August 1735 Jekyll told Wilson and Oglethorpe of his plans when Wilson presented him with a draft of his pamphlet *Distilled Spirituous Liquors the Bane of the Nation*. Jekyll personally paid for a thousand copies to be printed. He spoke to the Queen in an ultimately unsuccessful attempt to get the King to mention the issue in his speech to Parliament.[36] The essential character of the bill was probably determined by Jekyll. Certainly, his motions at the start of the debate set the parameters of the law, which was entirely directed at the regulation of retailers. This stress is not surprising, but it is striking that the distilleries themselves, so much the direct target of the pamphlet debate, were not singled out. Jekyll had told Wilson, however, that his legislation called for higher duties,[37] and these taxes were not meant to be imposed only on retailers. Thomas Secker, writing in his diary of the 1743 debate against repeal, noted that Jekyll's original intent had been to lay a 2 shillings per gallon tax at the still-head in order to cut production.[38]

Jekyll would re-affirm his original intention to tax production in December 1737, and sought to have James Vernon and the excise commissioners draw up such a plan.[39] There is no explanation for why Jekyll ultimately abandoned this element of his plan, but between August 1735 and February 1736 his most effective proposal disappeared. Just two weeks before the bill was introduced, Jekyll left a copy of his scheme with the Lords of the Treasury for their comment.[40] It seems quite possible that Treasury officials were unwilling to countenance direct economic meddling with the manufacturing end of the industry. The way in which the law would be enforced strengthens the notion that the government intended that the Gin Act should be no more than an exercise in cosmetic social surgery.

In Parliament, Jekyll's motions were made, and though some debate ensued, they were accepted almost unanimously. Walpole gave notice that while he was all for restraining gin-shops, any attendant loss in revenue had to be made good. The Commons resolved that the low price of liquors was the cause of their abuse, that no-one should sell them without licence, and that a duty should be laid on them. Jekyll pressed for a duty of 20 shilling per gallon on retailed spirits, but this was opposed by several members, notably William Pulteney, as amounting to a total suppression. Pulteney acknowledged the dangers of excessive use, but said abuse constituted the problem, and that industry at home and in the colonies would suffer if such a high duty was imposed. Supporters of the heavy duty replied that anything less would not answer the 'loud complaint presently made against these evils'. Clearly the public nature of the debate brought it home to Parliament that it could not be seen to leave the problem unregulated, and the 20 shilling duty passed without further debate.[41]

The Distillers Company did manage to get some concessions, but their efforts had little impact. The committee responsible reported that it would be in vain to oppose the bill in general, but did claim to have been responsible for the reduction of the minimum non-taxable quantity from five gallons to two and the postponement of the Act's coming into force from 24 June to 29 September.[42] They also were able to insert a clause allowing distillers to take up any other trade anywhere in the country, though they doubted this would be of much help to any except the younger members of the Company. The committee continued to lobby the Lords, but eventually decided against even making a petition.[43]

Most of the debate in the Commons was not on the merits of the bill itself, but on its consequences for the Civil List. Walpole argued that the annual loss from lower receipts of duty on spirits would be £70,000 (taking an average of the previous eight years), and insisted that this loss should be made good. Lengthy debate followed, the opposition questioning Walpole's use of those eight years, when production was at its height, and arguing that the eight years prior to George II's accession should be used, which would put the average at just £43,000. The opposition was easily defeated.[44] The only effort Walpole invested in the measure was towards gaining further revenue.

The law as enacted appeared impressive indeed; its most important clauses laid down that no person could retail any type of spirits in quantities less than two gallons without taking out an annual licence from the Excise costing £50. The penalty for retailing without a licence was £100. Licences were to be granted only to those keeping public victualling houses, inns, brandy-shops, etc., and each had to be approved by two or more justices. The retailer had to pay a duty of 20 shillings per gallon on all liquors sold in quantities under two gallons. Anyone who hindered an excise officer from searching was subject to a £50 penalty. Hawkers of spirits were to be fined £10 for each offence. If they were unable to pay, they were to be sent to the house of correction for two months' hard labour.

The ministry expected antagonism to the new law, and was prepared for extensive and violent reaction to the Act when it came into effect. George Rudé, however, has shown that the riots during the summer of 1736 were a reaction to the influx of Irish labourers, and that the government was more concerned with possible Jacobite backing of public disturbances than with the intentions of the distillers whose circular letters were intercepted.[45] The government's unease over Jacobite use of resistance to the law was exacerbated by the ingenious exploding parcel of handbills in Westminster Hall engineered by the non-juring priest Robert Nixon. The Gin Act headed the list of laws which were proclaimed to be injurious to the freedom and trade of the nation.[46] Although troops were stationed at various places in London and Westminster, the plans of the distillers proved essentially symbolic. One circular letter even referred to the demonstrations as 'the great drink' and specifically noted that there was 'no harm designed'.[47] Contemporaries agreed that the Act came into force quietly.[48]

One reason why the law did not engender opposition can perhaps be found by looking at the effectiveness of the statute in cutting the consumption of spirits. Using T.S. Ashton's production figures, it appears the distillers were not badly hurt. The pattern of production was quite similar to that following the 1729 Act, though the recovery was even faster. Certainly there was nothing but an extremely short-term decrease in demand for the product. While the law forced distillers briefly to reduce production, the industry did not face disaster. And although bankruptcies among both distillers and spirit-dealers increased during the 1730s, Julian Hoppit notes that this was due not to increasing rates of failure, but to new entrants flooding into an attractive business.[49]

The licensing fee for retailers had been designed to be prohibitive, but while the law was in force just twenty were issued. As to the duty levied on spirits sold in small quantities, it generated just over £500, and so was applied to less than 1/500 of 1 per cent of total domestic spirit production between 1736–42.[50] Jekyll's very high tax was to be imposed on those least likely to pay it, and although he may have believed it would be applied, for the government this provided a convenient way to appear to support the reformers without having to do so in reality. Given the appearance that official backing for the intent of the law was hollow, one should ask if its enforcement was equally perfunctory.

After the law's enactment, debate turned to an examination of the administration of the law, which became more contentious than its objectives. Enforcement was complicated by the involvement of two distinct institutional bodies. The excise commissioners were to punish unlicensed retailers while magistrates were to deal with hawkers. This division and the uncertainty it engendered was one of the issues attacked in the popular press. The excise jurisdiction was clear, but the clause empowering the justices stated they were to punish those with no fixed abode, and included a catch-all phrase that allowed them to proceed against offenders found 'in all other places'. Metropolitan magistrates, who had played a key role in promoting the law, effectively had an unlimited jurisdiction.

The unrestricted magisterial ambit had an important and unpleasant consequence for convicted offenders. Eighteenth-century legislation was becoming increasingly more likely to specify methods of enforcement and punishment, particularly regarding penalties under summary jurisdiction. Under the hawking clause, offenders had to pay the £10 fine in full, or be immediately imprisoned, whereas the excise commissioners could mitigate fines, and a warrant to seize and sell the goods of the retailer had to be executed before imprisonment. Reay Sabourn claimed the Excise had been purposely empowered to judge retailers in metropolitan London because Parliament had never intended the law to be enforced to the letter.[51] After examining the number and manner of prosecutions, such an interpretation has some merit.

Estimates of prosecutions were widely disseminated in the press. Reports claimed that through March 1738 within the Bills there had been over 12,000 prosecutions; 4,896 convicted by the excise, 4,000 claims by informers for rewards, and 3,000 £10 fines paid to avoid imprisonment.[52] These reports erroneously inflated the total by double counting – the reward figure was almost certainly a consequence of both sets of convictions, not a separate category. Nonetheless, this leaves 8,000 prosecutions, a figure which does not include commitments to houses of correction or acquittals. Extrapolating from JPs' reports discussed below, it would be reasonable to suggest that at least as many were committed as paid fines. The number of convictions thus rises to 11,000. According to these figures, the excise commissioners would have had to convict nine people every day for eighteen months, and metropolitan JPs about ten people a day over the same period. If such a scale of activity had been even close to accurate, this would have been one of the most invasive penal laws enacted during the early eighteenth century.

The reported totals of convictions under the Excise were, however, dramatically overstated. While no detailed excise proceedings appear to survive, conviction totals were recorded. Within the Bills of Mortality, only 435 people were convicted by the Excise through March 1738.[53] Between the Act's coming into force and midsummer 1742, there were 1,642 convictions under the excise jurisdiction in the entire country. This does not constitute a record of inattention. Indeed, by eighteenth-century standards of enforcement, the number of convictions is fairly impressive. Yet less than £9,000 was recovered in fines from those convicted. On average, those convicted paid just 6 per cent of the possible penalty.[54] Clearly, the Excise often substantially reduced fines. On 16 June 1737, for example, the commissioners were reported to have called in all those who had paid their fines and lessened them by 80 per cent. In some cases, offenders were actually told to apply for mitigation of a fine.[55] It was therefore very seldom that the full weight of the law fell on those tried before the Excise on licence violations. For most offenders prosecuted in this way, conviction must have been an unwelcome, but affordable, inconvenience.[56]

Before moving on to assess the use JPs made of their summary powers, we should examine some facets of popular reaction, public debate and legislative action that were bound up with this issue. Criticism of magisterial action was not limited to their perceived usurpation of the excise jurisdiction. JPs were also portrayed as corrupt. One writer accused justices of pocketing fines for themselves, an allegation which was not without foundation. Thomas Cotton, a Middlesex justice, was himself informed upon for taking unwarrantable 'fees' out of received fines. Half the fine was to be given to parish churchwardens, and scrupulous churchwardens' accounts list the exact amount he skimmed off from their share. The Middlesex bench was worried that such practices both discouraged prosecutions and led people to suspect many convictions were motivated by greed.[57]

But while justices were maligned, informers became the real villains of the 1736 Gin Act. The use of informers and rewards was a normal provision in excise laws, but the aims and targets of prosecutions under such regulations were different, and the Excise had a formidable army of officials to ensure compliance. The reformation of manners campaign from the 1690s had made use of informers, though they attempted to avoid the problems associated with the acceptance of rewards.[58] In the case of the

Gin Act, it was reported within weeks of its passage that there were gangs of 'professional' informers trying to earn a living through false accusations. In June 1738, Mary Pocock was convicted of perjury for this offence and sentenced to a year's imprisonment and a £10 fine. Another informers' strategy was to extort money by threatening to go to the authorities. Richard Shaw was convicted of defrauding Richard Wilkins of 1 shilling 6 pence on this account, and sent to the house of correction for two weeks.[59] Both practices happened with some regularity, and a rise in acquittal rates in Westminster during 1738 shows justices became unwilling to see informers as credible witnesses.[60] Reay Sabourn, author of *A Perfect View of the Gin Act*, actually advertised in *The Craftsman* asking for people to send their stories against informers to him so they could be exposed 'for the Benefit of the Public'.[61]

While Sabourn and his colleagues were undoubtedly creating polemics against the law, there is little reason to believe their accounts were fictional. His use of names and places was exact, and he identified people as informers who appear in JPs' reports and house of correction commitment calendars as informers.[62] Still, questions remain about the informers' practices: were there actually organized gangs, and did people try to make their living by being informers? Some conclusions about the behaviour of informers can be drawn from Middlesex JPs' reports sent to the Duke of Newcastle. These reports for the Tower Division cover only 76 cases, but list the names and parishes of informers, and those who backed up their informations by oath. It is clear that it was common for a person to make multiple informations. Almost three quarters of 149 informations and oaths were made by persons who had made at least one, and often many others. One extensive group can be detected: working in different combinations, this cluster of thirteen people made a quarter of all statements to the justices. With the frequent appearance of the same people in informations, it is not difficult to see how the perception of an organized trade was started.[63]

Informing was frequently attended with harassment. There was a long history of dislike of informers going back to the Conventicle Acts of the previous century. While it appears to have taken some time for popular resentment to get started, by midsummer 1737 mob action against informers began to grow. Although the press cannot provide a complete guide to the frequency of such events, the *London Evening Post* took a consuming interest in the law from its inception, and reported troubles ranging from a slight beating of an informer to full riots thirty times between 16 July 1737 and 25 February 1738. There was just one report of crowd violence of this sort before the first date, and only two after the last.[64] The treatment of informers was much the same accorded to any object of crowd action: beatings, being rolled through the kennels and streets, being pelted with dirt, and duckings in the Thames or a horse pond. A would-be informer at Bristol was tarred and feathered. One man was made the centrepiece of a kind of charivari, and put on an ass and led up and down Bond Street. Most survived their ordeals with only minor injuries, but several deaths were reported in the press.[65]

Though most incidents were small, several turned into large-scale riots. The most serious occurred in January 1738 when Thomas DeVeil ordered Edward Arnold committed to Newgate after he threatened to destroy an informer's house. Arnold brought a large mob to DeVeil's house in Soho, and proclaimed he would pull it down and kill the informers the magistrate sheltered. Reportedly over a thousand people assembled. DeVeil read the Riot Act, but was forced to send for troops. Roger Allen, who urged the crowd on, was tried under the Riot Act. The government took the trial seriously, employing both the Attorney and Solicitor General as prosecuting counsel. Treasury solicitor Nicholas Paxton, however, felt the Gin Act was generally viewed as too severe, and believed it would only inflame the populace to make it the cause of a capital prosecution. The ministry went ahead with the prosecution at DeVeil's insistence. Public order always came before public relations. The jury acquitted Allen, and the general dislike of informers may have played a role in the decision.[66]

The response to this verdict by both informers and officials responsible for enforcement shows that they were sensitive to crowd action. The high constable of Westminster told the justices that with Allen's acquittal the constables had become afraid to enforce the law. Edward Parker notified the bench that informers were too terrified to appear. The justices reacted by ordering a thousand broadsides detailing punishment under the Riot Act printed and put up on all church and chapel doors.[67] Gin consumption had ceased to be the primary concern of those in authority.

Having examined the issue of informers, we can now return to enforcement under summary jurisdiction. It is impossible to discover how many people were tried in this manner, but we can construct a representative trend for committals to Tothill-fields house of correction by Westminster justices between 1736 and 1743. From April 1738 to January 1739 there are also reliable totals for those who paid fines or were acquitted in Westminster.[68] The evidence for the first fifteen months is sporadic, but suggests there was very little enforcement. Unless all those convicted managed to pay the £10 fine necessary to avoid imprisonment, which is unlikely, it appears magistrates did not immediately enforce the 1736 law.[69] Prior to December 1737, with commitment calendars covering over half the period, just six offenders were imprisoned. Publicized figures on summary convictions before magistrates must therefore have been exaggerated. A report in August 1737 claimed that 127 persons had been sent to houses of correction in the London area since midsummer, yet only one had been committed to Tothill-fields.[70] Commitments increased in early 1738 and then grew spectacularly from April. This persisted until the autumn, after which commitments fell significantly.

The explanation for these fluctuations lies in the response of the central government to the increasing frequency of rioting from late 1737. On 8 March 1738 a royal proclamation declared that although the Gin Act had been effective, certain people had promoted riots to stop officers from executing the statute. The proclamation commanded justices, sheriffs and other officers to put the laws in execution against all offenders.[71] The excise commissioners sent copies of the proclamation to officers, exhorting them to 'endeavour to prevent a defeat' of the law.[72] The Privy Council took action, asking Newcastle, as *custos rotulorum* of Middlesex and Westminster, both to enforce the law strictly and ensure public disorder was dealt with effectively.[73] Newcastle wrote to the JPs in his jurisdiction, and the result was the sharp increase in magisterial activity in April. Procedures were regularized – justices scheduled regular meetings, normally three times a week, and complex rotations of constables and headboroughs were organized. In Westminster, a dozen constables were to attend every meeting. In order to discourage people hindering them, they were always sent out in teams of two to apprehend people. Though informations were often laid before one magistrate, judgement was to be made by the justices sitting together.[74] Not only was there safety in numbers, but decisions would take place in a more authoritative setting.

Along with the proclamation and instructions to justices, a new bill designed to make prosecutions easier was brought in by Jekyll and quickly passed. According to this law, almost anyone living in or near a domicile could be deemed a retailer, rescuing offenders or abusing informers became a felony, and magistrates could issue warrants without a summons being served. The new law permitted anyone to seize and hold a hawker until an officer could be found, and also attempted to reduce lax enforcement by justices.[75]

This unusual three-way central initiative – the proclamation, instructions to officials and the new law – was responsible for the great increase in summary prosecutions in 1738. Two important conclusions can be drawn from the trends in prosecutions. First, in normal times the government was willing to countenance minimal enforcement at the magisterial level, and instead relied on the excise's less stringent procedure against retailers. Second, contrary to the usual explanations given, mob action against informers did not lead to the failure of enforcement. The opposite was true: summary prosecutions increased because of the riots. Once the problem of disorder had ended, enforcement was gradually allowed to sink into its former lassitude on the magisterial level. Westminster justices soon tired of diligent attendance at the special sessions. An average of nine attended meetings in April–May, but this dropped to four by September, and often only one was present at the meetings in January 1739. As these reports were sent to the Duke of Newcastle and the Privy Council, one can assume the government acquiesced in this winding down of the magisterial machinery. Even the excise prosecutions fell off significantly.

William Hay, MP for Seaford, wrote in his diary in 1737 that 'there is scarce a law made but the people . . . immediately prepare to resist it . . . so that it is now become a question whether this Nation is for the future to be governed by a Mob or by the legislature'.[76] The King's Speech at the close of the 1736–7 parliamentary session echoed those sentiments, complaining that 'Defiance of all Authority, contempt of Magistracy, and even Resistance of the Laws' had become too general.[77] The one period of strict enforcement of the Gin Act was due to the desire of the government not to curb gin-drinking, but to restrain open defiance of the law and public disorder.

As contemporaries and historians have noted, the law became almost a dead letter by 1740, but debate re-emerged in 1743 when it became apparent that the new patriot ministry, led at the Treasury by Samuel Sandys, wanted to repeal the law. No one could really defend its record, but some MPs disliked the proposed replacement and argued against repeal until a better alternative could be found. Even those unhappy with repeal admitted the idea of prohibitive licence fees and high duties on retailers had been an impediment only to fair traders, not to the ones requiring regulation. They felt that the social dichotomy built into the law raised the indignation of the poor, making the law impossible to execute, and that the cure had caused problems, notably riot and perjury, which were worse than the disease.[78] There was thus considerable ammunition available to those who pressed for repeal.

The proposed new bill embodied the idea of a direct duty on the distilleries, but set the levies at very low levels ranging from 6 pence per gallon on spirits made from imported materials to just 1 penny per gallon on those made from domestic produce. Annual licence fees were lowered dramatically, to just 20 shillings, and only licensed victuallers or publicans allowed to take them out. The penalty for retailing without licence was decreased to just £10, and although hawkers could still be committed to a house of correction, whipping was abandoned. The government argued these changes would lead to an effective, if gradual, diminution of excessive drinking.

Despite an easy passage through the Commons, there was a concerted effort to stop the bill in the Lords. There is no need to discuss the lengthy debate in detail; old ideas were gone over again and again. It was argued that the new bill would not act to curb consumption. Instead, it would establish 'Iniquity by Law' and institutionalize vice. A contemporary ballad was entitled 'Drinking by Authority'.[79] Opponents claimed it would unleash an army of 50,000 retailers ready to plunge the populace into a mire of drunkenness.[80] The imposition of duties at the still-head was agreeable to most, but the duties were felt to be too low. Distillers and retailers, it was claimed, could absorb the duty between them and sell at the same low price as before. Chesterfield, stating that concern for revenue obviously overrode that for society, chided, 'We have various funds already, the aggregate, the sinking fund; this will be called the drinking fund.'[81] The government replied that the previous scheme had failed and a new experiment was needed. While conceding a large revenue would result, they said that it was impractical to attempt total suppression.[82] As had been the case with Walpole in 1736, it is far more likely that revenue was uppermost in the minds of the new government rather than laying down a workable social policy.[83] While there were ballads and broadsides levelled at the perceived treachery of Samuel Sandys, the response in the popular press was muted.[84] The bill eventually passed the Lords on a division, 82–55, despite Edmund Gibson's first appearance in the house for over a dozen years to vote against it.[85]

The 1743 law did result in a temporary drop in production, but after the initial reduction all that was achieved was a halt to the spiralling increase of the 1720s and 1730s. Since the law had few contentious elements, it occasioned little comment. Reasonably prosperous retailers had no difficulty in affording licences and the duties presented only a minimal deterrent to distillers. As to enforcement, there were reports of quite a few excise prosecutions in the newspapers, but there is no reason to believe these were any more onerous a burden than they had been under the 1736 legislation.[86] Summary judgement remained the method for dealing with hawkers, and the record here is one of inaction. According to a series of Middlesex house of correction commitment calendars covering over half the sessions between 1745 and mid-1751, just two persons were imprisoned for retailing spirits without a licence.[87] Sensitivity was low enough for Parliament to loosen licensing controls in 1747 without any real opposition.[88]

Renewed pressure for regulation erupted in 1751, when it was reported that there were more than 17,000 gin-shops within the Bills of Mortality, and that over 4,000 people had been convicted for retailing without a licence during 1750.[89] Press debate was significant, though not on the scale of the 1730s. Fielding's influential *An Enquiry into the Causes of the Late Increase of Robbers* singled out gin as a key element in the causation of crime, and Hogarth's graphic illustration of the evils of spirits was printed in February and almost immediately interpreted at length in the press.[90] The economic discussion was taken on by Josiah Tucker, arguing on the same lines as Thomas Wilson had in 1736, though perhaps with more accuracy.[91] Isaac Maddox, the Bishop of Worcester, discussed the moral and physical arguments in a pamphlet that went through several editions during the year.[92] The works of Hales and Wilson were held up as pioneering works of social commentary, but unlike the thirties, silence greeted this revived attack. Just one weak reply seems to have been attempted, arguing that the people, not the distilleries, needed to be restrained.[93]

The parliamentary campaign of 1751 was inaugurated by a petition from the City of London, and sixteen others followed within a month.[94] Thomas Potter suggested a duty of 2 shillings per gallon on domestic spirits, which was opposed by Pelham.[95] Loss of revenue continued to be a key concern, but Pelham bowed to pressure and introduced an increased tax of $4\frac{1}{2}$ pence per gallon, and doubled licence fees. The first bill in the entire series of regulatory measures that countenanced a real sacrifice in revenue was passed. Inexplicably, the Distillers Company was inactive during the 1751 debate. Perhaps they chose not to throw money away in a lost cause. Their lack of faith in lobbying was amply demonstrated in 1752, when they decided they no longer required a parliamentary agent.[96]

The forces behind the 1751 law merit further research. The broad based petitioning campaign almost certainly had some effect. Moreover, when the earlier drive for reform was pressed by activists, the government did not exert itself to address the complaints. The crime wave following the peace of 1748 certainly focused attention on its perceived causes, and Parliament in 1750 set up a committee to investigate the criminal law and find ways to suppress crime.[97] The regulation of spirits would have formed a natural part of such a movement. The foundations for specific arguments on the gin issue had been laid during the previous two decades, but the climate had never been sufficiently conducive to prompt a ministry to eschew revenue in pursuing social policy – 1751 was different.

As a first step, the 1729 Act had been understandably tentative, with uncontroversial aims and means, and pursued without vigour. It died a quiet death in 1733. The 1736 Gin Act was a legislative fudge that sought to allay the pressure from the moralist lobby without really harming the distilling industry. The law had been the work of a small group that helped to intensify a public debate present since the early 1720s. That intensity, along with the efforts of Jekyll, made some form of regulation almost certain. No matter what the reality of the situation was, the ministry would have found it hard not to support such legislation. The government, however, was never squarely behind the law, and while the distillers complained bitterly about the destruction of their trade, Jekyll's idea for direct taxation of the distilleries disappeared from the bill. The propaganda of the distillers in 1736 was far more effective than it seems on the surface. Just as important, the conventional dictates of contemporary economic wisdom weighed heavily against government legislating a healthy industry out of existence. During this period, economic and fiscal policy were the two most important domestic objectives of the state, and a social policy which was at odds with either of these was likely to fail. This does not mean Parliament was an unimportant institution, or legislation an untenable vehicle, for the implementation of social policy in the eighteenth century.[98] In this case, however, although moral reformers appeared formidable in the public debate, they were unable to push through an effective bill. The 1736 law was part of a continuing departure from active sponsorship of the domestic distilleries, but does not conform to the descriptions drawn of it by historians. Not an 'heroic' or 'draconian' law which failed, it was a law designed to assuage opinion, and do as little economic damage as possible while generating more revenue for the government.[99]

The 1736 law was not effective enough to answer the wishes of its promoters, but as informers had been chosen as its key instrument, it was adequate to engender violent opposition. The 1738 law was required for a short-term corrective, and was designed to solve a problem brought about by the patchwork nature of the one stitched together two years before: its brief period of relatively strict enforcement was intended not to establish a social policy concerning drunkenness, but to deal with disorder. The enforcement of the laws soon lapsed, and their repeal in 1743 had far more to do with raising revenue for the war than with cutting liquor consumption. The combination of very low rates of taxation and affordable licence fees was calculated to fill Treasury coffers, not put gin out of the reach of the poor. Only with 1751 was the first real step taken toward making sumptuary policy on spirits, so long a stated goal, an actual policy.

Notes

Versions of this essay were delivered to the Eighteenth-Century Seminar at Oxford University in March 1987 and to the Law and Society Seminar at the Institute of Historical Research in May 1988. I am grateful to John Brewer, David Hayton, Tim Hitchcock, Joanna Innes, Tim Keirn, Nicholas Rogers, Robert Shoemaker and John Styles for their helpful comments and suggestions on various aspects of this essay.

1   For a brief discussion of this earlier legislation, see M.D. George, *London Life in the Eighteenth Century* (1966 edn.), pp. 42–43. For a discussion of the rise of gin consumption and retailing, see P.A. Clark, 'The "Mother Gin" controversy in early eighteenth-century England' *Transactions of the Royal Historical Society*, 5th ser., xxxix (1988), pp. 64–66.
2   Clark, 'Mother Gin', pp. 67–71.

3 Clark, 'Mother Gin', p. 63.

4 For the growing respectability of the alehouse, see P.A. Clark, *The English Alehouse*, (1983), p. 222. For reformers' views see *A Dissuasive from the Horrid and Beastly Sin of Drunkenness* (1701), p. 2 and also Josiah Woodward, *A Dissuasive from the Sin of Drunkenness* (1711). For proportions of SRM prosecutions, see below, ch. 5.

5 Chandlers in this context refers not to tallow-chandlers but to small retailers dealing in a variety of goods. This figure is considerably higher than the 40.9 per cent Clark found in 1735–6 reports. See Clark, 'Mother Gin', p. 84.

6 GLRO MR/LV 34/3.

7 Clark, 'Mother Gin', p. 69. Clark notes Campbell's description of chandlers as all-purpose small retailers, but omits his excoriation of them for selling spirits, which Campbell believed made them 'the most obnoxious' dealers in London. R. Campbell, *The London Tradesmen* (1747), p. 280.

8 GLRO MJ/OC/3, ff. 41–3, 47. The physicians' petition is cited in E. Gibson, *An Earnest Dissuasive from Intemperance in Meat and Drinks, With a more particular View to the Point of Spirituous Liquors*, 15th edn. (1771).

9 See J.M. Beattie, *Crime and the Courts in England, 1660–1800* (Oxford, 1986), pp. 216–17.

10 *A Dissertation Upon Drunkenness, shewing to what an intolerable Pitch that Vice is arriv'd at in this Kingdom* (1727), pp. 12–13.

11 D. Defoe, *A Brief Case of the Distillers and of the Distilling Trade in England* (1726).

12 D. Defoe, *The Complete English Tradesman* (1726), ii, part 2, p. 80. Cited in George, p. 43.

13 *The Historical Register for the Year 1729* (1729), pp. 154–5.

14 Compound liquors were the result of flavourings, such as juniper berries, being combined with the produce of the malt distillers.

15 Guildhall Library MS 6207/1A, Court of Assistants of 25 March 1731.

16 HMC, *Egmont Diary*, I, p. 331.

17 In 1730 only 255 licences were taken out in London, and only 38 in the rest of the country. These fell to 23 and 0 respectively by 1732. Net receipts for the new duty were only £7500 during the first year of the law, falling to £1830 by 1732. M.J. Jubb, 'Fiscal policy in England in the 1720s and 1730s' (Cambridge Univ. Ph.D. thesis, 1978), pp. 274–8.

18 T.S. Ashton, *An Economic History of the Eighteenth Century*, p. 243. The accounts in Cambridge Univ. Lib. Ch(H) Papers 28/6 suggest a somewhat slower recovery, but do not substantially alter the trends. Sugar-planters and rum importers may have benefited from the law; rum imports rose 60 per cent between 1729 and 1730, and the amount of spirits drawn from molasses went up more than 20 per cent while it was in force. See Ch(H) Papers 28/18.

19 Guildhall Library MS 6207/1A, General Quarterly Court of 10 July 1733.

20 Caroline Robbins placed him among her 'True Whigs'. See *The Eighteenth Century Commonwealthman* (Cambridge, Mass., 1959). Jekyll was called the 'great promoter' of the Act by Edward Harley in his journal. Cambridge Univ. Lib. Add. MS 6851, p. 35.

21 For further discussion of the personnel in this context, see Clark, 'Mother Gin'.

22 S. Hales, *A Friendly Admonition to the Drinkers of Brandy, and other Distilled Spirituous Liquors*, 2nd edn. (1734), p. 15.

23 T. Wilson, *Distilled Spirituous Liquors the Bane of the Nation*, 2nd edn. (1736), pp. 35–7.

24 C.L.S. Linnell, ed., *The Diaries of Thomas Wilson, D.D.* (1964), pp. 139–40; 143–4.

25 Wilson, *Distilled*, pp. 14–20.

26 *A Supplement to the Impartial Enquiry into the Present State of the British Distillery* (1736), pp. 44–8.

27 *An Impartial Enquiry into the Present State of the British Distillery*, 2nd edn. (1736), pp. 16–17.

28 *Some Brief Considerations Upon the Prevailing ill Consequences and Dangers Arising from the Malt-Stillery* (1736), pp. 30–2.

29 *A Collection of Letters Published in the Daily Papers Relating to the British Distillery* (1736), Letter iii, pp. 14–22.

30 *The Case of the Sugar-Trade, with Regard to the Duties intended to be laid on all Spirituous Liquors, Sold by Retail* (1735).

31 Guildhall Library MS 6207/1A, General Court of 8 July 1735. This action also formed part of the Company's on-going attempts to get the powers of their charter reinstated.

32 *The Case of the Malt Distillers* (1735). See also, *An Impartial Enquiry into the Present State of the British Distillery* (1736), p. 2. The distillers of course denied their industry fell into such a category.

33 *Parliamentary History*, xii, 1219. The speech was ascribed to Chesterfield.

34 *Some Brief Considerations*, p. 5.

35 *Parliamentary History*, ix, 1043.

36 *Diaries of Thomas Wilson*, p. 143; HMC, *Egmont Diary*, II, p. 229.

37 *Diaries of Thomas Wilson*, p. 132.

38 BL Add. MS 6304, f. 159.

39 *Diaries of Thomas Wilson*, p. 220.

40 *Diaries of Thomas Wilson*, p. 148.

41 There was some dispute over the minimum quantity retailers would be allowed to sell at one time without having to pay the duty, another way to be certain small amounts could not be sold at low prices, and that the poor would not have access to the liquors. Jekyll, along with Thomas Winnington and others asked for a five gallon minimum; Perry, Sandys, and Sir John Cotton endorsed a one gallon limit. After some movement back and forth, Walpole's suggestion of two was adopted. HMC, *Egmont Diary*, II, p. 257.

42 There was a division on this amendment. The vote was 183–110. The tellers against were Sandys and Sir John Barnard. The latter had been voted thanks by the Company in 1729, but had obviously changed his position, possibly getting over what Wilson described as his 'fear of the Distillers in the next election'. *Diaries of Thomas Wilson*, p. 134.

43 Guildhall Library MS 6207/1A, General Quarterly Court, 13 July 1736.

44 *Parliamentary History*, ix, 1097.

45 George Rudé, '"Mother Gin" and the London riots of 1736', *Guildhall Miscellany*, x (1959), pp. 53–63.

46 PRO TS/11/1027.

47 Cambridge Univ. Lib. Ch(H) Papers 70/2/11.

48 See *Memoirs of the Times in a Letter to a Friend in the Country* (1736), pp. 14–19.

49 Ashton, *Economic History*, p. 243; J. Hoppit, *Risk and Failure in English Business 1700–1800* (Cambridge, 1987), pp. 88–90.

50 BL Add. MS 30,038, ff. 216, 221–2. There were about 30,000,000 gallons produced during that period.

51 He felt that the law against hawkers was meant to be taken more seriously. R. Sabourn, *A Perfect View of the Gin Act* (1738).

52 See for example, *A Short History of the Gin Act, or, an Impartial Account of the Conduct of some of those who have been intrusted with the Execution of it* (1738), p. 16.

53 An additional 213 were convicted in the rest of the country during the first fifteen months of the Act. PRO CUST48/13, p. 395.

54 The commissioners noted in their reports that nothing was paid into the Exchequer, all of it having been used for rewards to informants and incidental charges. PRO CUST48/13, p. 395.

55 *London Evening Post*, 16 June and 28 July 1737.

56 Not surprisingly, despite their considerable summary powers, the commissioners were seldom identified with perceived excesses in the law. By the 1750s there was some

questioning of the freedom of the excise to mete out punishment in a summary way, see J. Fitzsimmonds, *Some Free and Candid Disquisitions* (1751).

57   Sabourn, pp. 21–31. Victoria Library Archives, Churchwardens Accts A2106. GLRO MJ/OC/4, ff. 107–8.

58   See below, ch. 5.

59   *Old Bailey Sessions Papers*, October 1738, pp. 155–57. GLRO MJ/SBP/14, February 1739/40. Another was sentenced to two months' hard labour, or a fine of 14s. 6d. GLRO WJ/CP/P 54. For an example of reports in the press see *London Evening Post*, 26–29 November 1737; 28–31 January 1737/8; 27–29 April 1738.

60   PRO PC1/15/5.

61   *Country Journal or Craftsman*, 23 September 1738; Sabourn, p. 31.

62   His portrayal of Edward Parker, an excise officer, as corrupt is echoed in another pamphlet, and Westminster justices informed Newcastle that Parker had embezzled fines paid by those convicted. Sabourn, pp. 31– 6; *A Short History of the Gin Act* (1738), pp. 56–60; PRO PC1/15/5.

63   Middlesex (Tower division) reports in PRO PC1/15/5. Multiple informations can be found in Westminster as well. These reports and Tothill-fields commitment calendars show that women were frequently involved on both sides of prosecutions. In the Middlesex reports, for example, 61 per cent of informations were made by women, and 62 per cent made against them. The large proportion of women convicted illustrates their participation in spirit-selling. See Clark, 'Mother Gin', p. 70. The wives of men who owned taverns or dram shops might also have been the subject of prosecutions. Details of such a case can be found in King's Bench affidavits alleging a false information against Catherine Croft. PRO KB1/6 Mich. 13 Geo. II, bundle 3.

64   *London Evening Post*, 1737: 10 May; 16, 23, 26 July; 16, 18 August; 8, 22 September; 1, 11, 25, 27, 29 October; 17, 19, 24 November; 1, 3, 24 December 1738: 5, 7, 9, 10, 21 January; 4, 7, 9, 14, 18, 25 February; 6, 18 May.

65   *London Evening Post*, 18–20 August and 11–13 October 1737; 18–21 February 1737/8. See Beattie, pp. 134–5.

66   *Memoirs of the Life and Times of Sir Thomas Deveil* (1748), pp. 38–42. See also *London Evening Post*, 21–24 January, 18–21 February, and 9–11 May 1738.

67   PRO PC1/15/5.

68   GLRO WJ/CC/R; WJ/CC/B; PRO PC1/15/5.

69   In the Westminster sample almost equal numbers of those convicted were imprisoned as paid the fine.

70   *London Evening Post*, 16–18 August 1737. There were of course other houses of correction in Clerkenwell and the City, but Westminster should have had many more committed if this figure were accurate.

71   For the text see *The Political State of Great Britain* (1738).

72   PRO CUST43/75. Letter of 25 March 1738.

73   GLRO MJ/OC/4, ff. 104–5.

74   PRO PC1/15/5. Reports were made that justices were not following the procedure, and they were ordered to do so. GLRO MJ/OC/4, f. 113.

75   There had been a law passed during the previous session which attempted to encourage informations by allowing rewards to informers in cases where offenders could not pay the £10 fine. In these cases, the informer's share was to be paid out of excise prosecution fines. Another encouragement to payment was that those committed were to be whipped until bloody before their release. See 10 Geo. II, c. 17, clauses 7–12.

76   Northants. R.O., L(C) 1734, 3 February 1736/7.

77   HCJ, xxii, 21 June 1737, pp. 902–3.

78   See *Parliamentary History*, xii, 1198; 1242–3.

79   BL Add. MS 30,038, ff. 221–2. *Drinking by Authority. Now who'd be sober? A new Ballad* (1743).
80   This estimate was an exaggeration, but by 31 January 1744, there were over 22,000 licences paid for at the excise. PRO CUST48/13, p. 459.
81   BL Add. MS 6304, f. 160.
82   Over £92,000 had been received by 31 January 1744. PRO CUST48/13, p. 459.
83   *A Letter to a Friend in the Country in Relation to the New Law Concerning Spirituous Liquors* (1743).
84   Sandys had supported the law in 1736. See C.H. Williams, *S—s and J—l, A New Ballad* (1743) and *S—y's Budget open'd; or Drink and be D—'d* (1743).
85   BL Add. MS 6304, f. 168.
86   The only totals for Excise convictions are for the year following Christmas 1749. They cover Westminster and the parishes of St. Andrew Holborn, St. George the Martyr, St. George Bloomsbury and St. Giles in the Fields. There were 261 convictions. PRO CUST48/14, p. 354.
87   GLRO MJ/CC/R 4–31.
88   20 Geo. II, c. 39. This law allowed certain distillers within the Bills of Mortality to take out licences (at £5 per annum) to sell spirits.
89   *Gentleman's Magazine* (1751), pp. 89, 136. The figures on the number of retailers were surely exaggerations. See the constables' returns of 1750 in George, *London Life*, p. 54. The claims for convictions were no doubt highly inflated.
90   H. Fielding, *An Enquiry into the Causes of the Late Increase of Robbers with some Proposals for Remedying this Evil* (1751). *A Dissertation on Mr. Hogarth's Six Prints* (1751).
91   J. Tucker, *An Impartial Enquiry into the Benefits and Damages . . . from the present very great use of low-priced Spirituous Liquors* (1751).
92   I. Maddox, *An Epistle to the Right Honourable the Lord-Mayor, Aldermen and Common-Council, of the City of London . . . concerning Spirituous Liquors* (1751).
93   *The Consequences of laying an additional Duty on Spirituous Liquors, candidly considered* (1751).
94   *HCJ*, xxvi, pp. 55, 77, 84–5, 94, 106–7, 114, 117, 133.
95   H. Walpole, *Memoirs of King George II*, John Brooke ed., I (1985), pp. 49–50.
96   Guildhall Library, MS 6207/1A, 14 Jan. 1752.
97   Beattie, *Crime and the Courts*, pp. 220–21.
98   For a recent examination of this issue, see Joanna Innes, 'Parliament and the shaping of eighteenth-century English social policy', *Transactions of the Royal Historical Society*, 5th ser., xl (1990).
99   The first of these epithets was bestowed on the law by Dorothy George, in *London Life*, p. 47, and the second by Peter Clark in 'Mother Gin', p. 63.

Part Two: Crime

3

London Crime and the Making of the 'Bloody Code', 1689–1718

John Beattie
University of Toronto

The criminal law and its administration changed strikingly in England in the half-century after the Revolution of 1689. On one side there began in this period the significant broadening of the scope of capital punishment, the construction of what came to be known in the eighteenth century as the 'bloody code'.[1] But along with the extension of capital punishment, the decades after the Revolution of 1689 also saw several other innovations of equal importance, innovations that were designed, like capital punishment itself, to increase the deterrent capacities of the criminal law. They included, perhaps most importantly, the establishment of the first non-capital punishment that the courts could impose on convicted felons, in the form of transportation to the American colonies. They included, in addition, a variety of measures designed to encourage victims of robbery and other crimes to go to the trouble and expense of bringing prosecutions, a matter of the greatest significance in a system of justice that put the burden of prosecution entirely on the victim of the crime. It was also in this period that a fundamental alteration was made in trials for felony, for it was only in the 1720s and 1730s that lawyers began to appear in the criminal courts, authorized for the first time to act as counsel for the defendant as well as the prosecutor. Such developments transformed the administration of the criminal law and laid the foundations for the more recognizably 'modern' system of criminal administration that was to come into being in the nineteenth century.

Until very recently those changes have not much registered in historical accounts of this period. Discussion of the eighteenth-century criminal justice system has turned very largely on capital punishment, its meanings and consequences, and on the debates over the reform of the law. Other important transformations – including what it is not too fanciful to call the achievement of penal stability in the early decades of the century – had been little noticed even before the eighteenth century was reduced to stasis under the neo-Tory gaze of so-called revisionism. The reason for this neglect seems clear. These changes did not stir a great deal of contemporary discussion. They were not accompanied by the kind of public debate in the press and Parliament that was to mark the late eighteenth century as an 'age of reform'; there was no similar early eighteenth century airing of views on crime, prosecution, and punishment, no body of literature to draw attention to the changes taking place in the law and the practice of the courts, or to articulate ideas in the process of formation. Indeed, the later movement of 'reform' acted to obliterate any memories there might have been of earlier developments, for those who sought change after 1770 in the criminal law, in the condition of the prisons, in policing arrangements, or in forms of punishment, invariably characterized the system they attacked as the unthinking product of an unenlightened and more barbarous past. To the reformers, the legacy of the early eighteenth century appeared to be simply a bloody-minded enlargement of the scope of capital punishment. For them, as for succeeding generations whose views were shaped by the reform discourse, the gallows were the dominant image of eighteenth-century criminal justice, and terror its major weapon. The early part of the century came to be seen mainly as a time in which Parliament had given free rein to the personal interests of individual members and, by inattention and thoughtlessness, had allowed statutes to be had for the asking that would extend the threat of capital punishment to forms of property as yet unprotected.[2]

That view has dominated discussions of the criminal law in the eighteenth century until very recently. It shapes the work that established the modern foundations of the subject, that of Sir Leon Radzinowicz, whose magisterial account of the history of the criminal law begins with the onset of the 'movement for reform' in 1750 and is driven by the story of the reform enterprise and the efforts to overcome resistance to it. The deficiencies of this as an account of the eighteenth century – and even more as an account of the transformation of the English criminal justice system between the seventeenth and nineteenth centuries – become clear when one looks beyond the texts of the late eighteenth century reformers to the actual day-to-day administration of the law at the county assizes or the Old Bailey. An examination of the courts 'from below' makes it clear that other very significant developments besides an extension of capital punishment were underway before 1750. A system that appeared from the point of view of the reformers to have been a bundle of unchanging administrative practices inherited from a long past can be seen in fact to have been changing and adapting in significant ways and under a variety of influences, particularly in the late seventeenth and early eighteenth centuries.[3]

Many of those changes were effected by statute. Capital legislation was only one aspect of a more complex set of parliamentary initiatives, and indeed the objectives behind the extension of hanging, at least in the early eighteenth century, are only fully revealed when they are placed in that wider context. That is my subject. I want to try in this paper to characterize the range of legislative proposals to deal with property crime introduced into Parliament in the generation after the Revolution of 1689, setting out in broad terms the effort to establish more effective forms of punishment, non-capital as well as capital. I will go on to examine several of the most important – and notorious – of the capital statutes in more detail, especially those that made shoplifting and servants' theft hanging offences. To ask why these statutes were passed in the reigns of William III and Anne, who introduced and supported them, what interests they represented and what intentions they expressed, may reveal some of the impulses behind the extension of capital punishment in this period. I hope that it might also shed some light on more general issues surrounding the promotion of legislation. As we will see, there was very little direct official involvement in the making of the criminal law: for the most part, criminal legislation was introduced by private members, though it is possible that members interested in a piece of legislation would consult ministers, and that ministerial support was necessary for success. It is clear that the views of the judges were often sought when legislation was debated in the House of Lords, especially capital legislation. But these matters are only imperfectly understood. The process of legislation remains obscure in large part because the sources are so poor. There are no records of debates, and even the more official parliamentary records are fragmentary.[4] I hope that my discussion of the making of a number of criminal statutes might illuminate these more general matters. But my main intention is to place the capital statutes of the reigns of William and Anne in the context of the range of innovations pressed forward in this period to enlarge the deterrent capacities of the criminal law.

Changes in the law and in administrative practices in the generation after the Revolution were too piecemeal and unco-ordinated to have been the product of a coherent plan. But they clearly reflect a conviction in Parliament, in the courts, in the government, and in some important social groups that crime and the social disorder it sprang from required a much firmer line than the authorities and the courts were taking. In broad terms, this programme – if I may beg the question and call it that – was the indirect product of the Revolution of 1689. It sprang in part from convictions about the threat of immorality in society released by the events of the Revolution, and from the effect of warfare on patterns and perceptions of crime in the generation after the Revolution. Ultimately, many of its most important features were the product of a more powerful executive and of the intrusion of the State into criminal administration.

But most directly, it was encouraged and made possible by the regularity of parliamentary sessions after 1689.

The criminal legislation introduced into Parliament between the Revolution and the early years of George I's reign can be divided broadly into four areas: (1) measures removing benefit of clergy from specific offences, designed to discourage these crimes by making them subject to capital punishment; (2) measures aimed at introducing various forms of secondary punishment; (3) measures to prevent crime by improving surveillance, and by encouraging the apprehension and prosecution of offenders; (4) measures taken to strengthen the courts. Nearly a hundred bills dealing with such subjects were introduced in the reigns of William III and Anne and in the early years of George I, and they led to the passage of about a dozen significant statutes.[5] Such extensive activity was made possible by the frequent meetings of Parliament after the Revolution. But the important question is why were men looking to take advantage of opportunities to introduce the measures they did? What were the problems, and why were these particular options and solutions put forward?

One answer lies in the character and experience of crime, and in perceptions of the causes of crime. Among the legislation proposed soon after the Revolution, for example, was a series of measures designed to encourage the apprehension and prosecution of highwaymen. Robberies on the highway did not of course alarm people for the first time in this period; highway robbery had been one of the first offences removed from benefit of clergy in the sixteenth century, and in the 1650s and after the Restoration a variety of means were proposed to encourage the discovery and prosecution of such offenders.[6] But robberies on the highways may have been especially common in the early 1690s; certainly, the problem was very much on people's minds soon after the Revolution. A London man, who was acting as an agent for a country gentleman in this period and who regularly included crime news along with other interesting occurrences in his correspondence, reported dozens of attacks in the streets of the capital in the 1690s.[7] There was sufficient anxiety that the government took several steps to encourage the apprehension and prosecution of robbers. In May 1689, the keeper of Newgate gaol was given a royal warrant that authorized him to arm his turnkeys and other servants and to patrol the highways from time to time to 'apprehend such robbers' as he should meet with and take them before the nearest JP.[8] The central government took a variety of further steps to counter robbery in the capital. A Privy Council committee was appointed in 1691 to 'consider expedients for the better securing of the streets from robbers, preventing burglaries, and redressing the disorders and abuses that are daily committed, as well in St James Park as in the streets'.[9] And those same concerns were expressed in initiatives taken in Parliament. They lie behind the introduction of bills into the House of Commons in 1690 and 1692 'to encourage the apprehending of highwaymen', and behind the Act passed in 1693 for that purpose.[10]

That statute was part of the early renewal after 1689 of a practice established in the sixteenth century of extending capital punishment to particular offences by the denial of benefit of clergy. But this 1693 statute was particularly significant in that it introduced a principle into criminal administration that was to have fundamental effects in the eighteenth century and after. The statute authorized a reward of forty pounds to be paid by the sheriff of a county to anyone who apprehended and then successfully prosecuted a highwayman. Rewards had been paid before on the authority of royal proclamations; and for a brief period in the 1650s they had been authorized by law.[11] But for the most part, earlier rewards had been *ad hoc*, usually for the particular offences named in proclamations or advertisements. Rewards now became an established feature of the criminal justice system, with payment guaranteed by statute – a guarantee that the conviction of a highway robber would be worth forty pounds to those who brought the prosecution. Later statutes added rewards in the form of certificates that excused a man from holding parish office; and a forty pound reward was added in 1706 for the conviction of burglars.[12] But the statute of 1693 was the important enactment. It made the apprehension and conviction of robbers an extremely profitable activity and it clearly encouraged private-enterprise policing.[13]

There is no reason to think that concern about robberies was confined to the capital: on the contrary, there is evidence of alarm from around the country. The keeper of Warwick gaol was given the same warrant as the keeper of Newgate in May 1689, for example, presumably in the wake of an outbreak of highway robberies in that county.[14] And some of the provisions in the legislation submitted to Parliament in the 1690s suggest that robberies in the countryside were partly responsible for the panic that seems to have gripped some Members of Parliament – proposals for example to reconstitute and revivify established institutions like the hue and cry and to reaffirm the responsibility of the hundred to indemnify victims of robberies.[15] But it seems clear that robberies by footpads in the streets of London and attacks by mounted men on the roads leading into the capital were thought to be particularly common and particularly brutal in the last decade of the seventeenth century, and measures were taken in the city itself, as well as by Parliament and the administration, to bring such attacks under control.[16] One response in the City, for example, was an attempt to improve the lighting of the streets, for it was clear that darkness encouraged robbery by making it comparatively easy for the attacker. By 1692, sufficient lights had been set up to allow the contractor to claim some success in preventing robberies.[17] Violent crime was a concern around the country, but it seems clear that the anxiety caused by such offences in the metropolis in these years after the Revolution was particularly important in stimulating the variety of efforts to deal with it.

Robbery and burglary were to be met by improved surveillance and by more certain prosecution. But the main weapon remained, as it had always been, the terror of the gallows. It was a fundamental assumption that some offenders were such a threat to the community that their execution was essential; and that the sight of men and women being hanged provided the only effective means of deterring others. But crime, and particularly crime in London, consisted of more than violent depredation. There was also a very large number of more minor offences, offences that did not threaten a victim in the way that robbers did or that burglars might, but that were nonetheless damaging, costly, and deeply irritating. Such offences as shoplifting, theft from stalls and wagons and ships in the Thames, the picking of pockets, and theft by servants and other employees were particularly pervasive in London. They arose from the sheer size and density of the population and from the circumstances of life and work in the capital – no doubt from the opportunities provided for theft, but also from the relative independence of much of the working population and the desperate circumstances they found themselves in from time to time. Crimes against property appear to have been common at all times in London, but they also fluctuated strikingly. There were moments throughout the late seventeenth and eighteenth centuries when crime seemed particularly threatening – certainly when prosecutions were very numerous, the prisons crowded, the court calendars packed, and the gallows very busy. Such moments came regularly at the conclusions of wars, a sharp fall in prosecutions having always taken place during the war itself.[18]

The problem of crime brought periods of serious anxiety in London. But the nature of crime in the capital, its pervasiveness as well as its violence, made it a common and continuing problem and placed it frequently on the public agenda. It was for this reason that considerable efforts were made in the late seventeenth and early eighteenth centuries not only to deter violent property offences more effectively, but also to find ways of combatting all forms of theft and pilfering. These initiatives are of the greatest significance, for while the determination to deter violence reinforced and extended established methods of deterrence, the efforts to eradicate more minor forms of property crime led to new approaches, and to the emergence of new ideas about crime prevention.

One problem attacked in a variety of ways in this period was the absence of an established non-capital punishment. Felonies, including crimes against property, were all capital offences at common law. In practice the device of benefit of clergy saved vast numbers of convicted felons from the gallows. But clergy did not substitute another punishment: those granted its privileges were branded on the thumb, but more as a record than a punishment. In the late seventeenth century some convicted felons were hanged, but most were granted clergy and immediately released. Clergy operated as a rough way of controlling levels of capital punishment. But the lack of an alternative punishment for those eligible to apply for clergy – a number that grew in significant ways in the late seventeenth and early eighteenth centuries[19] – had become irksome to judges and some parliamentarians and no doubt to others. Certainly, there is a great deal of evidence that the penal choices available to the courts were thought to be entirely inadequate by the last decades of the seventeenth century. That evidence is not to be found in public debate or in pamphlets, but rather in a variety of *ad hoc*, piecemeal attempts, some through legislation, to find a solution to that lack of choice.[20]

The centre of the problem seems certainly to have been the lack of a non-capital punishment that would deter property offenders, and especially that would diminish and control the numbers of petty crimes. One can see that in the efforts made in Parliament in the 1660s to establish transportation to America as a punishment for clergyable felony: two bills were introduced soon after the Restoration to authorize the courts to transport felons, but both failed. The search for a non-capital punishment was taken up again in Parliament after the Revolution of 1689. What was seen as the inadequacy of clergy was revealed most directly in a clause of a 1699 statute that we shall return to in a moment that shifted the branding from the thumb to the left cheek to make it more terrifying and thus a more effective deterrent.[21] More significant than this desire to heighten the terror of the law along old lines were several attempts to establish non-capital punishments on a new basis, punishments that would work not by deterrence alone, but by reformation and rehabilitation. In the wake of the drive in the early 1690s that resulted in the establishment of the forty pound statutory reward for the successful prosecution of a highwayman in 1692, for example, the Member of Parliament who had introduced that legislation and chaired the committee, John Brewer, a backbench lawyer, also introduced a bill that would have taken another approach to the problem of robbery on the highway. Brewer chaired a select committee of the Commons in 1694 that reported in favour of the introduction of a bill that sought 'the more effective apprehending and punishment of highwaymen, by changing the present punishment of death; and, instead thereof, to confine them to hard labour, with marks of ignominy.'[22] About this bill a contemporary observed that 'The Commons have fallen on many excellent points lately, whereof one is, that there bee a middle punishment for highway men, betwixt hanging and acquitting [i.e. clergy], viz. exposed to labour, and that workhouses be set up for that purpose. . . .'[23]

A middle punishment – between hanging and the ineffective branding of clergy which seemed to this man as to so many others tantamount to acquittal – is clearly what many contemporaries sought. And, as in this 1694 bill, the punishment that seemed to some MPs likely to be most effective both as a deterrent and as a means of training and rehabilitating offenders was hard labour. This bill got no further than leave to submit. Nor did another attempt to introduce a non-capital punishment in place of hanging for serious property offences when, in 1698, in a bill to introduce a ten pound reward for the conviction of house-breakers, a motion to instruct the committee to which the bill was sent after second reading to 'consider of some other Punishment than Death for Burglars and Highwaymen' was rejected.[24]

Little evidence has survived about these attempts to introduce a non-capital punishment for at least some of the offenders convicted of what were regarded as the most serious property crimes. It seems reasonable to think that they got nowhere in the House because those offences *were* regarded so seriously; and that no doubt also explains the defeat of a bill 'for the more effectual punishment of felons and their accessories' introduced in 1702 by Sir Robert Clayton and Sir William Ashurst, both aldermen and past mayors of London and both members for the City.[25] The bill, which was rejected at second reading, has not survived, but its main point is made clear in the diary of Sir Richard Cocks who noted under the date on which the bill was turned back: 'some bills were read and amongst the rest the alteration of the law as to felons, viz. to transport them to our plantations instead of hanging them. . . .'[26] But the City was to lead a more successful campaign in the next few years to institute a non-capital punishment, a campaign that was successful perhaps because it concentrated more clearly on the target Brewer, Clayton, Ashurst and others like them seem to have had in mind all along: not capital punishment, but clergy, or rather the consequences of the granting of clergy. That is borne out by the successful attack on clergy in the early years of Queen Anne's reign, an attack centred on less serious offences than robbery and burglary, and instigated by the City of London.

A fundamental change in the consequences of benefit of clergy had been effected in 1699, as we have seen, when the branding it entailed – the record in effect of its having been granted – was moved from the thumb to the cheek. Within five years that alteration was seen to have had disastrous consequences. In December 1704 a petition to the House of Commons from 'the Grand Jury, Citizens, and Shopkeepers of the City of London' argued that branding felons on the cheek 'hath been found by Experience not to have the intended Effect' since the permanent and visible stigma made it impossible for them to find employment and thus 'made them desperate' and confirmed them as thieves. The petitioners urged that as an alternative, clergied felons should be 'kept to hard labour' for a year for their first offence, for two years for the second, and put to death if they were convicted for a third time. A bill to this effect was presented by Sir Gilbert Heathcote, an alderman, lord mayor, and MP for the City of London, but got no further than second reading.[27] Another bill to the same effect failed in the House of Lords early in 1706, but was passed at the third attempt in the 1706–7 session, having again been introduced in the first place in the House of Lords. Why it was introduced in that House is unclear. It is possible that the purpose was to seek the approval and support of the judges for such a major change in penal policy, a possibility suggested by the Lords' order, when the bill was introduced, that the judges be asked to attend at second reading.[28] The statute that received the royal assent in February 1707 (6 Anne, c. 9) did not include the penalties for second and third offences originally contemplated, but it did include the central suggestions in the City of London petition, and indeed the petition was quoted verbatim in the preamble. As a result, the branding of clergy was returned to the hand, and the judges were authorized at their discretion to sentence clergied felons to a period of six months to two years at hard labour in a house of correction or workhouse. That provision was immediately employed in a significant number of cases in several jurisdictions.[29]

Hard labour and the discipline of the house of correction appealed to the authorities of the City of London in this period for the same reasons that were to make the penitentiary such a promising instrument of social order at the end of the eighteenth century. Such a punishment, it was said in 1706, would be 'a proper meanes to breake [offenders] of their idle and wicked course of life. As also by the Example thereof to deter others from the like course and ill practices.'[30] But in fact another form of non-capital punishment was clearly preferred for felons. This was transportation to America, a punishment that could be seen as serving the interest of society, the criminal justice system, and the offenders themselves in that it punished seriously without killing, without burdening domestic institutions, and while giving offenders a chance to re-establish themselves and contribute to the imperial economy. Transportation had been practised fitfully for a century by Anne's reign, mainly as a condition of pardon for felons condemned to death. But it had not flourished. Attempts were made after the Revolution of 1689 to establish transportation as a punishment that could be openly employed by the courts. In 1702, as we have seen, leave was sought by two MPs for the City of London to bring in a bill that was described as altering 'the law as to felons viz. to transport them to our plantations instead of hanging them'. It was rejected on second reading, perhaps because it was perceived as an attempt to replace rather than to supplement capital punishment.[31] But transportation was nonetheless a favoured remedy for what clearly continued to be a serious problem for those engaged in the criminal justice system and those concerned about issues of public order. And it was to be established firmly and successfully in the new political circumstances that followed the Hanoverian succession. It succeeded then because it was not left to private Members of Parliament to shape it as they chose, nor entirely to private enterprise to administer. It was a piece of government business, and the system set up – though run by merchants – was paid for out of the public purse.[32]

The origins of the Transportation Act are not easy to trace, and little evidence has survived of a debate in or out of Parliament. But the interest of the City of London in its passage seems clear. Certainly, the City was well represented among the sponsors of the 1718 Act. It was brought in by a group of MPs that included two London aldermen, one of them, Sir William Lewen, the sitting lord mayor, the other, Sir John Ward, who would become the lord mayor in the following year. But, perhaps most significantly, it included Sir William Thomson, who was both Solicitor General and Recorder of the City. He clearly acted on behalf of the administration in his former capacity – a crucial matter for a transportation programme that was to be made to work with public money – and in the interests of the City in the latter. In fact, the Recorder of London had become an important link in criminal matters between the metropolis and the central government over the previous twenty-five years. Early in the reign of William III he had begun to appear in person before the cabinet after the eight annual sessions of the Old Bailey to bring the list of men and women convicted of capital offences and to receive orders about who among them were to be hanged and who pardoned.[33] He brought the government in this way much more closely than it had been before into contact with crime in the capital, at least as that was revealed in the character and the number of offences prosecuted in this most important court. His new role also placed the Recorder in a position to pass on the advice and the concerns of City authorities. That the Recorder and two aldermen served on the drafting committee suggests that the City was strongly supportive of the transportation policy. Thomson also managed the bill through the House of Commons and through a long and difficult dispute with the House of Lords about the inclusion of a clause – resisted in the Commons – that would have empowered courts of quarter sessions to transport deer-stealers.[34] At any event, the Transportation Act at long last provided what the City authorities – and no doubt many other interests – had wanted for some time: a penal sanction short of hanging that the courts could impose on convicted felons, particularly property offenders. That was a fundamental turning point in English penal history. Because it came to be paid for by the public purse the transportation of convicts to America also brought the central government into the administration of the criminal law in a new way. And because it was taken up and used extensively by the courts it came to have important implications for the entire system of justice – for the gaols, for trial procedure and jury practice, for attitudes towards punishment itself. It was in truth as significant a development for the history of criminal justice in England as the statutes that would later create systems of incarceration.

The emergence of secondary punishments for felonies over the late seventeenth and early eighteenth centuries seems to have enjoyed wide support in the country, at least among those who administered the law at quarter sessions and assizes. One thing is clear about this process of law-making: it was not the work of the government. Apart from the special case of the Transportation Act, and the occasions on which the advice of the judges was sought, there is little evidence of any official involvement in the criminal legislation as it passed through Parliament. It resulted largely from the initiative of MPs with a personal interest in reshaping the law, or perhaps of MPs whose constituents had such an interest. If one takes as the central group of parliamentary supporters of legislation dealing with penal issues (and parallel efforts to encourage prosecutions, or to make improvements in the night watch) those who brought in bills, or who chaired committees and reported bills, served as tellers, or carried bills from the Commons to the Lords, a group of several dozen members seems to have been actively involved. In the reign of William III close to fifty MPs supported criminal legislation in these ways, many of whom were the kinds of back-benchers Joanna Innes has identified as promoters of what she has called the general domestic legislation of the eighteenth century, that is legislation dealing with a variety of social problems like poverty or vagrancy, the imprisonment of debtors, or the criminal law and its administration.[35] Not surprisingly, about sixteen of these men were lawyers. Of course, many MPs besides lawyers would have had experience as magistrates of the administration of the criminal law, but some of the lawyers were particularly well qualified to speak to such matters: men like John Brewer, who was involved in half a dozen bills in the early 1690s, and who was Recorder of New Romney. An even larger number, perhaps as many as nineteen, can be identified as supporters of some aspects of the moral reform legislation against blasphemy, drunkenness, gambling and other forms of vice and immorality that the Societies for the Reformation of Manners and the SPCK promoted so actively in the reigns of William and Anne.[36] That provides a clue to some of the anxieties that encouraged the search in this period for punishments that might be thought to attack the roots of crime rather than simply terrorizing offenders into obedience by the bloody example of the gallows. For vice and immorality were widely agreed to be the breeding grounds of crime: what began as blasphemy or dishonoring the Sabbath or drunkenness, it was frequently said, would almost certainly lead, if unchecked, to pilfering and theft and then on inexorably to the most serious offences. Punishments that might interrupt this downward moral spiral, that might reform and restore, had an increasingly strong and natural appeal. And such ideas had perhaps a particular appeal in London where crime was so pervasive, and where the Societies for the Reformation of Manners were particularly active.

It is difficult to uncover in any detail the motives at work behind the criminal legislation introduced into Parliament in this period. There was very little debate or public argument, at least little that has survived. But the overlapping interest of MPs in moral reform and criminal law reform suggests at least one of the contexts within which changing penal ideas were forming. Further evidence of the way those links might have worked is provided by the views of a body of men who regularly expressed opinions on matters affecting the community: the grand jury of the City of London. The presentments of the grand jury were declarations of matters the jurors thought required attention, addressed to the magistrates at the Guildhall sessions, or to the bench at the eight annual sessions of the Old Bailey. Thirty-one such presentments from the City jury survive in the Old Bailey sessions papers from the reigns of William III and Anne.[37] Grand jurors were men of some substance in the City. If they were rarely the very wealthiest of its merchant princes, they were nonetheless – as merchants and shopkeepers and substantial tradesmen from the upper reaches of the rate-paying population – men who could speak with authority. They were also men of very considerable experience, both of jury service and of service in all the offices of ward and parish government in the City. Many were members of the Common Council. City grand jurors were leading citizens, civic-minded and active. They were also much more representative of their community, much closer to its problems and its ideas and attitudes, than were the grand jurors of the counties. By the late seventeenth century, county grand jurors, at least at the assizes, were being drawn from a narrow range of the county elite – from the upper reaches of the gentry.[38] Perhaps because of that, and because the county grand jury always included by then a substantial number of magistrates, their presentments tended to become briefer and more pro forma by the eighteenth century, except when they commented, as they did from time to time, on an urgent issue in national affairs. But the presentments of the grand juries of the City of London continued to speak in direct and detailed ways about matters of importance to the local community well into the eighteenth century.

The London grand jury presentments dealt with a wide range of issues, some very specific, some more general. In the reigns of William and Anne, they turned frequently to the issues that animated moral reformers and those who sought a more effective criminal law, and their presentments provide evidence of the way opinion was shaping on those matters in an important segment of an influential community. They frequently encouraged the City's magistrates to take action against the profanation of the Sabbath, against Sunday trading or public drinking, against gambling, blasphemy and obscenities of various kinds, including public stage plays, 'musick houses', and the excesses of St Bartholomew's Fair.[39] Such general concerns were also commonly linked to more specific recommendations, some of which were within the province of the criminal law. One of them that exercised the reformers and focused attention on the criminal law was concern about the attitudes and behaviour of young people in London. The corruption of youth, and in particular the dire consequences of the corruption of the morals of servants and apprentices, was frequently on the minds of the grand jurors, most of whom, as shopkeepers and craftsmen, were employers of young people. Immorality, they were certain, bred crime; indeed, the connection seemed so natural that when prosecutions for serious crime diminished in London during the War of Spanish Succession (as they always did during wars) several grand juries saw in this the good effects of the reform campaign. The 'visible success' of the Queen's proclamation against vice and immorality and the good work of the city magistrates, they declared in May 1703, could be seen 'in the inconsiderable number of Criminals in the list of this and divers former Sessions'.[40] Later in the war, the great reduction of offences was linked to the success of the London Corporation of the Poor, and particularly to the workhouses in which 'blackguard children' had been given work and training. Even more extensive use of workhouses, grand jurors thought, would result in further reductions of beggary and vice, enabling men to 'enjoy their possessions without fear of rapin and theft and other molestation'.[41]

But as one would expect, the grand jurors more often than not saw crime on the increase. They blamed this on a variety of problems, apart from the corruption of youth. Several juries commented disapprovingly on the temptations that many public houses presented their customers by serving drink in silver tankards.[42] Others were persuaded that a large proportion of property crime was being committed by people who came to London to find work, failed to do so, and were thrown destitute upon society. Several presented particular alehouses or lodging houses that they alleged were harbouring and protecting gangs of thieves and robbers. Another theme that recurs in the grand jury presentments of this period is the connection between serious crime – robbery and burglary in particular – and the failure of constables and the watch to maintain adequate surveillance.[43]

For the most part, grand jurors called upon magistrates and other officials to fight crime in London by enforcing the laws on the books. But on occasion they recommended that new legislation be sought. The great influx into London of 'loose and disorderly persons', the grand jury said at the January sessions in 1694, 'having noe visible estates or honest way to mainteyne themselves doe turn Robbers on the highway, Burglarers, pick pockets and Gamesters that follow other unlawful wayes to support themselves'; and they went on to suggest that the Court of Aldermen should 'endeavour the obtaining an effectual Law to compell' young men who came to London and were not working to join the army. This would be 'a greate meanes', they suggested, 'to prevent Robberies, Fellonies, Burglaries, and other Crimes and Misdemeanors which doe daily abound in and neere this City', and which, they concluded, 'bring many young and able persons to untimely ends by the hands of Justice'.[44] Another jury suggested that magistrates needed additional powers, so that after examining men who lived by pilfering and begging they could send them to the army. Women and 'blackguard' boys should, they thought, be sent to the plantations. That same grand jury also called for new laws against clipping.[45]

The clearest example of a grand jury pressing for significant changes in the criminal law came at the December 1704 session, at which the jurors devoted their presentment to the weaknesses of the secondary punishments available to the courts – to the inadequacy of clergy, the counterproductive character of burning on the cheek, and the failures of transportation as it was then established. They did so, they said, following complaints 'by many Eminent Tradesmen' in the City that the laws in force did not sufficiently discourage serious crime against property, and following a similar presentment to the Court of Aldermen at the previous session of the Old Bailey from the justices of the peace of Westminster. Although this grand jury was willing to leave it to the aldermen to take such action as they 'thought most proper and expedient', it was clear that what they wanted above all were more effective ways of punishing thieves short of death. It was this presentment that led to the petition from London to the House of Commons that resulted in the important statute in 1706 which altered the criminal law by returning the burning of clergy to the thumb, and authorized the courts to imprison clergied offenders for a period of six months to two years at hard labour in a house of correction or workhouse.[46] The value of hard labour as a means of punishing and reforming petty offenders was clearly an idea with considerable appeal to the shopkeepers and tradesmen and small masters of the City. I do not intend to argue that all changes in the law in this period can be traced to the influence of the City of London. But many of the changes being urged and being tried out in the courts and in Parliament seem to me to have been responding to the convictions about crime and punishment that the grand jurors in the City expressed – the strong sense that crime was enlarging and out of control, that old methods had failed, and that there was an urgent need for a non-capital punishment as a supplement and alternative to the gallows.

The establishment in the early eighteenth century of imprisonment at hard labour, and of transportation, as punishments for convicted felons was an important departure in English criminal administration. But it did not signal a principled opposition to capital punishment. Indeed, the complex parliamentary responses to crime in this period also included a number of capital statutes, three of which are particularly important and revealing. These were the statutes that extended capital punishment to housebreaking (1691), shoplifting (1699), and theft by servants (1713).

These statutes were the first for a very long time to remove clergy from crimes against property, and they can be seen as part of the first wave of the legislation that was to enlarge the 'bloody code' in the eighteenth century. But, unlike the Tudor legislation that had removed benefit of clergy from several forms of property crime (including burglary and robbery on the highways), they were addressed to relatively minor forms of theft, particularly the shoplifting and servants statutes. And – as a result – they were not very strictly enforced in subsequent decades. Such statutes have come to exemplify the thoughtlessness and bloody-mindedness of Parliament in this period, and to demonstrate the ease (it is often said or assumed) with which such statutes were accepted by Parliament.[47] Why then were these statutes introduced after the Revolution? Why were they thought to be necessary, and why did they take the form they did? What lay behind the threat of capital punishment for shoplifters and pilfering servants?

There seem to me to be two broad answers to this last question. One we have already touched on: the absence before 1718 of a non-capital punishment for felonies that the courts could award directly and that was widely accepted as appropriate and effective. These capital statutes were passed when the absence of a secondary punishment was being strongly felt in the courts and when efforts to remedy the lack of such a punishment had persistently failed. This was also the period in which benefit of clergy – the consequences of which were in effect simply discharge from the courts – was extended to all convicted offenders equally, a fundamental change that could only have served to underline the weakness of the penal system. That may have been one reason why some men thought it necessary and useful to extend capital punishment to additional forms of property crime.

A second answer lies in the character of crime, and perhaps, in particular, crime in the metropolis of London. These statutes can be explained as part of the attack on the more minor yet pervasive crime of the capital. They were directed at offences that were typically urban, not only in the obvious and straight-forward way that they sought to prevent shoplifting and theft by servants, but in another and more important respect: one of their main targets was a problem becoming increasingly identified in this period as a fundamental source of crime to the city – the activities and lack of controls over receivers, especially pawn-brokers. It was argued, for example, in the statute of 1691 that removed clergy from the offence of breaking and entering into a house during the day (3 Wm & Mary, c. 9) that such offences were encouraged by the 'great number of persons [who] make it their trade and business to deal in the buying of stolen goods'. That receiving stolen goods was merely a misdemeanor was emerging as a matter of major difficulty. The punishments imposed even on the few receivers who were caught and convicted were thought to be inadequate. This statute made receivers of stolen goods accessories after the fact and thus made it possible for them to be punished as felons (s. 4). As accessories, however, they could not be tried until after the principal was convicted and thus continued frequently to escape punishment altogether. Dealing with receivers was to remain a nagging problem.[48]

Receivers seem also to have been much on the minds of those who pressed for more effective ways to punish theft from shops in 1699, but the removal of clergy from shoplifting goods of more than five shillings in value – making it a capital offence – may have happened almost by chance. The statute (10 & 11 Wm III, c. 23) had a rag-bag quality in that it dealt with a number of quite different matters. That was not in itself unusual: virtually all bills of this kind – bills dealing with domestic legislation – were introduced by private members who may or may not have sought expert help.[49] And even if they began as bills dealing coherently with one subject, they were always open to amendment and to the addition of clauses that could easily turn them into patchwork statutes. That seems to have happened on this occasion. The statute began as a bill to establish rewards 'for the encouraging the apprehending of house-breakers, horse-stealers, and other felons'. It is likely – though there is no evidence of this – that the bill was a response to the level of such offences around the country, for in the years following the end of the war in 1697 there was a strong sense that serious crimes against property were increasing dangerously.[50] If it was this climate of anxiety that had suggested a bill to persuade victims of such crimes to carry on prosecutions, it may well have been the particular circumstances of crime in London that explain why this bill was expanded to encompass a number of other matters, including shoplifting. For while the statute that emerged did indeed introduce new rewards, numerous amendments and additions were proposed, some of which were accepted. The text of the original bill does not survive, nor are the details of all the amendments noted in the Journal of the House. But it is clear that amendments were proposed on at least five occasions and that the bill seems to have provided a convenient hold-all for members with ideas about how the crime problem should be dealt with. One of the amendments that failed would have required that witnesses for the defendant in a criminal trial give their evidence on oath – the point being to undermine what was thought to be the often perjured testimony given on behalf of thieves at their trials by receivers and others who encouraged them to steal.[51] But several other amendments were successful, and they changed the character of the bill considerably. It was by way of amendment that it came to include two very important clauses: one that moved the branding of clergy from the thumb to 'the most visible part of the left cheek nearest the nose' (s. 6); and a second that turned out to be the central matter of the statute as it was finally passed, to make shoplifting a capital offence.[52]

These additions seem to have been directly inspired by an intervention from the City of London, where, as elsewhere in the metropolis, crime was causing a good deal of anxiety in the post-war years. The shift in direction followed the addition of several members to the original committee that took up the bill after second reading, several of whom were City members or men with London connections. And what may have been a decisive influence was the publication of a broadside addressed to Members of Parliament. Entitled 'The Case of Traders, relating to Shoplifters, for the Bill against House-breakers, Shop-lifters etc. now depending in the Honourable House of Commons', the broadside called for the kinds of measures that were added to the bill in committee.[53] Shoplifters deserved much severer punishment, the authors of this 'case' argued, because shoplifting in London had increased to such an extent that it exceeded in value 'all other Robberies within this Kingdom'. It was also well-organized, backed by receiving networks, by bullies to rescue thieves if they were apprehended, and solicitors to help them if that failed. It was also common, they thought – anticipating in this, as in other aspects of their argument, the views of later law reformers – because victims failed to prosecute, preferring often to compound for the return of their goods rather than bring charges. But what was particularly to be blamed, the authors argued, was the lightness of the punishment suffered by the few who *were* caught and convicted. Some offenders, they said, were merely confined briefly in the house of correction without being indicted.[54] Even if they were sent to trial at the Old Bailey and convicted of felony, shoplifters were granted clergy, merely branded in the hand and then discharged from the court to go back to their business with impunity. The authors of this broadside left the solution to Parliament. But it was surely criticism of this kind that led directly to the harsh additions to the bill as it made its way through the House of Commons: the shifting of the brand of clergy from the thumb to the cheek; and the removal of benefit of clergy altogether from the offence of theft from shops over the value of five shillings, making it a capital offence.

It is clear that the perception was widely shared that shoplifting was very common and that the authorities, especially in London, were unable to deal with it.[55] This may well reflect the development in the late seventeenth century of retail outlets in London. It is also the case, as we have seen, that in the late 1690s crimes against property in general increased sharply across the metropolis in the wake of the peace signed in 1697 and demobilization of the armed forces. But a panic about the state of crime and the weakness of the courts does not explain the character of this statute, especially the making of shoplifting a capital offence. If the more effective punishment of shoplifters had been the central issue, one might have expected that the clause in the Act moving clergyable branding from the thumb to the cheek would have been given a try first. At least part of the answer might be that shoplifters themselves were not the only target, perhaps not even the central target of this swingeing legislation. It seems likely in fact that the new massive powers given to the courts were aimed at uncovering and prosecuting receivers, and at limiting theft in shops by deterring those suspected of encouraging it.

The petitioning shopkeepers were certainly persuaded that the rash of thefts arose in considerable measure from the stimulus and encouragement of receivers. And this no doubt explains why a large number of cases of shoplifting were brought before the London magistrates in the two years before the Act was passed and why the lord mayor and other city magistrates appear from the depositions they took in those cases to have made a particular effort to uncover the names of receivers. In February 1698, for example, Alderman Geffery, a city magistrate, recorded the confession of one Charles Cooper in which Cooper listed ten thefts from shops that he had committed with three other men in various combinations, and in each case the receivers they had sold the goods to – all of them different.[56] Of course, shoplifters and other thieves were frequently caught because they sold something that was subsequently recovered or because they tried to sell something and were challenged: the receiver or intended receivers were then naturally named in depositions because they were part of the evidence against the accused. But if they confessed to the theft, the accused need not have named the receiver in their examinations before the magistrates. Yet they very commonly did so in cases brought to the Old Bailey in these years, as though that information was valued not merely as part of the evidence against this particular accused, but part of the reason for the prosecution. And that may have been the point of adding the death penalty for shoplifters – not merely to frighten prospective offenders with the gallows, but to induce those who were caught to disclose their links with the criminal underworld by the threat of death and the prospect of mercy.

There is another reason to think that that was a matter of calculation, and that the capital provisions of the statute were seen as providing the authorities with such a flexible weapon. Section five of the Act laid it down that anyone accused of shoplifting – or burglary, house-breaking or horsetheft – who revealed the identity of two or more of their accomplices and gave the evidence that convicted them would be entitled to the King's pardon. That was clearly aimed against gangs, including gangs of shoplifters. To earn such a pardon, the evidence had to be given before the accused was actually committed to trial, that is the accused would have to confess to the examining magistrate and divulge the names of his or her accomplices.[57] Making shoplifting a capital offence similarly provided magistrates with immense powers to induce accused offenders to name the receivers who it was widely believed were responsible for a great deal of theft.

It seems likely then that from the beginning there was a conviction in Parliament and in the courts that the statute would do its work more by threat than performance, that there would be no need for dozens of shoplifters to be executed. There is thus no reason to think that the failure of the courts to administer the new statute to the letter would have surprised or dismayed parliamentarians. Indeed, since they defined the offence to be removed from clergy by the value of the goods stolen (five shillings or more) and not merely by the character of the act, it seems that those who drafted the bill aimed in fact to allow juries to impose the death penalty when they thought it appropriate and to remove it when they chose. They certainly must have anticipated that both judges and juries would have interpreted the five-shilling limit as an invitation to use such discretion. And the trial juries at the Old Bailey made it immediately clear that they would do so. In the three years following the passage of the Act in May 1699, thirty-eight men and women were indicted for shoplifting in the City of London under the statute. Seven were convicted and sentenced to death: how many of them were hanged is unclear, but it is almost certain that most were pardoned. Of the rest, five were acquitted, and twenty-six – two-thirds of the total – were found guilty by the jury of the reduced charge of theft under five shillings and were granted clergy.[58]

The third offence excluded from benefit of clergy in this period was another form of larceny: the theft of goods worth forty shillings or more from a house. This was a much more straight-forward statute than the shoplifting Act; it was introduced in the Commons in 1713 and passed quickly through both Houses with only minor amendments, emerging as a statute with essentially only one clause.[59] It was entitled 'an act for the preventing and punishing robberies that shall be committed in houses', but despite its apparently wide range the statute was in fact aimed at servants who stole their masters' goods, a point made explicitly in the preamble.

Why the statute was introduced and passed when it was is not entirely clear. But, as with the shoplifting act, its timing was almost certainly related to the level of prosecutions for property crime in the country and especially in London. In 1713, the end of a war was again marked by a sharp increase in the numbers of cases before the Old Bailey. But why servants? There is perhaps some clue in the kinds of cases being prosecuted in London in the few years before the statute was passed. In 1711 and 1712, a larger number (and what seems to have been an unusually high proportion) of the cases brought to the Old Bailey involved servants.[60] A high prosecution rate could mean that such crimes were in fact very common or simply that employers chose for some reason to prosecute their servants more readily than they might have earlier. In either case the figures are revealing; and equally revealing is the fact that, as in shoplifting cases in the late 1690s, the magistrates were clearly intent on getting these accused servants to name the receiver to whom they had sold the stolen goods. Elizabeth Huddlestone, for example, confessed in May 1711 that a woman she named had encouraged her to remove a piece of cloth from her master's shop and to throw a larger and better piece out of an upstairs window;[61] and George Knight told how he had stolen three to eight pairs of shoes from his master's shop each week for two years at the instigation of a man he named.[62] Many other servants made similar confessions in 1711 and 1712, and it seems clear that the cases that were pressed forward to trial, again as with shoplifting, were those in which a receiver could be identified, especially when there was a suspicion that the receiver had led the servant into the crime in the first place. There was a sufficient number of such cases certainly to persuade the grand and trial jurors who heard them at the Old Bailey, as well as those who attended the trials or read the accounts of them in the *Old Bailey Sessions Papers*, that the law was failing to prevent such offences.

But there was also clearly a common view that servants were not themselves as trustworthy as perhaps they once had been. Ample confirmation of that, for those who sought it, could have been found in the Old Bailey cases in 1711 and 1712. Several servants were alleged to have taken new posts in order to steal: Ann Ward, for example, who left a new mistress after a week, taking fifty pound's worth of silver with her; or Margaret Floyd who stayed only a day or two with the baker who had hired her on a yearly contract before making off with a silver tankard and spoon.[63] Even more alarming no doubt were the cases in which servants confessed to letting friends or lovers or gangs of men into their masters' houses at night to rifle them.[64]

The corruption of servants had been complained about on several occasions over the previous two decades in the presentments of the London grand jury.[65] And there had been at least twelve attempts in the reigns of William and Anne to get legislation that would have regulated servants in some way, mainly by forcing them to register with a central agency and to bring a testimonial from their previous master or mistress to any prospective future employer. The Court of Aldermen of the City were clearly interested in this legislation. In 1704 they prepared a bill to be introduced into the next session of Parliament – 'at the humble Petition of the Lord Mayor and Commonaltie of the City of London' – which makes it clear that the point of the registration of servants was to control theft. One great cause of crime, the bill asserted, was

> the ill Conduct of unwary housekeepers in the hiring and Retaining Men Servants and Maid Servants into their Service having no knowledge or good Account of them and who oftentimes prove persons of evil dispositions and shift from place to place 'till they have opportunity to put into practice their wicked designs. . . .

To prevent that in the future the bill called for the creation of a public office at which all servants within the Bills of Mortality (except those of the nobility) would have to be registered and from which they would require a testimonial before being hired.[66] A broadside printed in London in 1708 in support of another such bill spoke of the special need for such controls in London where, it claimed, employers 'are frequently robbed by Servants who belong to the Gang of House-Breakers . . . who oblige them to rob the House, or let some of the Gang in to do it. . . .'[67]

Such long-standing anxiety about servants was perhaps heightened by the apparent increase in property offences in general at the end of the war in 1712 and 1713. And that, along with the continuing deficiencies in the sanctions available to the courts, could well explain the demands for a change in the law that underlay the statute of 1713. The experience of the metropolis alone may not have created this panic about servants and the crime it was thought they were responsible for. But it does seem likely that there was particular anxiety about servants' loyalty in the metropolis where domestic servants changed posts regularly.[68] And there is no doubt that this statute addressed a problem that was at least thought to be acute in the city. It is this sense of anxiety that surely explains the capital provisions of the statute. It also explains the fixing of the non-clergyable offence at forty shillings or above, for that level of theft makes it clear that the statute was aimed not at the petty pilfering of servants, but at more sizeable and more threatening offences in which servants were allied with outside forces. And, as in the shoplifting act, the suggestions are that the new capital powers were intended to be used instrumentally or at least selectively. Certainly, the statute was no more stringently enforced than the 1699 act. In six Old Bailey sessions I have examined in the three years following the passage of the Act, fifteen men and women were accused under the statute, of whom seven were acquitted, four were convicted of a lesser charge by the jury reducing the value of the goods involved to less than forty shillings, and four were convicted and sentenced to death, though it is likely, given the common practice in the eighteenth century, that some of these were eventually pardoned.

Several initiatives were thus pursued in the generation after the Revolution of 1689 to find more effective ways to prosecute and punish offenders. A variety of options were taken up in Parliament, in the courts, in the central government. These did not flow from a set of agreed principles, nor from a coherent policy; indeed, they were in some respects contradictory. But the changes introduced after the Revolution in *ad hoc* and piecemeal ways had far-reaching effects. Not every path opened up in the 1690s and after was being taken for the first time; nor was each of massive importance on its own. But the sheer number of ideas developed and options explored, their overlapping character and their wider influences, made the generation after the Revolution a period of significant transformation in the criminal justice system.

There could surely be no single and simple answer as to why so many initiatives were pursued in this period to make the criminal law more effective, why the opportunities presented by the annual session of Parliament were seized in the reigns of William and Anne. But, without ruling out other explanations, the influence of London seems to me to be clear. Crime in the metropolis was more extensive and more violent and better reported than elsewhere, and it was at least perceived to be increasingly less amenable to control by established methods. That was especially true of the crime perpetrated by gangs and by what was conceived to be a growing army of predatory receivers. It seems apparent that much of the evidence that the law was failing to deter crime and the determination to find alternative weapons arose from the metropolis. The legislation of the early eighteenth century was not simply the last gasp of an old, bloody-minded, irrational, criminal justice system inherited from the long past, but at least in part a set of new responses from an urban world that was finding the problems of crime and social order increasingly difficult to contain. The response was muddled in that it combined old habits and new ideas. But it included what one can only call, in the language of the future, ideas of 'reform'. When men argued for the virtues of hard labour as a punishment for felons, or when shopkeepers complained, as they did in 1699, that very few shoplifters were being discovered, that of those arrested not one in ten was prosecuted, that of the few brought to trial not one in ten was punished, and that what was required therefore was a more effective system of prosecution and punishment, they were forming some of the central ideas that would underlie the more coherent and wide-ranging proposals of the criminal law reformers of the late eighteenth century.

Notes

I wish to express my gratitude to Alan Darnell for research assistance; and to David Hayton, Joanna Innes, John Langbein, John Styles, and my colleagues in the early-modern English history group in Toronto for their helpful comments and suggestions. I am grateful for financial support to the Social Sciences and Humanities Research Council of Canada and to the Ministry of the Solicitor General of Canada through its Contributions Grant to the Centre of Criminology, University of Toronto.

1 Sir Leon Radzinowicz, *A History of the English Criminal Law and its Administration since 1750* Vol. I (1948); E.P. Thompson, *Whigs and Hunters: the Origin of the Black Act* (1975); Douglas Hay, Peter Linebaugh, E.P. Thompson (eds.), *Albion's Fatal Tree: crime and society in eighteenth century England* (1975); J.M. Beattie, *Crime and the Courts in England, 1660–1800* (Princeton and Oxford, 1986), ch. 5.

2 For the reform discourse, see Radzinowicz, *A History of English Criminal Law*, I, parts III and V.

3 Beattie, *Crime and the Courts in England*, ch. 9.

4 For an illuminating discussion of the process of social legislation in the eighteenth century, see Joanna Innes, 'Parliament and the shaping of eighteenth-century English social policy', *Transactions of the Royal Historical Society*, 5th ser., 40 (1990), 63–92.

5 This total gives a slightly misleading impression because it includes similar bills introduced into several sessions before finally being successful or being dropped, and it includes some measures that may have been stimulated more by concern for the civil rather than the criminal courts – those dealing with juries for example. On the other hand, it does not include the large number of proposals dealing with the poor law or vagrancy or with vice and the reformation of manners, some of which bore in a broad way on the concerns of criminal legislation.

6 A ten-pound reward was established by act of Parliament in 1652, renewed in the following year, for the prosecution and conviction of highwaymen, burglars and housebreakers. See C.H. Firth and R.S. Rait (eds.), *Acts and Ordinances of the Interregnum, 1642–1660* (3 vols, 1911), II, pp. 577–8, 772–3. For initiatives taken in Parliament and elsewhere in the 1660s, see Beattie, *Crime and the Courts*, p. 51.

7 Russell J. Kerr and Ida Coffin Duncan (eds.), *The Portledge Papers: being extracts from the letters of Richard Lapthorne, Gent, of Hatton Garden London, to Richard Coffin Esq. of Portledge, Bideford, Devon from December 10th 1687 – August 7th 1697* (1928).

8 The keeper was also authorized to search houses suspected by him of harbouring felons (PRO, SP44/338, pp. 313–4; the warrant was re-issued in April 1693: SP44/343, p.

533). These thieftakers were to be given as a reward the money found on the robbers at the time of their arrest as well as their horses and arms. Further rewards for all those who apprehended and convicted a group of named robbers were added by royal proclamation in July 1689, and a further proclamation offering a twenty-pound reward for the arrest of members of a particular 'Party and Knot' of robbers was issued in October 1690 (*CSPD, 1689–90*, p. 181; PRO, PC2/74, ff. 23–4).

9   PRO, PC2/74, f. 66v.

10   4 & 5 Wm and Mary, c. 8. Another Act in 1691 had removed benefit of clergy from robbery in dwelling houses and from the offence of removing goods from a house when there was someone present in the house and put in fear: 3 Wm and Mary, c. 9.

11   See above, n. 6.

12   Successful prosecution of a burglar brought a certificate that excused the holder from parish office for life – known popularly as a Tyburn ticket – by 10 & 11 Wm III, c. 23 (1699); to that was added a reward of £40 by 6 Anne, c. 31 (1706).

13   Statutory rewards did not create thief-taking; private *ad hoc* rewards had been offered earlier; and there had long been other ways to profit from crime besides prosecuting offenders. But it is surely likely that the size of the parliamentary payment for the conviction of highway robbers (and the free gift of the offender's horse, weapons and equipment which the statute also authorized) encouraged men to engage in thieftaking. Thieftakers can be found at work in London by the late 1690s and they were to become familiar if rather shadowy figures in the metropolitan landscape in the eighteenth century (see Gerald Howson, *Thief-Taker General: The Rise and Fall of Jonathan Wild* (1970); and Ruth Paley, 'Thieftakers in London in the age of the McDaniel gang, c. 1745–1754', in Douglas Hay and Francis Snyder (eds.), *Policing and Prosecution in Britain 1750–1850* (Oxford, 1989), pp. 301–41.

14   PRO, SP44/338, p. 331.

15   For the continuing relevance and effectiveness of the hue and cry, see John Styles, 'Print and policing: Crime advertising in eighteenth-century provincial England', in Hay and Snyder (eds.), *Policing and Prosecution in Britain*, pp. 55–112.

16   For one contemporary view of the extent of the problem in the last years of the decade, see *Hanging Not Punishment Enough* (1701).

17   PRO, SP44/235, p. 297. Numerous bills to bolster the forces of watchmen in London parishes and to light the streets of the City were also introduced into Parliament in the reigns of William and Anne.

18   Beattie, *Crime and the Courts in England*, ch. 5; Douglas Hay, 'War, dearth and theft in the eighteenth century: The record of the English courts', *Past and Present*, 95 (1982), 117–60.

19   Fundamental changes in the character of benefit of clergy took place in this period. Before the Revolution the privilege of clergy was limited: the only women eligible were those convicted of theft below ten shillings in value; men could qualify only by proving their literacy by reading a verse from the Bible in court. Those restrictions were entirely removed after 1689. Clergy was extended fully to women in 1692: that is, if clergy was available in a particular offence, women were now as eligible as men to apply for it, and they would be granted it without having to prove their literacy. This surely explains why the literacy requirement was abolished for men in 1706. Henceforth, and for the first time, all convicted felons were treated alike. If their offence was within clergy they were granted its privileges; if not, they were sentenced to death. On the development of clergy see Beattie, *Crime and the Courts*, pp. 141–6.

20   For further discusion of these points see Beattie, *Crime and the Courts*, ch. 9.

21   10 & 11 Wm III, c. 23, for which see below, pp. 56–7. The argument in favour of branding on the face must have been that men and women would think twice about

committing an offence if they had to carry such a visible mark of shame for the rest of their lives. It was very quickly apparent that such harshness had entirely failed as a deterrent, both because the courts in fact soon began to evade the law's requirements; even more, because it was clear that men so branded were forced to turn to regular thieving because they could not find work.

22 *HCJ*, 11 (1693–97), pp. 95–6.

23 *The Portledge Papers*, p. 170.

24 *HCJ*, 12 (1697–99), p. 196.

25 *HCJ*, 13 (1699–1702), pp. 777, 781, 783.

26 The vote against second reading was 113 to 104. Cocks added that he thought 'half of the house did not know what they divided about'. Cocks's Parliamentary Diary, Cocks MS, Bodleian Library, MS. Eng. hist. b. 210, f. 7v. (I am grateful to the History of Parliament Trust for permission to read their transcript of this ms.).

27 *HCJ*, 14 (1702–4), pp. 463, 487–8, 526, 992.

28 *HLJ*, 18 (1705–9), pp. 184, 194, 202, 203, 232, 236; *HCJ*, 15 (1705–8), pp. 252, 270, 273, 281, 282. Not all criminal legislation was introduced in the House of Lords, but the judges were commonly consulted when that House considered important bills. By the end of the century it seems to have become an established custom that the opinion of the judges be sought on all criminal legislation. (Innes, 'Parliament and the shaping of eighteenth-century social policy', pp. 78– 9). That may not have been quite as clearly established in the early decades of the century, but it was certainly common, and it is possible that the judges were always consulted when major changes were contemplated, and especially changes involving capital punishment. Indeed, when the housebreaking bill of 1691 (3 Wm & Mary, c. 9) – for which see below, p. 64 – was under consideration by the House of Lords, the lord chief justice and another judge were specifically named to a committee to draw a clause that would deny benefit of clergy to servants who ran away with their masters' goods; and the judges were consulted later in the debate on an amendment relating to theft from lodgings. (*HLJ*, 14, pp. 638–9; *Historical Manuscripts Commission: MSS of the House of Lords (1690–91)*, p. 284). A copy of the bill that made theft by servants a capital offence in 1713 (12 Anne, c. 7) – for which also see below, p. 67–70 – was sent to the judges after second reading and they were asked to attend the committee of the whole house that would take it into consideration (*HLJ*, 19 (1709–14), p. 574). The judges were similarly sent a copy of the transportation bill in 1718 when it received first reading in the House of Lords and were asked to attend at second reading (*HLJ*, 20 (1714–18), p. 593). The judges do not, however, appear to have been consulted on the bill that made shoplifting a capital offence in 1699 (below, p. 64–7) which received very rapid passage through the Lords. (*HLJ*, 16 (1696–1701), pp. 455, 456, 460).

29 Joanna Innes, 'Prisons for the poor: English bridewells, 1555–1800', in Francis Snyder and Douglas Hay (eds.), *Labour, Law and Crime: an Historical Perspective* (1987), pp. 88–90; Beattie, *Crime and the Courts*, pp. 491–2.

30 These revealing intentions or hopes were expressed in an exchange of correspondence between Sir Charles Hedges and the lord mayor of London early in 1706 about the difficulties being experienced in transporting a group of women who had been pardoned from capital sentences on condition they be sent to the colonies, but who remained in Newgate because no colony would agree to receive them and no merchant would take them. Such difficulties were not new in this period: both the American and West Indian plantations resisted taking English convicts, especially women, and the arrangements for actually transporting felons were inadequate (see Beattie, *Crime and the Courts*, ch. 9). The problem was no doubt compounded by the difficulties of arranging shipping during the war. Early in 1706, Hedges proposed that the mayor and aldermen find an alternative, and particularly that they consider sending these women to houses of

correction to be kept at hard labour. The city authorities were only too willing: indeed it is likely that they had in fact proposed this to the government since they had for some time been pressing Parliament to enact a hard labour bill. Their suggestion was that London women who were pardoned should be sent to Bridewell, and women from Middlesex to the county house of correction. It was in the course of this correspondence that their intentions in pressing for hard labour in the house of correction as a sanction for some convicted felons were revealed (CLRO: Rep. 110, f. 68v.– 9, 75–6). It is possible that a hard labour act was eventually passed in 1706 because the administration gave it some support.

31 See above, text at n. 27.

32 By 6 Geo I, c. 23.

33 J.M. Beattie, 'The cabinet and the management of death at Tyburn after the Revolution of 1689', in Lois Schwoerer (ed.), *The Revolution of 1688–9: Changing Perspectives* (Cambridge, 1992).

34 *HCJ*, 18 (1714–18), pp. 667, 671, 675, 684–6, 691, 763–5, 768; *HLJ*, 20 (1714–18), pp. 586, 593, 600, 610, 632, 641, 648–52, 657–8, 660, 662.

35 Innes, 'Parliament and the shaping of eighteenth-century English social policy', pp. 80–90; and see T.K. Moore and H. Horwitz, 'Who runs the House? Aspects of parliamentary organization in the later seventeenth century', *Journal of Modern History*, 43, (1971). My identification of members in the passages that follow has been made possible by the kindness of the History of Parliament Trust. I am grateful to Eveline Cruickshanks, editor of the forthcoming volumes of the *History of Parliament, 1689–1715*, for allowing me to read the biographies of MPs already prepared and to use the materials gathered for that project; and to David Hayton for his advice.

36 For the Societies for the Reformation of Manners, see Shoemaker, ch. 5 below; I owe to David Hayton the identification of MPs as moral reformers: see his 'Moral reform and country politics in the late seventeenth-century House of Commons', *Past and Present*, 128 (1990), 48–91.

37 The same grand jury, normally sixteen strong, acted at both the sessions held in the Guildhall by the mayor and City magistrates for the adjudication of minor offences, and the gaol delivery sessions at the Old Bailey at which these officials were joined by several high court judges to deal with the cases of accused felons from the City and Middlesex held in Newgate. These sessions were held in the same week, one after the other. The grand jury could make two presentments if they chose, one at their dismissal in the Guildhall, the other at the Old Bailey, but they seem normally to have been content with one. For the timing and procedure of these London courts, and the composition of the grand jury, see J.M. Beattie, 'London jurors in the 1690s', in J.S. Cockburn and Thomas A. Green (eds.), *Twelve Good Men and True: Perspectives on the English Criminal Trial Jury, 1200–1800* (Princeton, 1988).

38 Norma Landau, *The Justices of the Peace, 1679–1760* (Berkeley, 1984), pp. 54–9; Beattie, *Crime and the Courts*, pp. 313–30.

39 See, for example, the presentments of February 1695, January 1696, September 1697, October 1698, July 1703; CLRO, Old Bailey Sessions Papers – i.e. the manuscript papers of the sessions, not the printed accounts of the Old Bailey trials which are commonly given that title (cited henceforth as Sess. Papers). Why the juries took up the matters they did is unclear. The members may simply have brought the issues that troubled them and their neighbours, or more formal means of tapping opinion may have been at work – through the wardmote inquests, for example. On the other hand, the presentments appear to have been written by the foreman of each jury, and those men may well have shaped their contents.

40 CLRO: Sess. Papers, May 1703.

41 CLRO: Sess. Papers, May 1706.

42 CLRO: Sess. Papers, July 1689, January 1690, December 1692.
43 CLRO: Sess. Papers, Dec. 1699.
44 CLRO: Sess. Papers, January 1694.
45 CLRO: Sess. Papers, February 1695. Several grand juries also called for improvements in the London gaols: one wanted an end to garnish, for example – the oppressive demands for fees when a prisoner first arrived in gaol (July 1699); another, in 1698, anticipated demands that were to be common in the future by complaining about the way prisoners in Newgate became hardened and lacked remorse – even at the place of execution – and called upon the aldermen to appoint gaolers who would oversee the 'reformation and instruction' of the inmates (February 1698).
46 5 Anne, c. 6 (1706).
47 For a critical assessment of this view, see Joanna Innes and John Styles, 'The crime wave: Recent writing on crime and criminal justice in eighteenth-century England', *Journal of British Studies*, 25 (1986), 380–435.
48 It was presumably the difficulty of convicting receivers that explains the passage of two statutes in Anne's reign that confirmed that receiving could also continue to be treated as a misdemeanor, so that even if the principal was not arrested and convicted a receiver could still be punished to some extent (1 Anne, st. 2, c. 9 (1702); 5 Anne, c. 31 (1706). On the laws dealing with receiving see Francis Hargrave, *A Review of the Laws against the Knowingly Receiving Stolen Goods: and a Proposal for making a New Law on that Subject* (London, 1770). The urban character of the 1691 Act is also suggested by section 5 which made theft of goods from a rented lodging a felony for the first time.
49 See Innes, 'Parliament and the shaping of eighteenth-century English social policy', pp. 76–90.
50 The author of *Hanging Not Punishment Enough* (1701) wrote in alarmist terms about the level of violent depredations that he blamed on demobilized soldiers and sailors. It was certainly the case that prosecutions for property crimes rose strongly at the Old Bailey and in other courts in the last years of the century; the level of reported crime was such that in the summer of 1699 the lords chief justice were called into the cabinet and ordered to instruct the judges on the eve of their going on circuit to make sure they dealt adequately with convicted highwaymen, housebreakers and other felons (*CSPD*, 1699–1700, pp. 237–8).
51 That clause was passed into law in 'An Act for punishing of accessories to felonies, and receivers of stolen goods': 1 Anne, st. 2, c. 9 (1702).
52 For the parliamentary history of this statute, see *HCJ*, 12 (1697–99), pp. 497, 525, 540, 541, 556, 607, 625, 659, 669, 671, 675, 681. The House of Commons was occupied with this bill on and off for three months; the Lords on the other hand, despite its inclusion of capital provisions, approved it in three days, though it was in the Lords that the words 'nearest to the nose' were added to the branding clause, and the further instruction that the branding be inflicted in open court in the presence of the judge, 'who is hereby directed and required to see the same strictly and effectually executed'. The judges do not appear to have been specifically consulted on the bill (*HLJ*, 16 (1696–1701), pp. 455, 456, 460, 465).
53 The full title at the head of the one-page broadside is '*The Great Grievance of Traders and Shopkeepers, by the Notorious Practice of Stealing the Goods out of their Shops and Warehouses, by Persons commonly called Shoplifters; Humbly represented to the Consideration of the Honourable House of Commons*'. The title quoted in the text is on the reverse. The broadside is undated. The British Library dates its copy ?1720, but internal evidence would place it in the spring of 1699.
54 This was almost certainly a reference to a common practice of London magistrates in this period (including the lord mayor) who very often labelled men and women accused of minor property offences as 'pilferers' and sent them to a term in the house of

correction under a form of summary jurisdiction rather than committing them to gaol to stand trial for larceny. This practice is revealed in the lord mayor's 'Waiting Book', a record of the mayor sitting as a magistrate (CLRO).

55   The real level of shoplifting, or of any other offence, is unknown. Even the level of *prosecuted* shoplifting cases is impossible to establish because before the 1699 Act theft from a shop was indicted simply as larceny, without the place of the offence being specified in the formal record. The character of many of the offences indicted as simple larceny can be uncovered, however, from supplementary evidence – from depositions of victims and witnesses, examinations of the accused, recognizances, printed accounts of the trials, and (for the identification of the victim as a shopkeeper) tax records. Such evidence suggests that in well over half the larceny cases from the City of London prosecuted at the Old Bailey in the 1690s the victims were in wholesale or retail trades, the largest number of them shopkeepers, and that at least a quarter of simple thefts were described as having taken place in shops. Those figures are based on an examination of all the available evidence of the year 1694.

56   CLRO: Sess. Papers, Feb. 1698.

57   For the importance of such pardons in eighteenth-century criminal procedure, see John H. Langbein, 'Shaping the eighteenth-century criminal trial: The view from the Ryder Sources', *University of Chicago Law Review*, 50 (1983), 1–136; and Beattie, *Crime and the Courts*, pp. 430–49.

58   One of the reasons why relatively few shoplifters were hanged, even in the years immediately after the Act was passed, may well have been because so many of the accused were women. But that is not the fundamental reason: while women were for the most part treated more leniently than men in this period, certainly for crimes against property, the courts were ready enough to hang women when their offences were heinous enough. See Beattie, *Crime and the Courts*, pp. 436–9.

59   12 Anne, c. 7 (1713); apart from the one main matter, a second clause excluded apprentices under the age of fifteen from the captial provisions of the Act, and a third clarified a point about burglary, extending it to include the offence of entering a house during the day for the purpose of committing a felony and then breaking out at night.

60   The relationship of the offender and the victim in a felony is not revealed in the indictment, but the depositions and examinations taken by magistrates often make that clear. Not all such documents have survived in the Old Bailey sessions papers in this period, but those that are available for City of London cases in 1711 and 1712 reveal that about a quarter of all property crimes involved thefts by servants. That is an unusually high level compared to previous periods examined.

61   CLRO: Sess. Papers (deposition 24 May 1711).

62   CLRO: Sess. Papers (deposition 14 July 1711).

63   CLRO: Sess. Papers, May 1711 (Ward); April 1712 (Floyd).

64   CLRO: Sess. Papers, Feb. 1712 (Rigby); April 1712 (Audry); Feb. 1713 (Roberts).

65   CLRO: Sess. Papers, October 1694; Feb. 1698.

66   CLRO: Papers of the Court of Aldermen, 1704 (18 September, 16 November, 1704). The bill was prepared at the request of the Court of Aldermen and examined by a committee of three of their number who in the end found it 'not serviceable', for reasons not given.

67   *A Proposal for the Due Regulating Servants, which will be Beneficial for the Kingdom in General, and to Private Families in Particular, and no ways Obstructive to honest Servants . . .* (?1708).

68   J.J. Hecht, *The Domestic Servant Class in Eighteenth-Century England* (1956; repr. 1981).

4

Confronting the Crime Wave:
The Debate over Social Reform and Regulation, 1749–1753

Nicholas Rogers
York University, Toronto

The frequency of audacious Street Robberies repeated every Night in this great Metropolis, call aloud on our Magistrates to think of some Redress; for, as the Case is now, there is no Possibility of stirring from our Habitations after dark, without the Hazard of a fractured Skull, or the Danger of losing that Property People are sometimes obliged to carry about them, which an honest industrious Family may be some Months, if not Years, working for again. These Villains now go in Bodies, armed in such a Manner, that our Watchmen, who are generally of the superannuated Sort, absolutely declare, they dare not oppose them. If, therefore, any person can think of a Proper Scheme for the Preservation and Safety of his Fellow Subjects, which carries with it, any Air of Probable Success, and will send it to our Publisher, it shall be inserted in this Paper.[1]

Written in early 1749, this notice in the *Whitehall Evening Post* addressed the anxiety men of property felt about the surge of street robberies that beset the metropolis and its environs in the aftermath of the War of Austrian Succession. In the next few years social commentators would propose a variety of measures to curb the crime wave that had so captured the public imagination, and a parliamentary committee would be formed to give some of them legislative effect. It is the purpose of this essay to explore this debate and its social, even political ramifications in order to understand perceptions about crime, punishment and the policing capabilities of mid-Georgian society; not simply by highlighting those precedents that subsequently informed the reform of the criminal law and new modes of punishment, on which a good deal has already been written,[2] but with an eye to the ways in which knowledge about crime and criminality was constructed and embedded in social and political discourses.[3] If, as Durkheim suggested, penality is in some sense a defining character of the social order, what do the penal and legal discourses of this crime wave tell us about the reproduction of class division and domination in mid-eighteenth-century England?

Historians have characterized the mid-century crime wave as a demobilization crisis. Both John Beattie and Douglas Hay have suggested that the rise of property crime in urban areas followed the rhythms of war and peace.[4] In 1749 approximately 70,000 men were discharged from the armed forces. Brutalized by war, without jobs and frequently suffering from arrears in pay, these men sometimes resorted to burglary or street or highway robbery to make ends meet, contributing significantly to a soaring rate of prosecuted crime. Indictments for theft in Staffordshire and Surrey rose dramatically in the years following the war, resulting in a striking increase in the number hanged.[5] Even in London and Middlesex, for which we have no recorded evidence before 1749, the numbers committed for burglary, housebreaking and highway robbery were significantly higher in the immediate aftermath of the war than they were in the war years of 1756–63, reaching a peak (as in Surrey) in 1751.[6] Here it is clear that a disproportionate number of those hanged were servicemen; over half in 1749.[7]

Contemporaries, of course, did not have the hindsight of historians. Nor did they have the means to measure crime with any accuracy. The first statistical account of those capitally convicted of crime, and one which offered some compelling evidence about the relationship of crime to war and peace, did not appear until 1772.[8] Subsequently reprinted by John Howard as an appendix to his classic study of prisons,[9] it heightened public awareness of the social dislocations of demobilization and its reverberations through the courts.[10] Prior to this, contemporaries gleaned their knowledge of crime impressionistically. If they did not attend trials themselves, they were reliant upon the reports in the newspapers,[11] supplemented by royal proclamations, sermons, pamphlets and digested commentaries in the monthlies.

Not all newspapers were especially intrigued by crime, save in its most sensationalist mode. But there were some that made it a special priority. Among these was the tri-weekly *Whitehall Evening Post*, which from the mid-1740s onwards consistently reported incidents of serious crime under the categories of 'Robbed' and 'Committed'. Regular readers of this newspaper were treated to a fare of violent crime: of footpads stealing watches, wigs, and purses from passers-by; of highwaymen haunting the heaths and roads to London and terrorizing travellers; of gangs creating sham disturbances in order to commit hit-and-run robberies, or impersonating lightmen in order to entrap theatre-goers. One theme of these reports was the impunity with which such acts were carried out. Robbers were seldom apprehended. More likely they made off in 'triumph', beating

Table 5.1
PROPERTY CRIMES REPORTED IN THE
WHITEHALL EVENING POST[13]

	1748		1749		1750		1751	
	Jan./ Feb.	June/ July	Jan./ Feb.	June/ July	Jan./ Feb.	June/ July	Jan./ Feb.	June/ July
Crimes reported (N=)	58	43	95	86	69	80	50	100
Highway robbery (%)	10.3	32.5	20.0	5.8	4.3	30.0	26.0	35.0
Street robbery (%)	48.3	46.5	54.7	53.5	73.9	47.5	48.0	40.0
'Violent' crimes (%)	58.6	79.0	74.7	59.3	78.2	77.5	74.0	75.0

and even wounding those who attempted to call out for help.[12] Indeed, as Table 5.1 shows, there was not only a significant rise in the number of robberies reported in the *Whitehall Evening Post* in the aftermath of the war, but a noticeable increase in those robberies accompanied by violence, beginning in the months following the signing of the peace preliminaries on 30 April 1748. 'The streets of this City, and the Suburbs thereof', the *Post* lugubriously concluded in late 1750, 'are greatly infested with a Number of Villains confederating in small companies to rob, and, on the smallest Opposition, to maim and murder the Passengers'.[14]

If newspapers chose to focus upon violent crime, they also chose to emphasize the vulnerability of the wealthy. Certainly poor men and women were sometimes cited as the victims of street robberies: servants; shop assistants; sailors, especially those flush with prize money; workmen on pay nights; and street higlers like Mary Hewitt, a seller of eggs and butter at Leadenhall market, who was accosted by two 'ruffians' on Highgate hill as she was returning home.[15] Yet, as the Table 5.2 suggests, the poor were under-represented as the victims of property crime, even if we cast the many anonymous men and women in that category. In the columns of the *Whitehall Evening Post* they became less conspicuous over time.

Partly this was the result of eighteenth-century reporting. Robberies of the rich and influential were more likely to capture the attention of the newspapers, either through Bow Street or word of mouth.[17] But partly it was a consequence of criminal activity. Robbers were sometimes discriminating about whom they targetted, preferring to steal from the propertied classes rather than the poor out of compassion as well as expediency. When two sailors robbed a dozen passers-by at Newington Butts in the summer of 1749, they returned the few farthings they took from an old woman 'who pleaded poverty', and added another so that she could get 'a Pint of Beer at the next House she came to'.[18] Such charitable treatment towards the less fortunate was understood by the coachman of Dr. Cox, of Burlington Street, whose chariot was held up by two highwaymen on Parson's Green. When they discovered the carriage was empty, the highwaymen robbed the coachman of four shillings and nine pence, upon which the coachman declared, 'he thought they never robbed Servants'. The highwaymen replied, 'It was very low with them, and if his Money was lucky, they would return it him again'.[19]

In view of the risks involved, men of property were the most desirable targets, at least for the more spectacular robberies that drew public attention. Among those reported in the *Whitehall Evening Post*, we find farmers, graziers, brewers, distillers, maltsters, hopfactors, merchants, corn dealers and silk manufacturers, men whose cash transfers made them especially vulnerable. Together with the attorneys, surgeons, apothecaries, the stewards of the gentry and the respectable tradesmen, they made up a third or more of the victims reported in the *Post*. Equally significant were the gentlemen and women whose conspicuous consumption marked them out as enviable prey, even from the apparent safety of their coaches. Gentlemen of quality, after all, were expected to bring in a good haul: a good cape, wig, watch, a pair of silver buckles, and a fat purse. On a good day robbers might generously forsake the clothes and buckles; 'We only take Watches and Money Tonight', declared several footpads to a gentleman in Chelsea fields in February 1750.[20] But those who did not live up to their class expectations were suitably denounced. 'You ought to have your Throat cut for not having a watch', two footpads told an apothecary whom they had robbed in Cavendish Square. 'D—n you', exclaimed a highwayman upon discovering a gentleman in Epping Forest with only a few shillings on his person, 'what signifies shooting twenty rascals such as you, who have the Figure of a Gentleman without

Table 5.2
VICTIMS OF CRIMES REPORTED IN THE
WHITEHALL EVENING POST[16]

		1749		1750	
		Winter	Summer	Winter	Summer
Crimes reported	(N=)	72	42	52	67
Women	(%)	6.9	4.8	7.7	14.9
Gentlemen/women	(%)	36.1	28.6	53.8	46.2
Middling sort	(%)	33.3	52.4	36.5	44.8
Other	(%)	30.6	19.0	9.6	8.9

any Money in your Pocket'.[21] In the canting language of the day, neither had been a 'stanch cull'.[22]

Contemporary understandings of criminality were strongly conditioned by these images. Although we do not know how much incidental theft accompanied the social dislocations of war and to what degree, as French historians have surmised in other contexts, this involved intra-class stealing, this is not how contemporaries saw the crime wave of 1749–52. They were disturbed by the ubiquitous and audacious character of street and highway robbery, its accompanying violence, the impunity with which casually-formed gangs were allowed to operate, and the threat it posed to the security of property and the maintenance of social order. The wealthy seemed especially vulnerable to these depredations, to a point that the crime wave appeared as a form of class retribution. The poor 'starve, and freeze, and rot among themselves', commented Henry Fielding in 1753, 'but they beg, and steal and rob among their betters'.[23] Such anxieties were not viewed in the abstract. They were personally experienced by men and women of wealth and influence, fuelling fears in the highest circles. Henry Pelham's eldest daughter was so troubled by the reports of street robberies that upon one scheduled Court appearance she hid her diamond earrings under the seat of her hackney chair, 'for fear of being attacked'.[24] Among those confronted by footpads and highwaymen in these years we find the Reverend Dr. Terrick, the prebend of Windsor, soon to be promoted to an episcopal see; members of the nobility such as the Earl of Leicester, the Countess of Albemarle, and her son and daughter-in-law, Lord and Lady Bury.[25] Prominent bankers such as Sir Thomas Hankey were not left out of the account, either; he and his lady were held up on Clapham Common.[26] Nor was Horace Walpole. In November 1749 he recalled: 'as I was returning from Holland House by moonlight, about ten at night, I was attacked by two highwaymen in Hyde Park, and the pistol of one of them going off accidentally, razed the skin under my eye, left some marks of shot on my face, and stunned me. The ball went through the top of the chariot, and if I had sat an inch nearer to the left side, must have gone through my head'. A year later he was bemoaning the fact that 'Robbing is the only thing that goes on with any vivacity', and reported that dining out was as dangerous as a military sortie 'owing to the profusion of housebreakers, highwaymen and footpads – and especially because of the savage barbarity of the two latter, who commit the most wanton cruelties'.[27]

Ruling-class anxieties about the high incidence of crime abounded in the years following the War of the Austrian Succession, but such anxieties required further sharper definition if solutions to the crime wave were to be

found. Among those who contributed significantly to the debate was
Henry Fielding. Already well-known as a playwright, novelist and
political journalist, Fielding had been appointed to the Westminster
bench through the recommendation of his patrons, George Lyttleton and
the Duke of Bedford, in October 1748. Within a month, thanks again to
Bedford's intervention, Fielding had acquired the property qualification to
sit on the Middlesex bench, taking up residence in Bow Street.[28] As the
most active magistrate in the vicinity, responsible for the routine
administration of law, the detection of crime and the maintenance of the
public peace, Fielding was well placed to comment on the prevailing crime
wave.

Fielding's credentials were not impeccable. He was, after all, a trading
justice, one whose livelihood was partly sustained through the fees of
office, and he never entirely lived down the taint that such 'professionalism' carried in an age that habitually linked impartial justice to
independent wealth.[29] His promotion also smacked of political favouritism. As opposition critics rightly recognized, his magistracy was a reward
for services rendered in the defence of the treaty of Aix-la-Chappelle and,
more generally, in the trenchant satire of government opponents, whom
he had regularly smeared as Jacobites, republicans and disloyal scoundrels
in newspapers and pamphlets.[30] Such partisanship, as his role in the
tumultuous Westminster by-election of 1749 was to reveal, did not
disappear with his appointment to the bench.[31]

Fielding's credentials as a spokesman on social problems were nonetheless vindicated in July 1749 upon the publication of his charge to the
Westminster Jury the previous month. 'This ingenious author and worthy
magistrate', the *Monthly Review* commented, 'has, in this little piece, with
that judgment, knowledge of the world, and of our excellent laws, (which
the publick, indeed, could not but expect from him) pointed out the
reigning vices and corruptions of the times, and the legal and proper
methods of curbing and punishing them'.[32] In his tract Fielding did not
deal with property crime directly; rather he urged jurymen to curb 'the
licentious and luxurious Pleasures' of the times – brothels, gaming houses,
fairs, masquerades – especialy those vices that promoted idleness and
immorality among the 'lower sort of people'.[33] This quite conventional
call for a reformation of manners set the scene for an extensive inquiry
into street robbery some eighteen months later, which in turn coincided
with the formation of a parliamentary committee to investigate the
pressing problem of crime.

Fielding's *Enquiry* received considerable public attention when it first
appeared in January 1751. It was generously summarized in the monthlies
and more frequently cited than any other social pamphlet during the early
fifties.[34] Josiah Tucker thought it a 'very seasonable and judicious treatise'

and at least two members of the 1751 committee, William Hay and Charles Gray, commended some of Fielding's proposals for countering crime.[35] To be sure, Fielding's literary prominence has led some to inflate his importance. His influence over the parliamentary committee, for example, was not as great as has been claimed.[36] Nonetheless, it is clear that his *Enquiry* was a substantial intervention in the debate over crime.

Fielding's pamphlet was not only important for the detail of its recommendations. It was also significant for its salient silences. Like other authors, Fielding did not analyse the crime wave as principally a product of demobilization. Despite the continual references in the newspapers to sailors or men in 'sailor's habits' robbing men and women on the streets and highways, despite the well-known riotous activities and petitions of sailors for their arrears of pay, social critics by and large declined to link crime to the social dislocations of war, even though they must have privately admitted its importance.[37] Those who sympathized with the seamen's plight certainly alerted the public to this problem. One public 'petition' reported that the sailors, 'driven into Despair through mere Necessity', had 'run headlong into Malepractice [sic], purely to keep themselves from starving', making 'their Exits at the Gallows'.[38] Others acknowledged that demobilized servicemen might be 'turned adrift, without a visible way of livelihood, and without the least degree of thought and prudence to find any (employment) . . . that is good and useful'.[39] Indeed, legislators devised schemes to address this predicament, most notably the settlement of Nova Scotia and the creation of a British herring fishery. The former offered every demobilized soldier and seaman fifty acres of land rent free for ten years, with an additional grant of ten acres for every member of their family they took with them.[40] The latter was intended to provide Britain with a valuable nursery of seamen in time of war and to bring work to discharged seamen. Otherwise, one advocate asserted, seamen might sail in foreign fleets or be 'reduced to the sad Alternative, either of begging from Door to Door; or of plunging into Crimes that may bring them to a fatal End, of which we have already had many melancholy Instances'.[41] Here, as elsewhere, the seaman's plight was conceded; its potential links with crime admitted. Yet in the larger discourse upon crime it was marginalized.

It is conceivable that the promotion of the settlement plan and the fishing industry so absolved the conscience of the rich that demobilization was denied as a *pressing* social problem. If servicemen had opportunities to accommodate themselves to civilian life, then taking to the road could not be a product of need, but rather of the deplorable dissoluteness of the lower orders. Such a line of reasoning reinforced the conventional explanations of crime which centred upon the idleness, insubordination and immorality of the poor and the threat such vices posed to the protection of property and the social order by deflecting the poor from honest labour. Such labour, one clergyman affirmed in 1750, was 'the main Support of the Advantages and Blessings of higher life, and a Common Benefit to all'. Consequently, 'Such Members as are unemployed, or employ'd in Mischief, are a common Burden and Nuisance, wasting the Public Stock which they are, by their Rank and Station, fitted to augment'.[42] In this way the question of crime became umbilically linked to the question of regulating the poor, to monitoring its manners, morals and pauperdom.

In the *Enquiry*, Henry Fielding addressed these linkages squarely. The principal causes of crime, he averred, were the 'luxurious' habits of the poor and the maladministration of the poor laws. The growth of trade and the consequent commercialization of leisure had created tastes and expectations among the 'lowest sort of people' that were not only socially inappropriate but publicly damaging. 'To be born for no other purpose than to consume the fruits of the earth is the privilege . . . of very few' Fielding opined. 'The greater part of mankind must sweat hard to produce them, or society will no longer answer the purposes for which it was ordained.'[43] Public diversions, gin and gaming had destroyed industry and morality in favour of idleness and crime. Furthermore the poor laws, one of the cornerstones of social regulation in eighteenth-century society, had failed to arrest this trend. Originally designed to inure the able-bodied poor to labour as well as to provide for the aged and infirm, they had been compromised by administrative indifference, neglect, and misplaced charity.

Fielding clearly believed that there were enough laws on the statute book to begin to address these problems, for he listed a whole battery of legal sanctions to control the poor. Cast, as Malvin Zirker has reminded us, in a conservative mould,[44] Fielding's commentary consistently evoked the image of the *unfree* labourer, whose wages should be regulated, mobility restricted, and leisure time supervised. Despite the erosion of paternalist controls and the usefulness of readily available mobile labour to agrarian capitalism and manufacture, Fielding continued to cherish a patriarchal vision of society.[45] He deplored the freedom many workmen had over the labour process, to which he attributed 'the idleness of the common people' in London; and he lamented the fact that the settlement and vagrant laws had ineffectually restricted the mobility of labour, generating rookeries of depravity and crime in the heart of the metropolis.[46] 'The wonder is', he reflected, 'that we have not a thousand more robbers than we have; indeed, that all these wretches are not thieves must give us either a very high idea of their honesty, or a very mean one of their capacity and courage'.[47]

Fielding's analysis of crime was quite conventional, but in one respect he went further than his contemporaries. Whereas most social critics used the crime wave to advance their pet project – whether it be tighter controls over brothels, gaming, gin-drinking or better-regulated workhouses – Fielding contextualized the crime wave as a *structural* crisis of order. In the preface to the *Enquiry* he saw the long-term erosion of vassalage and the concomitant rise of independent labour as fundamentally altering the balance of forces in English society, creating a crisis of governance. In the more libertarian, commerical environment of the mid-eighteenth century, Fielding argued, the powers of government were weak; too weak to contain the licentious, insubordinate habits of the common people, of which the rising crime rate was but one manifestation. Hence his call 'to rouse the civil power from its present lethargic state'.[48] Hence also his proposals for a range of legislative interventions to enhance the prosecution of crime and respect for law and order.

Many of these proposals emanated from Fielding's practical experience as a magistrate. He advocated tougher laws against receivers of stolen goods and an extension of the Vagrancy Act of 1744 to allow magistrates to arrest suspicious persons. He also wanted greater weight given to the evidence of accomplices in cases of theft, a revision of the rule that interested parties should not be sworn in as witnesses. Disturbed by the public's reluctance to prosecute felons on account of the cost, he recommended that the state reimburse the plaintiff. Above all, Fielding wanted to streamline the prosecution of property offences by removing the prejudice against thief-takers, advising juries against 'downcharging' indictments, and restricting the number of pardons. In his view, such acts of clemency had mitigated the terror of the law and rendered deterrence ineffectual. As, indeed, had the ritual processions to the gallows. Like Mandeville, Fielding believed that Tyburn had become a festival in which the intrepidity of the victims rather than their crimes preoccupied the crowd. To restore the solemnity and awful nature of the death sentence, he recommended that the condemned be hanged soon after sentencing, upon a gallows before the Old Bailey.

In addressing these last issues, Fielding must have recalled, as presumably did his readers, the tumultuous events of 1749 with which he was so intimately involved. During July, a large body of sailors had ransacked several brothels on the Strand in retaliation for the theft of thirty guineas and more from two of their comrades.[49] At a late stage in the disturbances, Fielding returned to town to suppress the disorders, calling in the troops and taking several rioters into custody. In the trial that ensued, three men were indicted under the terms of the Riot Act for 'feloniously and riotously' assembling to pull down The Star. One was acquitted, but the other two, John Wilson and Bosavern Penlez, neither of them seamen, were sentenced to death for their part in the proceedings, despite the very dubious evidence mustered against them. Vigorous efforts were launched to secure them a pardon,[50] including entreaties to Lord Trentham, Bedford's son-in-law and the parliamentary candidate in the up-coming Westminster by-election. But only in Wilson's case was the sentence respited at the eleventh hour. On 18 October, Penlez was hanged at Tyburn before a tense and bitter crowd that included sailors armed with cutlasses and bludgeons. Had the sheriff, Stephen Theodore Janssen, not dismissed the troops sent to reinforce his already formidable civil guard and denied the surgeons the bodies of the condemned for public dissection, an explosion of popular fury might have ensued.

Fielding defended the course of justice with respect to Penlez in the following month, partly to vindicate his own conduct, but also to exonerate Lord Trentham, his patron's relative, for whom the affair had become a public embarrassment. In his account of the Strand riot he emphasized the threat it had posed to law, order and property. While admitting that brothels were a public scandal, Fielding denounced the fact that 'open illegal force and violence' had been used to remove them, especially when the perpetrators included 'thieves under a pretense of reformation'.[51] Indeed, 'The Cry against Bawdy-Houses might have been easily converted into an Out-Cry of a very different Nature', he warned, 'and Goldsmiths might have been considered to be as great a Nuisance to the Public as Whores'.[52] This explanation can only have convinced those panic-stricken by the crime wave. Although both Wilson and Penlez were found with stolen goods on their person, other accounts emphasized the sailors' discouragement of theft during the disturbances. According to 'a Gentleman Not Concern'd', nothing was embezzled 'except an old Gown or Petticoat, thrown at a Hackney Coachman's Head, as a Reward for a dutiful Huzza as he drove by'.[53] To many it must have appeared ironic, if not hypocritical, that a magistrate who had so roundly condemned bawdy-houses before a Middlesex grand jury, should five months later be defending their property rights and railing at their violent suppression.

Fielding was satirized for his response to the Strand riots in the Westminster by-election of 1749, but his conduct had a broader relevance. It testified to his growing aversion to plebeian self-assertion: its surliness on the streets of London,[54] its capacity for direct action in defence of its customary liberties, its raucous presence at elections and political meetings. In 1747 Fielding had roundly condemned the assault upon his patron, the Duke of Bedford, at the Lichfield races, when the tory clans of Staffordshire had reviled the defection of Bedford's cousin, Lord Gower, in a rollicking Jacobite festival replete with toasts to the Pretender and treasonable songs.[55] Four years later he was still struggling with the whiffs of disaffection that accompanied popular opposition to the Court, this time pertaining to the street demonstrations in favour of Alexander Murray, who had defiantly refused to apologize to the

Commons for his critique of the Court party's conduct during the Westminster by-election. In June 1751, he committed a hawker to Tothill Fields bridewell for selling a defence of Murray about the streets and had the offending pamphlet burnt before his door.[56] Such efforts to curb popular protest, and by extension, what Foucault would have termed 'popular illegalities', were also manifested in other contexts: in his public and active support for the Duke of Richmond's campaign to clean up Sussex smuggling;[57] and in his condemnation of the counter-culture of Tyburn fair, with its mock-gaiety, victuals, gin and beer, its fierce struggles to save the bodies of the condemned from public dissection at the hands of the surgeons. 'Instead of making the Gallows an object of Terror', he reflected in 1752, 'our Executions contribute to make it an Object of Contempt in the Eye of the Malefactor; and we sacrifice the Lives of men, not for the Reformation, but for the Diversion of the Populace'.[58] Like many of his propertied contemporaries, Fielding strongly disapproved of the way in which the judicial terror of the London gallows had been undermined by popular anger and irreverence. He also bemoaned the degree to which the 'Mob' had become a power unto itself, a veritable 'Fourth Estate', commanding public space and compromising the policies of its superiors. 'None of the other Orders can walk through the Streets by Day without being insulted', he claimed in the *Covent Garden Journal*, 'nor by Night without being knocked down'. Were it not for the magistracy and the military, the crowd would 'have long since rooted all the other Orders out of the Commonwealth'.[59]

Fielding's aversion to plebeian culture was in some sense a part of his personal agenda, concurrent with his gravitation towards the whig establishment since the early 1740s. But his fears about plebeian insubordination and disorder undoubtedly resonated throughout the propertied public during the crime wave of 1749–53, when reports about street robberies were accompanied by accounts of turnpike riots in the West Country, keelmen's strikes on the Tyne, and unruly revels at the London fairs, where, it was said, 'the common people are so audacious, insolent and ungovernable'.[60] A few spokesmen, it is true, were perturbed by Fielding's neglect of upper-class luxury in his analysis of crime, seeing a revival of public service as the bedrock of social regulation. Writing under the *nom de plume* of Ben Sedgly, Richard Rolt, Fielding's most outspoken critic, felt that the Middlesex magistrate had exaggerated the need to augment magisterial powers, believing that it would enervate the spirit of liberty so essential to the welfare of free societies. Yet even Rolt saw the need to strengthen the deterrent effect of the law for serious crimes and to promote new measures to curb drunkenness and gambling. 'The idleness, the insolence, the debauchery of the common people of both sexes, with their natural and certain consequences, poverty, diseases, misery and wickedness', he declared, 'are the daily observations to be made in every part of this great metropolis'.[61]

In these circumstances it was not surprising that there was a large measure of consensus about some of the proposed strategies for social reform. Spokesmen agreed upon the need to arrest the gin epidemic that was widely seen as a contributory factor to the breakdown of social order. They also advocated new laws to monitor pawnshops, alehouses and places of amusement, only occasionally voicing a little concern that such regulation might be perverted for political ends. To counteract this, some writers proposed that all substantial men of property should be promoted to the bench, not simply those sympathetic to the government.[62] Such recommendations were hardly needed, for Henry Pelham and Lord Hardwicke had already begun the process of promoting tory landowners to the commissions of the peace, sometimes in the face of local Whig opposition. By the early 1750s, appointments to the bench were becoming increasingly non-partisan as the government sought to mobilize gentry resources to combat crime and disorder.[63] Indeed, it is quite conceivable that the crime wave furthered this trend.

Accordingly some of the measures to counteract the crime wave reached the statute book with a minimum of debate. This was true of 25 George II, c.36, the Act 'for the better preventing thefts and robberies', which licensed places of public entertainment in London and its environs, fined those advertising rewards for the return of stolen goods with no questions asked, allowed justices to hold 'suspicious persons' for up to six days, and facilitated the prosecution of bawdy houses.[64] It was also true of the Gin Act of 1751, which extended the compromise reached between fiscal interests of the state and the large producers some eight years earlier by pricing the liquor beyond the reach of the poor and policing its distribution.[65] And it also applied to the Murder Act of 1752, which sought to strengthen the judicial terror of the gallows by hanging murderers two days after their sentence had been passed, if necessary in chains, as well as allowing the Surgeons Company the right to dissect and anatomize those condemned to death at Tyburn. Although a few commentators advocated slavery as an alternative to hanging, largely on the grounds that it would strike more terror in a liberty-loving populace,[66] the general consensus was that chain gangs and galleys were punishments more appropriate to continental regimes than to the British system of justice.

Yet many of the resolutions of the 1751 committee never reached the statute book, despite the fact they were passed by the Commons. Sir William Yonge's efforts to tackle the issue of stolen goods in the pawnbrokers bill floundered at the committee stage, as did his dockyards bill, which sought to substitute hard labour for transportation. So, too, did the proposed amendments to the poor laws, which had they passed, would have completely overhauled the Elizabethan structure of poor relief and abandoned the Acts of Settlement.[67] Precisely why they failed will always be something of a mystery, for the minutes of the 1751 committee (or its sub-committees) have not survived; but it seems reasonable to infer from the pamphlet evidence that they exposed deep divisions within the propertied classes as to how the existing laws operated.

In the case of the dockyards bill it appears that contemporaries were far from convinced that hard labour in the ports was a useful alternative to the already well-tried punishment of transportation.[68] 'The Ends of punishment', wrote one pamphleteer, 'are, *in all cases*, to deter others from commiting the like Offences; and *in most cases*, to reclaim the Offender also'.[69] In his view, transportation to America allowed for a stricter supervision of felons than the cluster of contumacious convicts the authorities would inevitably confront in the dockyards. In the more open, smallholder society of the New World, moreover, there was a greater chance that convicts would be integrated back into society after their term, whereas in England the prospects of resettlement were fewer. Indeed, there was a real possibility that the concentration of convicts in the yards would simply generate a criminal sub-culture rather than a reformative atmosphere. It was only after the American War of Independence, when the option of transportation was temporarily closed, that reformers would reassess the punitive and rehabilitative sanction of hard labour, albeit in a more evangelical and panoptic environment.

With respect to the poor laws, the mid-century debate disclosed issues that had been raised since the late seventeenth century; that is, whether larger administrative units would provide a more efficient and economic system of poor relief than the parish. Advocates for change argued that larger unions would provide a better range of facilities to handle the different problems of poverty, whether that meant better provision for the sick and infirm, labour for the able-bodied, correction for the indolent and disorderly, or the reclamation of their progeny, potentially the next generation of criminals. They also claimed that the current system undermined the mutualities between rich and poor so essential to the social order and subjected the poor themselves to the vexatious rivalry of individual parishes and to the petty tyrannies of local officials, some of whom had misappropriated funds for their own ends. 'Every Parish is in a State of expensive War with the rest of the Nation', claimed William Hay, the MP for Seaford and resolute poor law reformer, 'regards the Poor of all other Places as Aliens; and cares not what becomes of them if it can but banish them from its own Society'.[70] These problems could only be resolved by abolishing the Settlement Acts and allowing JPs the opportunity to set up new unions, managed by propertied guardians, under

whose supervision new hospitals and houses of industry would be established. Only then, argued Hay, would the problems of crime, labour
discipline and itinerant poverty be brought under some semblance of
control and 'Examination, Passes, Duplicates, Certificates, Orders, Ap-
peals, and a thousand other idle Trumperies . . . dispersed like the Sybil's
Leaves'.[71]

Two bills were actually drawn up for this purpose in 1752, yet neither
got off the ground. Parliamentarians remained unconvinced that larger
institutions were necessarily more efficient or less corrupt. Even Charles
Gray, who chaired the committee which drew up the poor children's bill,
admitted that some corporations of the poor had not been successful.
While he applauded the administration of the Bristol corporation, he cited
others, including the one in his own constituency of Colchester, where
'party views and private purposes' had intervened.[72] He felt that the
promiscuous character of many large institutions was detrimental to the
morals of the poor, exposing the 'better sort' to the depravity of the
'vagabond and idle'. He also understood that such units were open to
legitimate libertarian and financial objections, to a deep-rooted suspicion
of new centres of power and to their problematic expense.[73] Such
scepticism from potential reformers was amplified by those who were far
from convinced that the poor laws were operating as disastrously as their
critics claimed; even in London, where the City parishes were said to be
competent managers of their poor.[74] 'The best, the safest, and the most
rational means' of employing the poor, one spokesman asserted, was to
continue the old policy of erecting local workhouses 'where the poor are
well looked to, kept industriously employed, and managed under all the
parishioners inspection in the most frugal as well as honest manner'.[75]
Indeed, one commentator claimed that the efficiency of poor relief was not
really a question of size so much as the fusion of self-interest and
benevolence within particular contexts. This was especially the case with
respect to pauper employment, which could only prosper where there was
a resilient demand for labour and a readily available stock of material. In
the eyes of this commentator, labour discipline could sometimes be better
instilled by contracting-out the poor than by subjecting them to mundane
tasks in parochial or county workhouses.[76]

These reservations sealed the fate of the two bills. The more radical, a
bill 'for the more effectual Relief and Employment of the Poor', sought to
substitute the county for the parish as the fundamental unit of poor relief,
to build multi-functional hospitals to accommodate the poor, financed
from a county rate, and to phase out the old system within two years. It
reached a second reading in March 1752 before it was ground down in
committee.[77] Gray's alternative attempted to meet some of the objections
raised against it by allowing for the contracting-out of pauper labour, and

by restricting the corporations to the maintenance and reclamation of poor children. These institutions could be established on the basis of a hundred rather than a county, but they were not to undermine those existing corporations that had been established by royal charter or act of Parliament. In contrast to the other bill, Gray's proposal also hoped to finance corporations from private as well as public sources, from charitable benefactions, voluntary contributions, and lotteries as well as from local rates.[78] In other words, the financing of these corporations did not fall entirely upon public sources; nor were many of the traditional functions of parish relief necessarily undermined. At the same time pauper children might be trained to pursue useful maritime or manufacturing employments and drawn away from a self-generating criminal sub-culture.[79]

Even so, the proposal satisfied neither reformers nor traditionalists. Thomas Alcock believed the poor children's bill was too 'narrowly bottomed'. In his view most parents would refuse to send their children to the House of Industry but 'would rub on without this assistance'.[80] Besides, workhouses without adjoining hospitals and houses of correction would hardly be worth the effort, especially since the Foundling Hospital and the charity schools already offered some provision for the children of the poor. Traditionalists, for their part, continued to believe that charity began at home, and baulked at the prospect of diverting their funds and committing their own poor children to large impersonal institutions over which they had limited control.[81] All that could be recovered from the reform drive of the early 1750s was two local acts establishing workhouses, one in Chichester and the other in Spitalfields, where legislators were assured that the poor could be more cheaply provided for and efficiently employed.[82] Efforts to launch a general scheme for larger workhouses or hospitals and to modify the Settlement Acts floundered in the face of localism and a scepticism of big government. With them went one of the central underpinnings of the regulatory drive to combat crime and disorder in the aftermath of the War of the Austrian Succession. Despite the warnings of Fielding, Hay and others that the war on crime could only be successfully waged by reforming the poor laws as well as the criminal code and the administration of justice, divisions within the propertied classes frustrated a broad legislative strategy.

Three themes deserve emphasis in a study of the crime wave of 1749 to 1752. The first pertains to the chronology of social reform in the eighteenth century. Conventionally that century has been viewed as one of social complacency if not stasis, the rhythm of reform only growing apace after 1780 when the impact of industrialization wrought profound changes upon an essentially agrarian society. As John Beattie, Joanna Innes,[83] and the essays in this volume reveal, this view clearly has to be modified. There were a series of regulatory drives throughout the eighteenth century, some of them synchronized to the dislocations of war and the problems of reintegrating servicemen back into society. During the mid-century, and again after the American war, the upsurge in property crime was the occasion for a broader assessment of the problems of social regulation, generating demands for a reform of the criminal code, the poor laws, and a reformation of manners. It was not accidental that the Gilbert Unions, policing and the penitentiary should form part of the social agenda during the final years and aftermath of the American war, just as public executions, incorporations of the poor, liquor licensing, and tighter laws against brothels, gaming houses, and the receiving of stolen goods formed part of the agenda at the mid-century. All formed part of the discourse of social regulation, impinging explicitly upon the social reproduction of labour and the patterns of domination that sustained the social order.

The mid-century crisis is also important for the light it sheds upon the course of criminal reform in the eighteenth century. Some years ago Sir Leon Radzinowicz depicted the 1750s as a crucial turning point in the revision of the criminal justice system, marking the first shift from a bloody code towards penal sanctions that emphasized preventive strategies and towards analyses of crime that stressed environmental factors.[84] Such an interpretation cannot be sustained. What the crisis illustrates was not the juxtaposition of traditional and 'englightened' discourses, but their intimate interconnection. Indeed, it might be more appropriate to say that the discourse of social regulation encompassed both deterrence and prevention. What was at stake was the particular mix of these features. In response to the mid-century crime wave, social reformers agreed on the need to vindicate the majesty of the law and to enhance the judicial terror of the gallows, which, in London at least, had been significantly undermined by the riots and the counter-culture of Tyburn fair. What proved more contentious was the combination of preventive strategies to instil deference and labour discipline and to curb those leisure preferences of the poor that were widely believed to be conducive to crime.

In the end the propertied classes opted for relatively conventional solutions: stricter licensing, local workhouse regimes, and so on. The most innovative features of the legislative thrust of 1751–2, apart from the Murder Act, were designed to facilitate the detection of offenders rather than inhibit the proclivity to crime. Although some reformers wished to enhance the visibility and efficiency of imprisonment, such initiatives floundered in the face of localism and public parsimony. The age of the penitentiary had yet to arrive, although the vision of a more intensive carceral regime was certainly present in some of the proposals for reform. Henry Fielding's recommendations for a county workhouse and a house of correction in Middlesex, for example, framed in the wake of the proposals for poor reform, certainly gestured in this direction.[85] With its salaried officials, its regimen of labour and religious instruction, its solitary cells and sex segregation, it hoped to mould the mind as much as punish the body of the reprobate and idle worker. To be sure, Fielding's proposal was not infused with an evangelical optimism about the regenerative potential of the religious conscience. Nor did his plan meet the three criteria so central to corrective institutions: a routine programme of solitary confinement; discretionary sentencing; and a notion of prison work as a source of character formation rather than revenue.[86] Fielding remained preoccupied with the economic viability of his workhouse and house of correction. While he recognized the usefulness of solitary confinement to bring the 'most abandoned profligates to reason and order', he did not envisage a continued and comprehensive routine of solitude to induce inmates to repent their sins. Rather he assigned the 'fasting room' to induct inmates to a regime of hard labour.[87] As for discretionary sentences attuned to each criminal's progress towards rehabilitation, such an individualizing mode of prison surveillance had yet to be conceived. Even so, Fielding's scheme signalled a break with the permissive, self-regulating prisons of the past and a shift towards more professional, centralized institutions devoted to reshaping the character of the criminal.[88] Such an emphasis would soon be taken up by other advocates of prison reform with a new vigour and intensity.

One other aspect of the debate of the mid-century crime wave is worth assessing, and that is the form that it took. Unlike earlier regulatory drives, the mid-century debate was conducted in a secular rather than religious idiom.[89] Although a few clergymen addressed the problem of crime, the principal thrust of the discussion was conducted in newspapers, periodicals and pamphlets rather than in sermons. It was, in a phrase, journalistic rather than homiletic. It was also noteworthy for its silence. The problem of crime was constructed in ways that inhibited any substantial discussion of the problems of demobilization. Its focus was rather upon luxury, not the luxury of the rich, although in reference to gaming that necessarily obtruded into the debate, but the luxury of the poor. Social reformers were alarmed that the economic priorities of the poor, their imprudent (though not necessarily irrational) habits of consumption, had generated expectations that enervated labour discipline, undermined class mutualities and promoted crime. The increase in property crime, in sum, was symptomatic of the degeneracy of the common people. Such an analysis obviated a thorough or penetrating examination of paternalist responsibilities or public services; in spite of the fact that the virtues of paternalist relations, albeit in small settings, were sometimes invoked to counter comprehensive schemes of social reform.

These concerns remained largely marginal to a debate that centred upon the profligacy of the poor and the need to bring them to labour.

Notes

1   *Whitehall Evening Post*, 14–17 Jan. 1749.
2   See Leon Radzinowicz, *A History of English Criminal Law and its Administration from 1750*, 5 vols (1948–86), i, ch. 12; J.M. Beattie, *Crime and the Courts in England 1660–1800* (Princeton, 1986), ch. 10.
3   On this question, see David Garland and Peter Young, 'Towards a social analysis of penality', in Garland and Young (eds.) *The Power to Punish. Contemporary Penality and Social Analysis* (1983), pp. 1–36, and Michael Foucault, *Discipline and Punish. The Birth of the Prison*, trans. Alan Sheridan (New York, 1977).
4   J.M. Beattie, *Crime and the Courts*, 213–45; Douglas Hay, 'War, dearth and theft in the eighteenth century: The record of the English courts', *Past and Present*, xcv (May, 1982), 117–160. For some scepticism of this interpretation, see Joanna Innes and John Styles, 'The crime wave: Recent writing on crime and criminal justice in eighteenth-century England', *Journal of British Studies*, xxv (October, 1986), 391–5.
5   Beattie, *Crime and the Courts*, pp. 213–22; Hay, 'War, dearth and theft', p. 125.
6   British Parliamentary Papers, xvii (1819), 296.
7   Peter Linebaugh, 'The Tyburn riot against the surgeons', in Douglas Hay et al., *Albion's Fatal Tree. Crime and Society in Eighteenth-Century England* (1975), p. 89.
8   Stephen Theodore Janssen, *Tables of Death Sentences* (1772).
9   John Howard, *The State of the Prisons in England and Wales* (4th edn. 1792), p. 482, first published in 1777.
10 See Hay, 'War, dearth and theft', p. 138; for a denial that demobilization was responsible for the high crime rate after the American war (but one which recognized it was publicly voiced), see William Man Godschall, *A General Plan of Parochial and Provincial Police* (1787), pp. 2–3.
11 For an analysis of the ways in which newspaper reporting in the eighteenth century could shape public perceptions of crime, see Peter King, 'Newspaper reporting, prosecution practice and perceptions of urban crimes: the Colchester crime wave of 1765', *Continuity and Change*, ii (1987), 423–54.
12 See, for example, the report of 'five fellows' who robbed the coaches, waggons and carts along Mile End Road in the *Whitehall Evening Post*, 18–21 Feb. 1749. See also the successful rescue attempt of a robber from the watch reported in the *Whitehall Evening Post*, 27–29 July 1749.
13 The figures are derived from the reports in the *Whitehall Evening Post* for January/February and June/July of each year. A few cases of housebreaking with violence are included in the 'street robberies' category.
14 *Whitehall Evening Post*, 4–6 Dec. 1750. See also the comment by 'Publicus' in the *Whitehall Evening Post*, 24–26 Jan. 1749.
15 For Hewitt, see *London Morning Penny Post*, 4–6 Sept. 1751. For sailors, see *Whitehall Evening Post*, 25–28 Feb., 16–18 Nov. 1749.
16 These figures are derived from the reports in January/February and June/July of each year. I have classified artisans as 'middling' wherever they were in genteel trades or had the prefix 'Mr.' before their names.
17 On the reporting of crime, see Patrick Pringle, *Hue and Cry. The Story of Henry and John Fielding and Their Bow Street Runners* (n.d.), pp. 100–2; Radzinowicz, *A History of*

English Criminal Law, iii, 11–62; John Styles, 'Sir John Fielding and the problem of criminal investigation in eighteenth-century England', Transactions of the Royal Historical Society, xxxiii (1983), 127–49.

18 Whitehall Evening Post, 25–27 July 1749.
19 Whitehall Evening Post, 7–10 Jan. 1749. For an example of a highwayman holding up a coach but giving the coachman two shillings to drink his health, see London Evening Post, 2–5 Feb. 1751.
20 Whitehall Evening Post, 6–8 Feb. 1750.
21 Whitehall Evening Post, 6–9 July 1751; London Evening Post, 10–12 Jan. 1751.
22 A man worth robbing. See Old Bailey Sessions Papers, 16–21 Jan. 1751, p. 45.
23 Henry Fielding, A Proposal for Making an Effectual Provision for the Poor (1753), in Complete Works, ed. William E. Henley (1903), xiii, 141.
24 Yale Edition of Horace Walpole's Correspondence, ed. W.S. Lewis (New Haven, 1960), xx, 114. She also left them there, with the result, Walpole reported, that 'The chairman have sunk them'.
25 Whitehall Evening Post, 16–18 June 1748; 25–27 Jan. 1750.
26 London Evening Post, 2–5 Feb. 1751.
27 Cited in Pringle, Hue and Cry, pp. 87, 90; see also The Yale Edition of Horace Walpole's Correspondence, xx, 99, 101, 106, 199.
28 For these appointments, see M.C. with R.R. Battestin, 'Fielding, Bedford and the Westminster election of 1749', Eighteenth-Century Studies, xi (1977/8), 143–54. See also, Pat Rogers, Henry Fielding. A Biography (New York, 1979), pp. 165–72.
29 Fielding's dependence upon legal fees was not total, thanks to the patronage of Bedford and to his novels, and he resented the insinuation that he was a corrupt, self-interested trading justice. See M.C. with R.R. Battestin, 'Fielding, Bedford and the Westminster election', 150–2, 175, Henry Fielding. A Life (1989), pp. 459–60, 532, and B.M. Jones, Henry Fielding: Novelist and Magistrate (1933), p. 119. For earlier criticisms of trading justices, see BL, Add. MS 35,601, ff. 261–2 and Sir Thomas De Veil, Observations on the Practice of a Justice of the Peace (1747), pp. 19–21.
30 See Thomas Cleary, Henry Fielding. Political Writer (Waterloo, Ontario, 1984), ch. 6.
31 For Fielding's role in this election, favourably interpreted, see Battestin, 'Fielding, Bedford, and the Westminster election of 1749', 154–85; for a more jaundiced view, see Nicholas Rogers, 'Aristocratic clientage, trade and independency: Popular politics in pre-radical Westminster', Past and Present, lxi (1973), 81.
32 Monthly Review, i (1749), 239–40.
33 Fielding, A Charge Delivered to the Grand Jury . . . 29 July 1749 in Complete Works, xiii, 197–219.
34 Monthly Review, iv (1751), 229–39; London Magazine, xx (1751) 64–7. I have discovered at least ten pamphlets and newspaper articles that mention the Enquiry.
35 Josiah Tucker, An Impartial Inquiry into the Benefits and Damages arising to the nation from the present very great use of low-priced Spirituous Liquors (1751), pp. 4–5; William Hay, Remarks on the laws relating to the poor (1751), p. vi; Charles Gray, Considerations on several proposals lately made for the better maintenance of the poor (1751), p. 14.
36 For a review of these arguments and a repudiation of them, see Hugh Amory, 'Henry Fielding and the Criminal Legislation of 1751–2', Philological Quarterly, l (1971), 175–92.
37 In a letter to Horace Mann in January 1750, Horace Walpole linked the high level of property crime to the 'disbanded soldiers and sailors' who had 'taken to the road, or rather to the street'. See Yale Edition of Walpole's Correspondence, xx, 111.
38 'Petition of British Mariners to the Nobility, Gentry and Commonalty of Great Britain', published in the London Evening Post, 17–19 January 1751.
39 London Magazine, xvii (1748), 292–3.

40 *Whitehall Evening Post*, 23–25 March 1749.
41 J. Lockman, *The vast importance of the herring industry &c. to these kingdoms* (1750), p. 25.
42 Charles Moss, *A sermon preached before the Right Honourable the Lord Mayor and the Governors of the Several Hospitals of the City of London* (1750), pp. 6–7.
43 Henry Fielding, *An Enquiry into the Causes of the late Increase of Robbers* (1751), in *Complete Works*, xiii, 24.
44 Malvin R. Zirker, *Fielding's Social Pamphlets* (Berkeley and Los Angeles, 1966), esp. the conclusion.
45 On the typicality and contradictory nature of this viewpoint, see E.P. Thompson, 'Patrician society, plebeian culture', *Journal of Social History*, vii (1974), 383.
46 Fielding, *Complete Works*, xiii, 70, 93–98.
47 *Ibid.*, 68.
48 Fielding, *Complete Works*, xiii, 17.
49 For the most comprehensive account, see Linebaugh, 'The Tyburn Riot Against the Surgeons', pp. 89–102.
50 The jury recommended mercy for the two men and over 800 parishioners from Westminster parishes petitioned for a pardon. See Linebaugh, 'The Tyburn Riots', pp. 93–4 and 'A Gentleman Not Concern'd', *The Case of the Unfortunate Bosavern Penlez* (2nd edn., 1750), p. 47.
51 Henry Fielding, *A True State of the Case of Bosavern Penlez* (1749), in *Complete Works*, xiii, p. 286.
52 *Ibid.*, pp. 284–5. The allusion to goldsmiths refers to the house of bankers, Snow and Denne, opposite The Star. Saunders Welsh, the high constable of Holborn, testified that had the mob burnt the contents of the brothel in the street, its flames might have spread to the Bankers' house. See *ibid.*, p. 278. Fielding insinuates that the bankers' house would have been pillaged as well.
53 *The Case of the Unfortunate Bosavern Penlez*, p. 22. For the purported thefts by Wood and Penlez, see GLRO, MJ/SR 2924.
54 For examples of barrow-women and draymen refusing to give way to genteel passers-by on the streets of London and abusing them in the process, see *Whitehall Evening Post*, 9–11 June 1748, 18–20 July 1751.
55 *Jacobite Journal*, 11 June 1747; Paul Kleber Monod, *Jacobitism and the English People, 1688–1788* (Cambridge, 1989), p. 199.
56 *Whitehall Evening Post*, 29 June–2 July 1751; Nicholas Rogers, *Whigs and Cities* (Oxford, 1989), pp. 173–4.
57 Mary M. Stewart, 'Henry Fielding's letter to the Duke of Richmond', *Philological Quarterly*, 1 (Jan. 1971), 135–140; Cal Winslow, 'Sussex smugglers' in Hay *et al.*, *Albion's Fatal Tree*, pp. 119–68; Battestin, *Henry Fielding*, pp. 465–6. The Duke of Richmond is referred to in the *Enquiry* as 'one of the worthiest magistrates, as well as of the best of men'. See *Works*, xiii, 77–8. On the notion of 'popular illegalities', see Foucault, *Discipline and Punish*, pp. 82–9.
58 *Covent Garden Journal*, 28 March 1752. See also 28 April 1752. For the counter-culture of Tyburn fair, see Peter Linebaugh, 'The Tyburn riot against the surgeons', pp. 66–9; for Tyburn as carnival, see Thomas W. Laqueur, 'Crowds, carnival and the state in English executions, 1604–1868', in *The First Modern Society: Essays in English History in Honour of Lawrence Stone*, eds. A.L. Beier, David Cannadine and James M. Rosenheim (Cambridge, 1990), pp. 305–55.
59 *Covent Garden Journal*, 13, 20 June 1753.
60 See *Whitehall Evening Post*, 1–3, 5–8, 8–10, 12–15 August, 2–5 Sept. 1749, 5–8 May 1750; *London Morning Penny Post*, 28–30 August 1751.
61 Ben Sedgly, *Observations on Mr. Fielding's Enquiry into the Causes of the late increase of*

robbers (1751), p. 22. For the attribution of the pamphlet to Richard Rolt, see Battestin, *Henry Fielding*, p. 521.

62 [Country Justice of the Peace], *Serious Thoughts in Regard to the Publick Disorders* (1750), pp. 50–1; Charles Gray, *Considerations on Several Proposals Lately Made for the Better Maintenance of the Poor* (1751), pp. 23–4.

63 BL Add. MS 35,601, f. 317; 35,602, f. 50; Norma Landau, *The Justices of the Peace, 1679–1760* (Berkeley & Los Angeles, 1984), pp. 98–145.

64 The Lords attempted to amend this bill by extending its application to England, and by facilitating the prosecution of gaming houses as well as bawdy houses. The Commons rejected the first amendment but agreed to the second. See *HLJ*, xxvii (1749–52), 686–9, 700; *HCJ*, xxvi (1750–54), 515; *London Magazine*, xxi (1752), 268–9.

65 See above, ch. 3 and Sidney and Beatrice Webb, *The History of Liquor Licensing, Principally from 1700 to 1876* (1903), pp. 28 et seq.

66 [John Campbell], *The Case of the Publicans, Both in Town and Country, Laid Open* (1752), pp. 17–19; *London Magazine*, xx (1751), 82–3; [Student in Politics], *Proposals to the Legislature for Preventing the Frequent Executions and Exportations of Convicts* (1754), pp. 26–38.

67 *HCJ*, xxvi (1750–54), 289, 345, 413–4, 490, 495, 500; Hugh Amory, 'Henry Fielding and the criminal legislation of 1751–2', 178– 84. For an abstract of the bill for 'the more effectual Relief and Employment of the Poor', see *London Magazine*, xxi (1752), 153–4.

68 On transportation, see Beattie, *Crime and the Courts*, pp. 470–83, 500–19.

69 Anon., *A Letter to a Member of Parliament* (1752), p. 1.

70 William Hay, *Remarks on the Laws Relating to the Poor, With Proposals for Their Better Relief and Employment* (1751), p. x. On Hay, see Joanna Innes, 'Parliament and the shaping of eighteenth-century social policy', *Transactions Royal Historical Society*, xl (1990), 85–6.

71 *Ibid.*, xi.

72 Gray, *Considerations*, p. 18; see also Sir James Creed, *An Impartial Examination of a Pamphlet Intitled Considerations* (1751), p. 29.

73 Gray, *Considerations*, pp. 3–5, 23.

74 Creed, *An Impartial Examination*, p. 22.

75 *London Magazine*, xx (1751), 502.

76 Anon., *A Letter to the author of Considerations* (1752), pp. 20–2.

77 *HCJ*, xxvi (1750–54), 500; *London Magazine*, xxi (1752), 153–4. The bill was not finally abandoned until 1754, when Pelham prevailed upon Lord Hillsborough not to pursue it any further, fearing a backlash of public opinion similar to the Jew Bill. See Innes, 'Parliament and eighteenth-century social policy', 79.

78 *London Magazine*, xxi (1752), 220–3.

79 For a similar line of argument, see Philonauta, *The Sailor's Happiness. A Scheme to Prevent the Impressing of Seamen in Time of War* (1751), pp. 19–27.

80 *London Magazine*, xxii (1753), 124, abstracting Alcock's pamphlet *Remarks on two Bills for the Better Maintenance of the Poor*.

81 *London Magazine*, xx (1751), 502–3, 549–51.

82 *HCJ*, xxvi (1750–54), 563, 643, 702. For precedents, see Tim Hitchcock, 'The English workhouse. A study in institutional poor relief in selected counties 1696–1750' (Oxford Univ. D. Phil. thesis, 1985).

83 Beattie, *Crime and the Courts*, esp. chs. 9–10; Innes, 'Parliament and eighteenth-century English social policy', 63–92.

84 Radzinowicz, *A History of English Criminal Law*, i, 399– 424. For a critique of this view, see Hugh Amory, 'Henry Fielding and the criminal legislation of 1751–2', 175–83.

85 Fielding, *A Proposal for Making an Effectual Provision for the Poor* in *Works*, xiii, 131–94.

86 On the importance of these criteria, see Foucault, *Discipline and Punish*, pp. 231–56. On
    Fielding's proposal, see Michael Ignatieff, *A Just Measure of Pain. The Penitentiary in the
    Industrial Revolution 1750–1850* (1978), pp. 45–6.
87 *Ibid.*, pp. 153–4, 183.
88 Fielding, *Works*, xiii, 183–7.
89 On the religious character of earlier reform campaigns, see Part III of this volume.

Part Three:
Poverty and Immorality

5

Reforming the City:
The Reformation of Manners Campaign in London, 1690–1738

Robert B. Shoemaker
University of Sheffield

England, it was argued in 1689 and 1690, had by Divine providence narrowly averted the disaster of a tyrannical Catholic monarchy, and in order to prevent actual Divine punishment for the country's sins a reformation of manners was necessary. The significance of the Societies for the Reformation of Manners, formed in several parts of the country from the autumn of 1690 and dedicated to the suppression of immorality, has largely been explained in the religious terms advanced by the Societies' founders.[1] Most recently, the campaign against vice has been seen as part of a radical millenarian movement, based on primitive Christianity and encouraged by the accession to the throne of William III.[2] Yet it is the argument of this essay that, viewed from another angle, the reformation of manners campaign was a response to concerns about social problems (poverty, crime, and disorder) in England's cities, particularly in London. This argument is not incompatible with religious explanations of the purposes of the movement, for in the early modern world religious reform often entailed attempts to reform society. It has been argued that behind the Puritan desire for a reformation of manners in the late sixteenth and early seventeenth centuries there was a concern to control the disorderly poor.[3] Similarly, Tim Hitchcock has argued that the millenarian movements of the late seventeenth and early eighteenth centuries spawned 'a large number of reform and social policy projects designed to discipline society at large'.[4] In this essay I wish to argue that the supporters of such projects were motivated not solely by spiritual considerations, but also by concerns to maintain social order. One of the main reasons why the inhabitants of late Stuart and early Hanoverian London welcomed a

campaign against vice was because it provided a method of clearing the
streets of prostitutes, beggars, street merchants, and other 'loose idle and
disorderly people'.

The first indication that the reformation of manners campaign was as
much about social reform as it was about religious reform is the fact that
reformers were far more active in cities than in the countryside. Although
in their propaganda the reformers argued for a 'national reformation', they
noted that cities, and especially London, were particular sites of 'common
wickedness'.[5] Thus, while the reformation of manners campaign was a
national, even international, campaign against vice, the Societies for the
Reformation of Manners were 'for the most part made up of residents of
cities and corporations': in England and Wales, societies were set up in at
least three dozen cities and towns, including Bristol, Coventry, Leicester,
Newcastle and Portsmouth.[6] The city which received by far the most
attention from the reformers was of course London. London is where the
reformation of manners campaign began, and where the reformers were
most active. At one point there were about twenty reformation of manners
societies active in the metropolis,[7] and the campaign in London lasted for
almost half a century. Annual reports of the societies' activities in London
were published until 1738, by which point, it was claimed, they had made
over one hundred thousand accusations of several types of vice. In
contrast, reformation of manners campaigns outside London were typically
short lived. In Bristol, where some of the best evidence of reformation of
manners activities survives outside the capital, prosecutions of vice lasted
only a few years; the reformers soon switched their activities to educating
the poor in charity schools.[8] The fact that the campaign was most active
in London is significant, because it was the fact that the campaign offered
the possibility of addressing some of London's social problems which made
it attractive to many of the informers, constables and justices of the peace
who supported it.

The late seventeenth century was a crucial period in London history, as
social problems threatened to multiply at a time when London's capacity
to cope with them decreased. Population growth led to rapid expansion of
the poorly governed suburban parishes outside the City: according to one
estimate the population of the suburbs north of the Thames increased by
76 per cent between 1660 and 1700.[9] The immigration that caused
population growth threatened to lead to social instability since many
immigrants had been driven from home by poverty, and much of the
available employment in the metropolis was casual and insecure. Most
immigrants settled in the suburbs, and, inside the City, two of the
institutions which had previously relieved distress, the wardmote and the
guilds, were in decline.[10] Economically, the decade in which the Societies
for the Reformation of Manners became established, the 1690s, was the

worst in a century, as high bread prices combined with wartime disruptions in trade and government manipulation of the coinage to drive large numbers of people to seek poor relief.[11] Awareness of the problems posed by poverty, crime and disorder was heightened by the outpouring of pamphlet literature which followed the expiry of the press licensing act in 1695. In this context many Londoners found a campaign against vice and immorality an attractive method of addressing the social ills of the metropolis.

In the early 1690s, a reformation of manners meant the suppressing of vice, debauchery, and profaneness, broadly defined. King William's proclamation against vice in 1692 mentioned blasphemy, profane swearing and cursing, drunkenness, lewdness, breaking the Sabbath, and 'any other dissolute, immoral or disorderly practice'.[12] As this last phrase suggests, no attempt was made to be specific about the offences that were to be prosecuted, because what was important was not the specific offence one might commit but the defect in one's character that led one to act immorally. In this sense, all forms of vice were connected – if one was so immoral as to swear or drink too much, one was also likely to fornicate or gamble. These concerns about vice were part of a wider critique of luxury in late Stuart England, a critique which saw lust, sensuality, and intemperance as products of a degeneration of the personality, in which reason lost control over the senses.[13] The anonymous *Proposals for a National Reformation*, published by one of the reformation of manners societies, demanded the suppression of playhouses as places which encouraged 'delight in idleness, excessive vanity, revellings, luxury, wantonness, lasciviousness, [and] whoredoms . . .', thus corrupting 'the natural vigour and manliness, prowess, and valour of our kingdom'.[14] Every character defect from idleness to 'whoredom', from luxury to a lack of 'manliness', was seen to be connected. As David Hayton has recently shown, opposition to vice was also connected with opposition to corruption in government. Edward Stephens, one of the earliest supporters of the campaign, advised the king to reduce 'needless and excessive salaries, pensions and expenses' in the preface to his pamphlet which described the origins of the societies, and the *Proposals for a National Reformation* complained about the 'universal corruption' of officers in the courts, who exploited the poor when they tried to file lawsuits.[15]

Although the concept of a reformation of manners encompassed a wide range of grievances, at the centre of the movement was the desire to suppress immorality, as perhaps the most visible and widespread symptom of the corruptions of the age. And, although all forms of vice were seen to be connected, there was a certain hierarchy of concerns about different types of vice in the language used by the most prominent supporters of the campaign, in which offences directly insulting to God, such as profane swearing and cursing and breaking the Sabbath, were given first priority. As John Tillotson explained, England faced Divine punishment for 'our horrible contempt of Religion . . . by our infidelity and profaneness'. According to Edward Stephens, 'among public offences judged worthy of the severest animadversions and punishment, profanation and contempt of . . . religion hath always been reckoned one of the first'.[16] Thus, proclamations and letters against vice written by the King, Queen, and Archbishop of Canterbury all mention the religious offences (blasphemy, swearing, breaking the Sabbath) first, with other offences such as fornication, gambling and drunkenness given less prominence and often referred to indirectly, under a vague rubric like 'all other lewd, enormous, and disorderly practices'.[17] This particular concern with direct insults to God is also reflected in the legislation of the period: the only legislation passed in support of the reformation of manners campaign concerned profane swearing and cursing and blasphemy; attempts to introduce new legislation against sexual offences (which, given the state of the laws, was even more necessary), failed.[18] (The reformers defined swearing as when the words God, Lord, or Jesus Christ were 'used plainly and lightly in the sense of an affirmation or negation', and cursing as 'any invocation of God or the devil for vengeance or harm'.)[19]

This priority given to the types of vice which were most religious in nature is hardly surprising, given that the roots of the Reformation of Manners Societies trace back to the religious societies founded by Anthony Horneck in 1678, and the fact that the reformation of manners campaign was originally promoted by several bishops and other divines in the court of William and Mary. Gilbert Burnet encouraged William and Mary to make religion 'the chief mark and measure of their whole government', and in an early letter encouraging 'a general reformation of all our subjects' William devoted half of the letter to methods for reforming abuses and corruptions among the clergy.[20] But this concentration on profanity is worth mentioning because it is much less evident in the activities of the members of the Societies for the Reformation of Manners on the ground – the informers, constables, and justices of the peace who actually set about trying to suppress vice in London.

The reason such a distinction (between the goals of the original promoters and the subsequent activities of some of the campaign's supporters) can be made is because the reformation of manners campaign was a very loosely organized movement. There were several societies in London alone, and it is a mistake to assume that all the reformers shared the same goals. By inviting the general public to join their campaign, the founders of the reformation of manners campaign in effect lost control of it. One of the most distinctive features of the campaign was its reliance on informers to make accusations, prosecute offenders, and supervise the activities of parish officers and even justices of the peace. In the sermons to reformation of manners societies, and in the reformers' printed propaganda, it was repeatedly proclaimed that in the war against vice one could not be neutral; all right-minded individuals were invited to act as informers. In her letter to the Middlesex justices, Queen Mary encouraged not only parish officers, but 'all other officers and persons whatsoever, to do their part in their several stations, by timely and impartial informations and prosecutions'. Making full use of the possibilities of the press, the societies printed and distributed several pamphlets and broadsheets encouraging people to inform, including copies of the King's proclamation against vice, Queen Mary's letter to the Middlesex justices, and proclamations by county Quarter Sessions, as well as books with abstracts of the laws against profaneness and immorality, advice on how to form societies, instructions on how to act as informers, and sample warrants.[21]

The propagandists and official supporters of the campaign encouraged informers to prosecute several types of vice – not only profane swearing and cursing and breaking the Sabbath, but also, since all forms of vice were seen to be connected, drunkenness, 'lewdness', and gambling, to name the most commonly mentioned offences. In effect, the activists who set about informing against offenders then made their own choices as to which sins to prosecute. Which offences did Londoners give priority to in the war against vice?

The answers to this question are to be found in Table 6.1, which provides the figures reported in the London societies' annual reports of their activities. It should be noted at the outset that these figures are not comprehensive. Most obviously there is a gap for the crucial early years between 1693 and 1700 for which annual reports do not survive, and the lists of offenders published until 1707 list only offences related to prostitution: 'lewd and disorderly persons' and keepers of 'bawdy houses'. Other evidence indicates that the reformers prosecuted several other offences in these early years.[22] In a short period in 1691, 563 persons were convicted for permitting tippling on the Sabbath, working on the Sabbath, drunkenness, and swearing and cursing; most of the convictions were for permitting tippling, and the justice responsible for the vast majority of the convictions was Ralph Hartley.[23] This pace was not maintained, however, because shortly thereafter Hartley was expelled from the Middlesex commission of the peace and the loss of their most active justice temporarily disillusioned the reformers.[24] In 1699, however, it was claimed that 'thousands of offenders . . . have been punished for swearing, drunkenness, and profanation of the Sabbath',[25] and it is clear from lists of convictions and prosecutions kept by the Westminster sessions and the societies that the reformers were prosecuting large numbers of people for swearing and cursing as early as 1695 and for Sunday trading from 1704.[26] Despite their absence from the printed accounts, offences other than prostitution were prosecuted in the early years.[27]

The reports up to 1707, therefore, refer to only one aspect of the activities of the societies, and, quite possibly, the activities of only one society.[28] From 1708, however, the reports include a wider range of offences. In addition, the format of the reports changed, to state the total numbers of offenders *accused* (not just those convicted). (By inflating the number of offences reported, the reformers hoped to improve their public image.)[29] Assuming that only a small number of the accused were discharged without punishment, it appears that the accounts after 1708 were also more comprehensive. Since the number of people in the societies' reports charged with offences punishable in houses of correction approximates the number of people actually committed to the metropolitan houses of correction, few prosecutions initiated by reformation of manners supporters can have been left out of the reports.[30]

Despite the incomplete nature of the evidence presented in Table 6.1, the patterns of prosecutions reported are significant, because they are quite different from what the stated goals of the reformers would lead one to expect. Profane swearing and cursing, one of the offences given greatest prominence by the leaders of the campaign, was only the third most commonly prosecuted offence, and prosecutions for this offence declined steadily from the first year that they were reported. Sabbath breaking, the other specifically religious offence in Table 6.1, resulted in a far greater number of prosecutions, in part because it was much easier to prosecute people working on the Sabbath than swearers and cursers, who, because they typically committed the offence on the streets, were difficult to locate when the warrant was issued to collect the fine. Sabbath breaking was very frequently prosecuted in the years 1708–9 and 1715, and was in fact the most commonly prosecuted offence in 1709. Nonetheless, like profane swearing and cursing, prosecutions soon started a steady decline which continued until the accounts ceased to be published after 1738.

The offence the reformers prosecuted most frequently was 'lewd and disorderly practices' – an average of 1,330 people per year were prosecuted for this offence in the years for which reports survive between 1708 and 1724. This is significant, because whatever the precise nature of the offences prosecuted under this rubric, this was not a vice given priority by the founding fathers of the reformation of manners campaign (though this is not to say that they would have disapproved of such prosecutions). What exactly were 'lewd and disorderly practices'? Lewdness had a very broad meaning during this period, but it most frequently referred in these

Table 6.1
PROSECUTIONS INITIATED BY THE SOCIETIES FOR THE REFORMATION OF MANNERS IN LONDON, 1693–1738

Year	Swearing & cursing	Sabbath breaking	Drunken-ness	Lewd & disorderly	Keep bawdy hse[1]	Gaming	Total
1693[2]				157	155		
1700				1063	102		
1701				1136	69		
1702				1077	80		
1704				1175	15		
1707				844	57		
1708[3]	626	1187	150	1255	51	30	3299
1709	575	1523	42	794	32	10	2976
1715	263	1066	46	1152	36	8	2571
1716	102	621	14	1066	9	8	1820
1717	400	524	25	1927	33		2909
1718	205	492	17	1253	31	8	2006
1720	114	615	11	1189	14	16	1959
1721	161	709	13	1197	15	4	2099
1722	201	653	8	1223	35	104	2224
1723	96	648	5	1622	36	42	2449
1724	108	600	12	1951	29	23	2723
1725							2506
1726							1060
1727							1363
1728							778
1729							1226
1730	22	424		251	30	15	754[4]
1731							895
1732	14	275		230	9		528
1733		395		89	3		487
1734		240		170			410
1735		268		318			586
1736							669
1737		393		95			488
1738		493		52			545

Source: Portus, *Caritas Anglicana*, Appendix V; Isaacs, 'Moral crime', pp. 252, 259; supplemented by the societies' annual accounts. The figures for 1693 are from *Proposals for a National Reformation of Manners*, pp. 34–5. The unit of analysis is the defendant.

[1] Includes disorderly houses.
[2] Year ending January 1694.
[3] In 1708, the societies began to report the number of defendants prosecuted, regardless of whether or not they were convicted. The figures up to 1708 are for convictions only.
[4] Includes 12 prosecutions for assaulting constables in the execution of their office.

contexts to sexual misconduct, or 'uncleanness'. And while 'lewdness' and 'uncleanness' referred to all forms of sexuality which took place outside marriage,[31] it is clear that in the societies' reports lewdness refers almost solely to prostitution. Not only were the vast majority of the people accused of 'lewd and disorderly practices' women, but a comparison of the societies' first 'blacklist' of offenders (for 1693) with London judicial records reveals that most were accused of 'nightwalking' and picking up men.[32] Moreover, the terms 'lewd and disorderly' were probably derived from house of correction calendars, where they were often used to describe women accused of soliciting, picking up men, and so forth. As is evident from Table 6.1, a small number of the keepers of 'bawdy' and other 'disorderly' houses, the houses frequented by 'lewd and disorderly' people, were also prosecuted throughout this period. There are several reasons why the number of keepers prosecuted was not larger, the most important of which is probably the fact that such prosecutions were expensive because they had to be conducted by in-dictment. Initially, more keepers were prosecuted, but the reformers soon realized that such prosecutions threatened to bankrupt the campaign.[33]

The reformers thus focused their efforts against sexual immorality on prostitution, and their efforts against prostitution on prostitutes and not their clients or the proprietors of brothels. Although the King's 1698 proclamation was directed against 'vice, immorality and profaneness in all persons from the highest to the lowest degree . . . and particularly in such who are employed near our royal person', the reformers focused their efforts against sexual immorality on poor women, for prostitutes committed to the house of correction were typically poor.[34] Why did informers devote so much attention to London's underclass of street prostitutes? A major motivation behind the reformation of manners campaign, hitherto overlooked by historians, was a concern to attack the problems of poverty, crime, and disorder in London, problems which appeared to be spiralling out of control in the 1690s and early 1700s. Street prostitution was perceived to be both a symptom and a cause of these problems, and was thus an obvious target of attack. We can see this connection between prostitution and other social problems both in the language the reformers used to describe the offences they prosecuted and in the concerns expressed by the members of London's first Reformation of Manners Societies.

Many women who were accused of prostitution and committed to houses of correction were suspected not simply of prostitution (for which the evidence was often limited)[35], but also of theft, vagrancy, 'idleness' (not having a lawful means of earning a living), or disorderly behaviour. Hannah Powell and three other women were charged in front of the Lord Mayor not only with being 'idle lewd persons and known to be common nightwalkers', but more specifically because they had been 'taken late last night [on suspicion of being] pickpockets'.[36] Mary Dickenson was committed to the

London Bridewell by the City's Recorder, 'charged on oath for being a lewd woman and for being picked up by a gentleman in the street late last night and [being] one that can give no good account of herself or her lawful way of living and hath no legal settlement but is a common vagrant'.[37] The small number of men included in the societies' prosecutions for prostitution (presumably as clients) were particularly likely to be suspected of an additional offence; Thomas Newton was committed to the Wood Street Compter in the City for being 'an idle disorderly person and taken late last night tippling in an alehouse and making a disturbance there and [is] suspected to be privy to the dispersing several libels in the streets'.[38] These examples, all of which involve people reported on the 1693 'blacklist' of offenders, illustrate some of the motives behind prosecutions for prostitution in London.

That prostitution was linked with broader concerns about the growth of poverty, crime and disorder in London is also evident from the language used by the men who launched the first sustained effort to prosecute vice in London after the Revolution of 1688. In the autumn of 1689, the churchwardens and overseers of the poor of St Martin in the Fields petitioned the Westminster justices to suppress brothels in the parish. The petition may well have been inspired by the minister of St Martin's, the supporter of moral reform and future archbishop John Tillotson, but the language of the petition suggests that it was very much a product of local concerns. The parish officers complained about 'a daily increase of poor' in St Martin's, and blamed this increase on 'people of evil fame who keep reputed bawdy houses in several by alleys and places in the said parish whereby several great disorders and misdemeanours are daily committed against the peace'. If prostitution was suppressed, the parish officers implied, levels of poverty and disorder in the parish would decrease.[39]

In response to the petition, two justices began to commit scores of offenders to the Westminster house of correction, not only prostitutes but also other 'loose, idle and disorderly persons'. Most of those committed were probably quite poor.[40] The idle (unemployed) poor were the target of prosecution waves like this because it was believed that they often led disorderly lives which led to law breaking. Referring to the poorest inhabitants of the City's outermost parishes, John Graunt wrote in 1662 that 'many vicious persons get liberty to live as they please, for want of some heedful eye to overlook them'.[41] Writing in 1712, the reforming magistrate John Chamberlayne (formerly secretary of the SPCK) expressed the belief that the unemployed were responsible for 'the sudden increase in whores, rogues, vagabonds, and sturdy beggars' in the West End. And in the words of Josiah Woodward, the reformers' most active propagandist, 'idle people . . . perplex the business of the more diligent, disturb their quiet, [and] pilfer their goods . . .'[42] The reformers' interest in suppressing prostitution, therefore, was part of a wider set of concerns to stop the growth of idleness, begging, and vagrancy in the capital.

As Josiah Woodward's comments suggest, worries about the level of crime in the metropolis were also an important motivation behind prosecutions of prostitutes and related offenders. Such concerns surfaced frequently during the period of the campaign, starting just before its inception in 1688 and running throughout the 1690s, and from 1712 through the 1720s.[43] In fact, the first formal reformation of manners society in London was set up specifically in response to a rather routine royal proclamation for the apprehending of highway robbers.[44] In late 1690 a group of parish officers and other inhabitants of the Tower Hamlets on the eastern edge of the metropolis concluded that 'the suppression of public bawdy houses in our several parishes and precincts . . . would be not only a proper means, but also a necessary expedient, to answer the noble ends of their Majesties' royal proclamation'. Brothels, the inhabitants argued, were 'not only the nurseries of the most horrid vices, and sinks of the most filthy debaucheries, but also (as we suppose them) the common receptacles, or rather, dens, of notorious thieves, robbers, traitors, and other criminals, that fly from public justice'.[45] To reduce the number of robberies in London it was necessary to prosecute prostitutes and bawdy house keepers, and that, according to the 'blacklists' of offenders summarized in Table 6.1, is just what the first reformers did. The link between prostitution and theft was made explicit in the 'blacklists': the only other offence besides prostitution mentioned before 1708 was pickpocketing, for which there were 57 convictions in five reports.[46]

The connection between vice and more serious crime is a common theme in the pamphlet literature of this period: serious crime, it was argued, was the inevitable result of irreligion, immorality, and idleness, especially among the poor.[47] Although by this reasoning all forms of vice and irreligion should be suppressed in order to prevent offenders from falling down the slippery slope to serious crime, prostitution was an obvious place to start, because it was so commonly associated with theft. Prostitutes were frequently accused of picking pockets and, as argued by the first Tower Hamlets society, prostitutes and thieves were thought to associate together in brothels and other disorderly houses. Moreover, it was feared that young people who frequented brothels would be tempted to defraud their masters or parents in order to pay for their vices.[48]

Motivations for prosecuting prostitution, however, were not restricted to concerns about its links with unemployment, vagrancy, and more serious crimes. Informers and justices were also persuaded to prosecute prostitutes and bawdy house keepers by pressure from local inhabitants, who complained of the noise and disruption caused by prostitutes soliciting and operating out of houses in their streets, especially late at night. Several inhabitants of Bridges Street near Covent Garden, for example, complained that prostitutes 'stop[ped] up the passages' to their houses and 'frequently obstructed and hindered [the residents] in their lawful callings'. People living near Drury Lane complained of 'frequent outcries in the night, fighting, robberies, and all sorts of debauchery committed . . . all night long', disturbances which threatened to force them to find another place to live in order to find peace and quiet and to avoid corrupting their servants and children.[49]

Such concerns clearly resulted from the fact that prostitution threatened to disrupt the social character of previously respectable neighbourhoods, and most of the neighbourhoods concerned were in London's West End. Prostitution occurred in several parts of the metropolis, but after the initial campaign by the first reformation of manners society against prostitution in the East End and the City, efforts to prosecute prostitution were concentrated in the West End. Prosecutions of prostitutes brought before the Lord Mayor peaked at 90 in 1694; in only two of the subsequent eleven years were more than a dozen prostitutes charged.[50] Within urban Middlesex, over 90 per cent of the commitments to houses of correction for prostitution and related offences came from Westminster and the urban Middlesex parishes of St Giles in the Fields and St Andrew Holborn.[51] Concerns about prostitution were greatest in the areas around Covent Garden and Drury Lane: this is the area where all of the petitions received by the Middlesex and Westminster sessions concerning brothels came from.

This area of London was experiencing significant social change at this time: as the newly-formed parishes of St Anne and St James in Westminster became the most fashionable places to live in the late seventeenth century, the social character of the inner West End parishes of St Giles in the Fields and Covent Garden started to decline. As wealthier inhabitants moved west, poorer inhabitants moved in, and brothels and gaming houses flourished. Thus, the hostility to prostitution in these parishes which resulted in so many prosecutions resulted at least in part from the changing social composition of these parishes, as older inhabitants attempted to protect the social respectability of their neighbourhoods from the threat posed by their new, poorer, and often 'disorderly' neighbours.[52] Since the informers who prosecuted prostitutes were relatively socially prestigious craftsmen, it is likely that they identified with the established housekeepers of these parishes rather than with the newer inhabitants. Two of the most active informers in the early 1690s lived close to this area, on the Strand: James Jenkins (a clock maker) and Bodenham Rewse (an embroiderer).[53]

More generally, the substantial efforts by the reformers to prosecute prostitutes and other 'loose idle and disorderly' persons reflect an attempt to preserve habits of social deference and subordination in London, which were thought to be under threat. This was the period when the word 'mob', with its connotation that the lower classes had become disorderly and ungovernable, was first used to describe rioting in London,[54] and there is a sense among some of the reformers that they wished to reinstate a lost discipline and hierarchy to social relations in the city. In reformation of manners propaganda the proliferation of vice was linked with a loosening of social bonds and a perceived decline in the authority of magistrates, ministers, masters, and parents.[55] Suppressing immorality, therefore, would provide 'a social cement', which would reinforce 'those ideas of subordination and submission that were necessary to make the nation secure and society orderly'.[56]

In particular, the reformers' efforts answered contemporary concerns about the behaviour of servants. In a sermon to the societies, Thomas Bray argued that the nobility and gentry, along with 'traders, parents, and masters' would benefit most from the elimination of vice, since servants and young people would then be less likely to pilfer or squander their property.[57] Concerns that servants were particularly prone to immoral behaviour (especially prostitution and gambling) were related to broader complaints, which were endemic during this period, about the growing unruliness and insubordination of servants in London. Demand for servants, especially female servants, increased considerably in the early eighteenth century, partly as a result of the increasing number of 'new gentry' taking up residence in the West End. These servants frequently switched jobs, and contemporaries found their independence and the lack of social supervision threatening. When out of work, they were frequently suspected of prostitution.[58] As a consequence, young women in the West End were particularly liable to be committed to the house of correction.[59] In sum, the campaign against prostitution and related offenders arose not simply out of fears of increasing poverty and crime, but also out of more general concerns about the growth of social indiscipline in London, particularly in the inner West End parishes.

There were several different Reformation of Manners Societies in London, and the set of motivations for reform which I have just described do not provide a complete explanation of the reformers' activities. Clearly, informers and justices of the peace did not all view the problem of vice in the same terms. Some London reformers, such as the City of London grand jurors in 1690, were most concerned about the profanation of the Sabbath, 'to the great reproach and scandal of the Protestant Religion and the good government of this renowned City',[60] and as a consequence some societies concentrated on the more strictly religious offences, profaning the Sabbath and swearing and cursing. As the interest of the first society (the Tower Hamlets society) in all forms of vice suggests, there was not a strict division of labour, but some societies did specialize. One early society, founded by five or six 'gentlemen of the Church of England', focused on swearing, drunkenness, and profaning the Sabbath, and another, composed of constables, focused on swearing.[61] According to John Chamberlayne, of the four reformation of manners societies in 1708, one, whose members were 'persons of eminency in the law, members of parliament, justices of the peace, and considerable citizens of London', focused on swearing, drunkenness and profanation of the Sabbath, and another, 'consisting of about fifty persons, tradesmen and others, have more especially applied themselves to the suppression of lewdness . . .'[62] The first of these societies may have been responsible for the several registers of accusations and convictions which survive; 97 per cent of the offences listed in the registers were Sabbath offences and the only other offences mentioned were swearing, cursing and drunkenness.[63] It could be argued that any prostitutes or related offenders apprehended by this group of informers would have been dealt with separately because the method of conviction and punishment (commitment to a house of correction) was different, but it appears unlikely that these particular informers actively prosecuted prostitutes: in the surviving records there is very little overlap between the informers who prosecuted prostitutes and those who prosecuted swearing and cursing and Sabbath offences.[64] Moreover, the informers whose activities are recorded in the registers were active in parts of London where prostitution was rarely prosecuted: large numbers of their prosecutions took place in the suburban parishes north and east of the City (especially Cripplegate, Shoreditch, Stepney, Aldgate, and Whitechapel) in addition to the West End.

Besides the obvious religious reasons, it is difficult to determine why informers were motivated to initiate so many prosecutions against people for working on the Sabbath. The biggest category of offenders was victuallers, whose real offence may have been selling ale during time of divine service. Like today, many of the other people working on the Sabbath were low-status shopkeepers who sold food, such as bakers, chandlers, butchers, and fruiterers. It has been suggested that the reformers focused on such low status offenders because 'they believed that ordinary people were the most vulnerable to corruption . . . from the twin allurements of profit and diversion'.[65] While this interpretation fits with the reformers' focus on the poor discussed earlier, there is another, more practical explanation for the concentration on low status offenders – like today, it may have been the smaller, less prestigious shops which were most likely to open on Sunday, and open shops were extremely easy to prosecute, since they were immobile. (It is not competition from their rivals which led to these prosecutions – no victuallers, chandlers, bakers, or fruiterers are recorded as acting as informers.) Higher status offenders, including gentlemen, surgeons, music and dancing school masters, and vintners, were prosecuted for swearing and cursing, so for religiously based offences informers were willing to prosecute more socially prestigious offenders.[66]

Although prostitution, Sabbath offences, swearing and cursing, and drunkenness were the offences most frequently mentioned in pamphlets published by the Societies for the Reformation of Manners, under the umbrella of the reformation of manners campaign Londoners attacked several other vices, or activities which promoted vice, which caused concern in the metropolis. These include sodomy, gambling, obscene and blasphemous books, music houses, masquerades, fairs, playhouses, shops which sold gin, wheelbarrow boys, and shoe blacks. The campaigns against several of these activities, like the campaign against prostitution, also derived (at least in part) from concerns about the growth of poverty, crime, and disorder in the metropolis. In particular, they reveal a recurring concern to keep the streets of the capital clear not only of prostitutes and vagrants, but also of fairs, street merchants, and other activities which caused potentially disorderly groups to congregate.

At the time that the Court of Aldermen in the City was preparing its response to Queen Mary's letter of July 1691 requesting stricter enforcement of the laws against vice, the Aldermen received several petitions from people living near Smithfield concerning Bartholomew Fair. The inhabitants asked the court to confine the fair to only three days of buying and selling of merchandise, instead of the two-week long 'riotous and tumultuous assembly' which they claimed it had become, in which a variety of disreputable entertainments took place, including drolls, lotteries, music booths, dancing, and obscene ballads. According to local inhabitants, not only did these entertainments corrupt the youth and other inhabitants of the City, but they led to 'very many murders, robberies and riots', they greatly inconvenienced nearby residents, and they presented a serious fire danger.[67] Although the Court acceded to the request to limit the fair to three days, repeated efforts to prevent entertainments from taking place at the fair were unsuccessful. Nonetheless, the attempt to clean up Bartholomew Fair is an example of how the desire to suppress vice could be channelled into an attack on a major nuisance and public order problem in the metropolis. Similarly, following an order of Common Council which once again limited Bartholomew Fair to three days in 1708, reformers among the Middlesex and Westminster grand juries and commissions of the peace attempted to suppress Mayfair, in Westminster, where a reforming constable had been murdered in 1702. As the Middlesex justices argued, the Queen's proclamation for the suppression of profaneness and vice could not be carried out 'if such notorious causes of [vice], as this fair is, be not removed'.[68]

Gambling was an offence which attracted considerable attention from the reformers in London, as an activity which took place not only at fairs, but also in the streets and in gaming houses. Wheelbarrow boys and shoeshine boys were accused of encouraging gambling on the streets; the former allegedly carried dice with them, which they used to entice unwary pedestrians and children to gamble for the goods on sale, especially oranges. There were, however, additional complaints against these street vendors.

'Shoe blacks' were accused of 'using at their games the most bitter oaths and execrations', and they were suspected to be vagrants and 'for the most part thieves or their spies'.[69] Wheelbarrow boys allegedly sold inferior goods, used false weights and measures, and obstructed the footpaths and streets. It is also likely that they deprived local businesses of custom.[70] By ordering constables to arrest these street merchants, the Middlesex justices hoped not only to suppress gambling, but also to clear London's streets of thieves, vagrants, and obstructions to traffic.

Although gambling was a topic of concern in the 1690s to Members of Parliament, London grand jurors, and Middlesex justices of the peace,[71] prosecuting gamblers and the keepers of gaming houses *per se* was not a major activity of the reformers until the early 1720s, as is evident from Table 6.1. These prosecutions were the result of a concerted campaign undertaken by the Middlesex and Westminster justices, in response to pressure from both the Lords Chief Justices and local inhabitants, to suppress gambling in Covent Garden. The reasons for focusing on gambling at this particular time are unclear, though the collapse of the South Sea Bubble may have led to less tolerant attitudes towards risk taking.[72] In any case, gambling was thought to be responsible for several social problems. Concerns were expressed that many people (especially young gentlemen) had been defrauded in gaming houses, thereby ruining themselves and their families. Moreover, gaming houses were, according to one account, 'thieving shops, for the reception of highwaymen, bullies, common assassins, and affidavit men, insomuch that the parts of the town that are frequented by these creatures are dangerously infected with robbers and knaves; and the streets as dangerous in the night as they are in Padua'. 'Divers riots, affrays, and bloodsheds' also occurred at gaming houses, most notably a major riot in December 1721, when constables attempting to close down a gaming house were attacked by men with swords, soldiers were called in, and a gambler was killed.[73] The challenge to public order posed by this attack probably stimulated the large number of prosecutions for gambling and keeping gaming houses in the following year.

Like gambling, the sale of gin was a late focus of interest of the reformation of manners campaign. The Middlesex justices began to investigate the problem in 1721, and over the next fifteen years they repeatedly complained about the ill effects of gin drinking in the metropolis. Reporting in 1726 that there were over 6,000 houses and shops that sold gin in London, the justices argued that gin drinking was 'one of the chief causes of the vast increase of thieves and pilferers of all kinds' in the metropolis, as well as 'one of the principal causes of the great increase of beggars and parish poor, notwithstanding the high wages now given to all sorts of workmen and servants'.[74] Justices sympathetic to the reformation of manners campaign provided some of the pressure which led to the passage of the Gin Act in 1736, but by that point the societies had virtually ceased to exist. Ironically it was the controversy caused by the use of informers to enforce the act which provided the death blow to the reformation of manners campaign in 1738; with informers discredited the reformers lost their strongest weapon against vice.[75]

Explaining the movement to limit the sale of gin, Peter Clark has argued that in public discourse in the 1720s and 1730s 'gin became the progenitrix of most of the socioeconomic problems afflicting the country', including the apparent increase in crime and disorder in London.[76] Much the same could be said of many of the other targets of the reformation of manners campaign: prostitution, gambling, fairs, wheelbarrow boys, and shoe blacks were all thought to contribute in one way or another to perceived increases in crime, disorder, poverty, and social instability in the metropolis. Although concerns about these social problems appear to have increased after 1688, it should be noted that they predate the revolution: we have seen that in 1662 John Graunt worried about the growth of poverty and 'vicious' behaviour in the extramural parishes of the City, and several Lord Mayor's proclamations in the period up to 1688 expressed concern over the growing number of rogues, vagrants, beggars, and other 'idle' persons on the City's streets.[77]

The reformation of manners movement tapped into an existing (and growing) set of concerns about the state of social relations in London, and Londoners who were worried about these problems used the rhetoric of the reformers and practical support provided by the Societies to address them. They were able to manipulate the reformation of manners campaign in this way because the original aims of the campaign were so open ended, and because the reformers invited magistrates and the general public to play an instrumental role in the fight against vice. Nonetheless, while many of the targets for reform in London were not part of the original aims of the movement, it is unlikely that the founding fathers would have objected to them. Although the reformation of manners campaign was a diverse movement, the participants were united in a common aim to make London a more virtuous and orderly city.

While initially the disparate groups of reformers were contained within one movement, from the early 1700s there is evidence of a growing split between the prominent supporters of the reformation of manners campaign, and the people on the ground in London who initiated prosecutions against vice. In the 1690s the societies had received encouragement and support from several bishops and other divines, and from its inception in 1698 the Society for Promoting Christian Knowledge helped coordinate reformation of manners activities in the provinces. In the early eighteenth century, however, both the church and the SPCK began to distance themselves from the reformation of manners campaign; the religiously inspired impulse for reform switched to charity schools and workhouses.[78] The Anglican establishment and others appear to have come to the conclusion that they had created a monster; the reformation of manners campaign had acquired a life of its own and could no longer be controlled or trusted. This distrust was due in part to the participation of dissenters in the campaign, but it was also due more generally to the fact that the reformers possessed so much autonomy in how they carried out their business.[79] With their efforts to supervise the activities of constables and justices of the peace (some of the reformers even reportedly tried to get immoral justices dropped from the commission of the peace)[80] and the fact that they totally bypassed the church courts, the societies appeared to undermine the authority of both state and church. This split between the church and the London reformers is reflected in the decline in the number of prosecutions for swearing and cursing and Sabbath breaking which set in sometime between 1709 and 1715 (while prosecutions for lewd and disorderly conduct continued at a high level), and in the increasing role taken by the Middlesex justices of the peace, especially in the 1720s, in initiating and conducting campaigns against street merchants, gaming houses and gin shops. These new targets of reform reflected the justices' pre-occupations with maintaining order in the metropolis rather than the original reformers' priority of punishing religious offences.

Recent research has demonstrated that the reformation of manners movement took on many forms and was used for many different purposes in the 1690s and early 1700s. Tony Claydon has argued that the attack on vice initially formed part of an ideological justification for the revolution of 1688. David Hayton has shown how the moral reform movement fed into the parliamentary 'country' critique of corruption in government in the late 1690s. As suggested below by Tim Hitchcock and Mary Fissell, the attack on vice also formed part of a more broadly based radical millenarian movement in the late seventeenth century.[81] And now I am arguing that there was a strong element of attempted social control (for lack of a better term) in the efforts to combat vice in London. The concept of a reformation of manners in the late seventeenth century thus brought together several disparate strands of ideas on religious, political, and social issues. The strength and diversity of the resulting movement exemplifies the strong impetus for reform found in English society after the Glorious Revolution.

Notes

An earlier version of this essay was presented to the Eighteenth-Century seminar at the Institute of Historical Research in London. I am grateful for comments and suggestions I have received from John Beattie, Tony Claydon, Penelope Corfield, David Hayton, Tim Hitchcock, Joanna Innes, and Paul Seaver.

1   Garnet V. Portus, *Caritas Anglicana: Or, An Historical Inquiry into those Religious and Philanthropical Societies that Flourished in England Between the Years 1678 and 1740* (1912); D.W.R. Bahlman, *The Moral Revolution of 1688* (New Haven, 1957); T.C. Curtis and W.A. Speck, 'The Societies for the Reformation of Manners: a case study in the theory and

practice of moral reform', *Literature and History* 3 (1976), 45–47; A.G. Craig, 'The movement for the reformation of manners, 1688–1715', (Edinburgh Univ. Ph.D. Thesis, 1980); Tina Beth Isaacs, 'Moral crime, moral reform, and the state in eighteenth-century England: a study of piety and politics', (Univ. of Rochester Ph.D. Thesis, 1979). For the roots of the reformer's providentialism in restoration Anglicanism, see John Spurr, '"Virtue, Religion and Government": the Anglican uses of providence', in Tim Harris, Paul Seaward, and Mark Goldie (eds.), *The Politics of Religion in Restoration England* (Oxford, 1990), pp. 29–47.

2   Tim V. Hitchcock, '"In True Imitation of Christ": The tradition of mystical communitarianism in early eighteenth-century England', in *Locating the Shakers: Cultural Origins and Legacies of an American Religious Movement* (Exeter: Exeter Studies in American and Commonwealth Arts, no. 3, 1990), pp. 13–25; below, chapters 6 and 7. See also Eamon Duffy, 'Primitive christianity revived; religious renewal in Augustan England', in Derek Baker (ed.) *Renaissance and Renewal in Christian History* (Oxford, 1977), pp. 287–300.

3   Keith Wrightson and David Levine, *Poverty and Piety in an English Village: Terling 1525–1700* (New York, 1979); William Hunt, *The Puritan Movement: The Coming of Revolution in an English County* (Cambridge, Mass., 1983), pp. 79–84, 228–29, 250–52; David Underdown, *Revel, Riot and Rebellion: Popular Politics and Culture in England 1603–1660* (Oxford, 1987), ch. 3. The connection between Puritanism and social control, however, has been questioned: see, for example, Margaret Spufford, 'Puritanism and social control?', in Anthony Fletcher and John Stevenson (eds.) *Order and Disorder in Early Modern England* (Cambridge, 1987), pp. 41–57; Robert von Friedeburg, 'Reformation of Manners and the Social Composition of Offenders in an East Anglian Cloth Village: Earls Colne, Essex, 1531–1642', *Journal of British Studies* 29 (1990), 347–85.

4   Hitchcock, '"In True Imitation of Christ"', p. 17.

5   Timothy Rogers, *A Sermon Preached to the Societies for Reformation of Manners in the Cities of London and Westminster* (1701), p. 26; [Edward Fowler], *A Vindication of a Late Undertaking of Certain Gentlemen in order to the Suppressing of Debauchery and Profaneness* (1692), preface; *An Account of the Societies for Reformation of Manners, in England and Ireland* (1699), pp. 76–77; David Hayton, 'Moral reform and country politics in the late seventeenth-century House of Commons, *Past and Present* no. 128 (1990), 53 and n. 16.

6   Gideon Harding, *A Sermon Preached before the Society for the Reformation of Manners: on Easter Tuesday, 1700* (1700), p. 35. For evidence of reformation of manners activity outside London, see *An Account of the Progress of the Reformation of Manners, in England, Ireland, and other parts of the World* (1701), pp. 4–5; Bahlman, *Moral Revolution*, pp. 38–39; Portus, *Caritas Anglicana*, pp. 125–27; *An Account of the Societies*, p. 26.

7   Josiah Woodward, *An Account of the Rise and Progress of the Religious Societies in the City of London, etc.* 2nd edn. (1698), pp. 82–83.

8   Isaacs, 'Moral Crime', p. 154; Bahlman, *Moral Revolution*, pp. 44–46; Fissell, ch. 6 below.

9   Roger Finlay and Beatrice Shearer, 'Population growth and suburban expansion', in A.L. Beier and Roger Finlay (eds.) *London 1500–1700* (1986), Table 2, p. 42. It has recently been argued that this figure underestimates the actual amount of growth in the late seventeenth century: Vanessa Harding, 'The population of London, 1550–1700: a review of the published evidence', *London Journal* 15 (1990), 123.

10 M. Dorothy George, *London Life in the Eighteenth Century* (1925; Harmondsworth, 1966 edn.), pp. 116–17; *The Case of the Parish of St Giles's in the Fields, as to their Poor, and a Workhouse Designed to be built for Employing them* [1722?], p. 3; Valerie Pearl, 'Change and stability in seventeenth-century London', *London Journal* 5 (1979), 25–27; J.R.

Kellett, 'The breakdown of gild and corporation control over the handicraft and retail trade in London', *Economic History Review* 2nd series 10 (1958), 384–89; Robert B. Shoemaker, *Prosecution and Punishment: Petty Crime and the Law in London and Rural Middlesex, c. 1660–1725* (Cambridge, 1991), pp. 11–13.

11   Stephen MacFarlane, 'Studies in poverty and poor relief in London at the end of the seventeenth century' (Oxford Univ. Ph.D. Thesis, 1983), pp. 15, 110, 123, 126, 258–62;*idem.*, 'Social policy and the poor in the later seventeenth century', in Beier and Finlay (eds.) *London 1500–1700*, pp. 253–54; BL, Loan 29/129 [Add. MS 70,216], John Chamberlayne to Lord Oxford (Robert Harley), 15 August 1712.

12   *By the King. A Proclamation Against Vicious, Debauched, and Profane Persons* (21 Jan. 1692).

13   Tony Claydon, 'Debauchery and the Revolution: the idea of luxury in late Stuart London', seminar given at the Institute of Historical Research, 14 March 1990. See also John Sekora, *Luxury: The Concept in Western Thought* (1977), ch. 2.

14   *Proposals for a National Reformation of Manners* (1694), p. 15. See also Rogers, *A Sermon Preached to the Societies*, pp. 18–29.

15   Hayton, 'Moral reform and country politics'; [Edward Stephens], *The Beginning and Progress of a Needful and Hopeful Reformation* (1691), preface; *Proposals for a National Reformation*, p. 12.

16   John Tillotson, *A Sermon Preached at Lincoln's-Inn Chappel. On the 31st of January 1688. Being the Day Appointed for Public Thanksgiving* (1689), p. 22; [Edward Stephens], *An Admonition to the Magistrates of England upon our New Settlement* [1689], pp. 5–6. See also *Proposals for a National Reformation*, preface.

17   See, for example, *A Proclamation Against Vicious, Debauched, and Profane Persons*; Queen Mary's letter to the Middlesex Justices (reprinted in *An Account of the Societies*, preface); [Thomas Tenison], *His Grace the Lord Archbishop of Canterbury's Letter to the Right Reverend the Lords Bishop of his Province* (1699).

18   Hayton, 'Moral reform and country politics', pp. 57–60.

19   SPCK Archives, 'Papers of Moment', f.97; Craig, 'Movement for the reformation of manners', pp. 133–34.

20   Gilbert Burnet, *A Sermon Preached at the Coronation of William III and Mary II* (1689), p. 19; *His Majesty's Letter to the Right Reverend Father in God Henry Lord Bishop of London* (1690).

21   *Account of the Societies*, pp. 27–28, 75–77, 87; Queen Mary's letter to the Middlesex Justices; Bahlman, *Moral Revolution*, pp. 50–56; *A Help to a National Reformation* (1700).

22   Woodward, *Rise and Progress of the Religious Societies*, p. 78. See also *Account of the Societies*, p. 11. The first blacklist refers to the 'several hundred persons that have been prosecuted by the society, this last year, for whoring, drunkenness, thefts, Sabbath-breaking, etc.', but only keepers of bawdy houses and prostitutes were actually listed: *Proposals for a National Reformation*, pp. 34–35.

23   Edinburgh University Library, Laing MS III, 394, pp. 315–22.

24   Craig, 'Movement for the reformation of manners', pp. 41–47, 85–89.

25   *Account of the Societies*, pp. 10–11.

26   GLRO, WC/R1, pp. 167ff.

27   Since the early accounts listed names of the offenders, it is possible that the reformers failed to include people convicted of swearing and cursing and profaning the Sabbath because they did not wish to embarrass respectable people who were convicted of these offences.

28   *Account of the Societies*. The first report was published by a society based near the Royal Exchange in the City: Laing MS III, 394, p. 510.

29   Craig, 'Movement for the reformation of manners', p. 128.

30 Between 1715 and 1721 (except 1719), an average of 1,297 people per year were
    charged with 'lewd and disorderly' conduct by the societies (see Table 6.1). In those
    same years, 1,395 people per year were committed to the Middlesex and Westminster
    houses of correction. Between July 1719 and July 1720, only a handful of prostitutes
    were committed to the London Bridewell: GLRO, MJ/SR 2240–2376; Bethlem Royal
    Hospital, Minutes of the Court of Governors of Bridewell and Bethlem (hereafter,
    Bridewell minutes).
31 A Short Dissuasive from the Sin of Uncleanness (1701).
32 The first blacklist was printed in the Proposals for a National Reformation. The names of
    the offenders have been compared with prosecutions for similar offences between July
    and December 1693 in the following judicial records: Mansion House Justice Room
    Charge Book (hereafter Mansion House Charge Book, which records appearances
    before   the   Lord
    Mayor), vol. 2 (CLRO); Bridewell minutes (which record commitments to the London
    Bridewell); indictments and recognizances in the City sessions rolls (CLRO); in-
    dictments, recognizances, and house of correction commitments in the Middlesex and
    Westminster session rolls (GLRO).
33 Shoemaker, Prosecution and Punishment, pp. 244–46.
34 By the King. A Proclamation. For Preventing and Punishing Immorality and Profaneness (24
    Feb. 1697/98); Shoemaker, Prosecution and Punishment, pp. 183–86.
35 Shoemaker, Prosecution and Punishment, pp. 179–82.
36 Mansion House Charge Book, 20 Aug 1693. See also the case of Elizabeth Thome,
    CLRO Sessions Roll, 5 Sept. 1693, recognizance no. 61; and Sarah Moore [or Moon]
    and others, Bridewell minutes, 24 Nov. 1693.
37 Bridewell minutes, 7 July 1693.
38 Mansion House Charge Book, 1 Sept. 1693.
39 GLRO, MJ/SP/August 1689, no. 10. See also, Occasional Paper, II, ix, (1718), p. 6.
40 Shoemaker, Prosecution and Punishment, pp. 183–84.
41 John Graunt, Natural and Political Observations . . . made upon the Bills of Mortality
    (1662), p. 58.
42 BL, Loan 29/129, John Chamberlayne to Lord Oxford (Robert Harley), 15 August
    1712; Josiah Woodward, A Sermon Preached before the Right Honourable the Lord Mayor
    (1697), preface. See also Timothy Nourse, Campania Foelix. Or, a Discourse of the
    Benefits and Improvements of Husbandry (1700), p. 226; Roger North, A Discourse of the
    Poor (1753) [written ca. 1688], p. 22; Josiah Woodward, Sodom's Vices Destructive to
    Other Cities and States (1697), pp. 14–15.
43 MacFarlane, 'Social policy', pp. 260–61; John Beattie, Crime and the Courts in England
    1660–1800 (Princeton, 1986), pp. 216–17, 500–01, 516; and the royal proclamations
    for apprehending street robbers and other offenders listed in PRO, SP 35/17, no. 383.
44 The proclamation did include a new clause claiming that murders, robberies, and
    burglaries were committed by 'lewd, disorderly, and wicked persons': A Proclamation for
    Apprehending Robbers on the Highway, etc (30 October, 1690).
45 Antimoixeia: or, the Honest and Joynt Design of the Tower Hamblets for the General
    Suppression of Bawdy Houses [1691]. See also Craig, 'Movement for the reformation of
    manners', pp. 20–23, and Bodleian Library, Rawlinson MS, D129, ff. 16–27.
46 Isaacs, 'Moral crime', p. 256.
47 Beattie, Crime and the Courts, pp. 421–22, 494, 624–25; above, ch. 3.
48 Thomas Bray, For God or For Satan: Being a Sermon Preached . . . before the Society for
    Reformation of Manners (1709), p. 28; Craig, 'Movement for the reformation of
    manners', p. 112.
49 GLRO, MJ/SBB/700, p. 24 (Westminster sessions, Jan. 1712); GLRO, WJ/OC/II, f.
    101d, 106 (April 1731).

50 Isaacs, 'Moral crime', p. 244. Not all prosecutions of prostitutes in the City took place before the Lord Mayor; records of appearances before him are merely indicative of the relative number of prosecutions which took place in different years.

51 This figure is based on 305 commitments from four sample years: 1693 (50% sample of the Westminster calendars), 1697 (50% sample of the Middlesex calendars) and 1712 and 1721 (33% sample of both). Since house of correction calendars do not identify the residence of the prisoners, this was inferred from the area of activity of the justice of the peace who made the commitment. Prisoners whose residence could not be inferred, who account for 13% of all commitments, were excluded from the calculation. GLRO, MJ/SR/1807–1822, 1884–1900, 2182–2200; 2358–2376.

52 Shoemaker, *Prosecution and Punishment*, pp. 292–96.

53 Evidence on the social status of informers is extremely limited because informers were rarely identified at all in the court records, let alone with their occupation and parish of residence. This evidence comes from the Mansion House Charge Book for July 1693–December 1694 and from the Bridewell minutes, City of London Quarter Sessions, and Middlesex Quarter Sessions, for July to Dec. 1693. Craig identified the occupations of 47 informers from the Wood Street society, and most were skilled craftsmen ('Movement for the reformation of manners', pp. 92–93). However, it is not clear what offences, if any, those informers actually prosecuted.

54 William Sachse, 'The Mob and the Revolution of 1688', *Journal of British Studies* 4 (1964–65), 23; Robert B. Shoemaker, 'The London "mob" in the early eighteenth century', *Journal of British Studies* 26 (1987), 273.

55 *Occasional Paper*, II, ix, (1718), pp. 4, 7; Edward Chandler, *A Sermon Preached to the Societies for Reformation of Manners . . . on . . . January the 4th, 1724* (1725), p. 13.

56 Bahlman, *Moral Revolution*, p. 42. See also Isaacs, 'Moral crime', p. 46; Craig, 'Movement for the reformation of manners', p. 213.

57 Bray, *For God or For Satan*, pp. 27–28.

58 Jean Hecht, *The Domestic Servant Class in Eighteenth-Century England* (1956), pp. 10–11, 23–26, 77–87, 90; Daniel Defoe, *Everybody's Business is No-Body's Business* (1725), pp. 4–24; [Idem], *The Great Law of Subordination Considered; or the Insolence and Unsufferable Behaviour of Servants in England duly enquired into* (1724); Peter Earle, *The World of Defoe* (Newton Abbot, 1977), pp. 170–77.

59 Shoemaker, *Prosecution and Punishment*, p. 297.

60 CLRO, sessions papers, 16 January 1689/90.

61 *Account of the Societies*, pp. 10–11.

62 John Chamberlayne, *Magnae Britannia Notitia: or, the Present State of Great Britain* (1708), 2 vols., I, pp. 277–78.

63 Rawlinson MS, D1396–1404; Isaacs, 'Moral crime', p. 252.

64 This conclusion is based on an examination of the activites of all the informers identified in the Mansion House Charge Book for July 1693–December 1694 and the City of London and Middlesex Quarter Sessions records for July to December 1693.

65 Craig, 'Movement for the reformation of manners', p. 142.

66 For the occupations of the accused, see Rawlinson MS, D1396–1404; GLRO, WC/R1, p. 167ff.

67 Laing MS III, 394, pp. 112–13, 153–57, 489–93; *An Account of the Last Bartholomew Fair, and the Late City Order for Regulating the Same* (1702); *Reasons Formerly Published for the Punctual Limiting of Bartholomew Fair* (1711); Craig, 'Movement for the reformation of manners', ch. 5; CLRO, Repertories, vol. 95, ff. 307, 318b (16 and 30 July 1691).

68 *Reasons for Suppressing the Yearly Fair in Brookfield, Westminster: Commonly Called Mayfair* (1709), esp. p. 11; GLRO, MJ/SP/Dec. 1708, no. 1; GLRO, MJ/SBB/666, p. 47 (Feb. 1709). Supporters of the reformation of manners campaign may also have been

behind efforts by the Middlesex justices to suppress or limit activities at other fairs in London and its environs during this period including those at Monmouth Street, Windmill Hill, Rosemary Lane, Bow, Tottenham Court, and Hampstead.

69 GLRO, MJ/SBB/677, p. 53 (Jan. 1710); GLRO, MJ/SP/October 1716, no. 18. See also GLRO, MJ/SP/Jan. 1715, no. 87; October 1716, no. 58.

70 For a similar complaint, see the London grand jury presentment for December 1692: CLRO, Sessions Papers, Dec. 1692.

71 Hayton, 'Moral reform and country politics', pp. 58–59; CLRO, Sessions Papers, 16 January 1689/90 and 16 January 1692/3; GLRO, MJ/SBB/551, p. 35 (Feb. 1698).

72 In addition, the Westminster justices had an ulterior motive for prosecuting gaming houses: to take business away from the rival Westminster Court of Burgesses, which appears to have tried to protect the gaming houses from being closed down: Shoemaker, *Prosecution and Punishment*, pp. 265–66.

73 GLRO, MJ/OC/I, f.46 (4 Dec. 1718) and ff. 107d–108 (13 Oct. 1720); GLRO, WJ/OC/I, ff.4–4d (5 Oct. 1720); *An Account of the Endeavours that have been used to Suppress Gaming Houses* (1722), p. 20 and *passim*.

74 GLRO, MJ/OC/III, ff. 41–43 (Jan. 1726).

75 Portus, *Caritas Anglicana*, p. 182; Peter Clark, 'The "mother gin" controversy in the early eighteenth century', *Transactions of the Royal Historical Society*, 5th series, 38 (1988), 80–82; Davison, ch. 2 above.

76 Clark, 'The "mother gin" controversy', p. 71.

77 BL, Printed Proclamations of the Lord Mayor, 17 Nov. 1676, 29 Nov. 1679, 15 June, 1680, 8 Nov. 1687.

78 Bahlman, *Moral Revolution*, pp. 76–99; Tina Beth Isaacs, 'The Anglican hierarchy and the reformation of manners 1688–1738', *Journal of Ecclesiastical History* 33 (1982), 400–03.

79 See, for example, the letter from Archbishop Sharp to Archdeacon Nicolson, Feb. 27, 1700, quoted by Bahlman, *Moral Revolution*, p. 57.

80 G.P.R. James (ed.), *Letters Illustrative of the Reign of William III . . . by James Vernon* (1841), II, p. 133.

81 Claydon, 'Debauchery and the Revolution'; Hayton, 'Moral reform and country politics'; Fissell, ch. 6 below; Hitchcock, ch. 7 below.

6

Charity Universal? Institutions and Moral Reform in Eighteenth-Century Bristol

Mary E. Fissell
Johns Hopkins University

Living in an early modern city meant constant exchanges between rich and poor, those verbal, visual and financial encounters again familiar to late-twentieth-century urban dwellers. The constitution of early modern urban poverty as a problem took a multitude of forms, from on-the-spot gifts of money to the foundation of formal, even bureaucratic, institutions. Not surprisingly, historians have tended to focus on the latter rather than the former, since few records of casual donations survive. However, apparent institutional continuities between eighteenth and twentieth centuries have sometimes served to obscure some of the peculiarities of the early modern construction of poverty and its remedies.

In particular, historians writing in the era of the welfare state have overlooked the specific role religion played in directing social reformers' varied efforts to solve the problems of poverty. Too often it is assumed that a general benevolence vaguely connected with the beliefs of a more religious era than our own underlay charity and welfare, an interpretation Donna Andrew labels the 'tradition of benevolence'. Recently, eighteenth-century social policy has been severed from religion entirely; both Roy Porter and Gordon Rupp have characterized philanthropy in this period as 'rational', the creation of hardheaded business types who emphasized value for money.[1] Andrew adds another dimension to this argument by suggesting that although writers on charity employed the language of religion, their vision was 'entirely practical'.[2] Piety, however, provided more than rhetoric; to overlook patterns of religious belief makes hospital donors, workhouse builders, and other social reformers oddly one-dimensional by ignoring one of their key motivations. The alliances of sect and congregation created unity within groups of benefactors, and, paradoxically, created tension and disunity amongst them. Religion, especially the politics of religious allegiance, helped to make social policy contentious and conflictual in an early modern English city. As Stephen Macfarlane observed, 'debates on the poor were as much about *who* ought to govern indigent or able-bodied paupers as *how* they should be governed'.[3] Casting these battles in terms of infighting amongst the urban oligarchy or as expressions of nascent party politics presents a foreshortened and simplistic picture of the complexities of urban government.[4]

This essay focuses on the tensions and divisions in early eighteenth-century Bristol over social reform projects. Two institutions are of particular significance: the city workhouse and the infirmary. Both derive, it will be argued, from an interest in the reformation of manners and a commitment to primitive Christianity. Often this commitment could serve to draw together disparate elements of the urban polity, but Bristol's elites were a divided group, and alliances forged from religious conviction were sometimes unable to withstand the stresses of faction.

Bristol was a wealthy place, the second or third largest city in England, a medieval cloth town grown up into a commercial and trading centre. Its riches came from the colonies and spawned a highly-elaborate provincial culture; the city was known for its hardheaded merchants but also for its unruly crowds, for its imports of sherry, slaves, and tobacco as well as its civic pageantry. Religious difference, even deviance, flourished. It was into Bristol that James Naylor blasphemously rode upon an ass, imitating Christ's procession; it was in Bristol in the 1650s that Quakers were possessed in the streets; and decades later, it was in Bristol that John Wesley would find many supporters.[5] As Jonathan Barry has recently elucidated, much of the city's civic life was structured by religious difference.[6] Tensions within the city's Anglican leadership were complicated by an abundance of dissenters: Independents, Baptists, Presbyterians and others met in the city. In the early eighteenth century there were proportionally more Quakers in Bristol than anywhere else in the country, and memories of Quaker sufferings in the 1670s and 1680s were too recent and too bitter to permit any real unity amongst the city's powerful merchant community.

Bristol's wealth meant that religious and political differences were reified in the bricks and mortar of charitable institutions. Like other cities of its size and complexity, Bristol enjoyed what Peter Borsay has termed an urban renaissance in the late seventeenth and eighteenth centuries.[7] Charity institutions provided an arena for the production and elaboration of this provincial urban culture. Not only were they sites for the display of social power and civic virtue through elaborate processions, banquets and church services. Charities were also the means for the direct exercise of patronage through the dispensing of favours to an individual's clients and dependants, in the same way that poor relief functioned on a parish level.[8] Hence political differences amongst philanthropists were played out in two arenas: that of civic ritual, and that of the individual patronage extended to specific clients.

Wealthy though the city's merchants were, many Bristolians experienced poverty. The 1690s saw cold winters, bad harvests, and the disruptions of war, all of which contributed to concern about the employment of the poor.[9] For instance, the Board of Trade at Westminster began a major investigation into poverty and unemployment in 1695–6. In Bristol, the situation of the weavers was especially grim, since they were doubly disadvantaged by a slump in trade caused by the war as well as a longer-term shift of the cloth industry out of the city to cheaper rural locations.[10] By the turn of the century, the city was becoming increasingly aware of the geographical segregation of poverty into the large suburban parishes; small wealthy inner-city parishes allocated some of their poor rates to the outer parishes.[11]

Many involved in combatting poverty in Bristol were connected through a commitment to a 'reformation of manners'; an early Society for the Reformation of Manners was founded in the city and interest continued even after the formal meetings lapsed. Such reformers believed that England's greatness impelled her subjects to lead godly lives, to manifest England's special providence in outward signs, virtuous behaviour and decent manners. These men (few women were recorded in these groups) also shared an interest in a return to a primitive Christianity, to religious worship untainted by modernity's trappings and conceits. The institutions these reformers created owed as much to this vision of a national providence and pure Christianity as to rational philanthropy.

Tracing the levels of connection amongst charitable institutions in Augustan Bristol reveals how deeply issues of religion shaped social policy. While party politics served as an occasional rallying point or line of division, religious ties and differences structured all forms of civic life, from trivial to profound. One of the sources of power and authority in Bristol's civil government lay in the alliances of congregation and meeting-place. Nor were religious divisions simple. The usual polarities of high church/low church, or Anglican/dissenter, do not do justice to peculiarities of local circumstance or varieties of religious difference.

Religion has also been left out of the history of English hospitals; historians of medicine have tended to see the provincial voluntary hospital movement in terms of its significance to medical professionals.[12] But an emphasis upon the early hospitals' medical aspects owes much to retrospection. In what follows, it is suggested that one of the first provincial infirmaries had much more to do with other institutions for the urban poor than it had to do with medicine. Recently, the provincial infirmary has been understood as a part of the development of urban culture, similar to lending libraries, assembly rooms and concert series.[13] While such an argument integrates hospitals into larger patterns of urban growth and differentiation, it suggests that these institutions were unproblematic extensions of civility. It ignores the relationship of the hospital to other institutions for the poor, and the potential for political contention inherent in many such foundations.

Although charity schools, hospitals and workhouses have usually been the subjects of separate histories, they were the product of the same impulses. All were fundamentally about work – providing it, training for it, healing for it. The founders and supporters of these charities saw the institutional setting as the ideal means to improve the behaviour of the poor and inure them to work. Likewise, all had an interest in the reformation of manners movement. As the word re-formation suggests, many of these individuals looked back to earlier models; some shared a vision of a primitive Christianity, others harked back to a former ideal of social relations. And many who sought reformation in an institutional context also shared a belief in inward religion.

In 1695, John Cary, a Bristol merchant, wrote an *Essay on the State of England* and started a campaign for a workhouse in the city. He drew upon a tradition of attitudes towards the poor that derived from mercantilist concern with England's population as well as a utopian vision of the reforming potential of institutional life. His own interest in the problems of poverty grew out of his economic thought; he testified to the Board of Trade and wrote pamphlets on aspects of political economy. Like earlier writers, the key to Cary's ideas about the poor was the provision of employment. He wanted to make 'multitudes of people serviceable who are now useless to the nation'.[14] The focus was on the children of the poor, teaching them to work, and then starting them off in employment as apprentices. Work was also provided for the unemployed. Both strategies were designed to benefit the nation by creating wealth.

Cary aired his scheme for a city workhouse in a public meeting, and the result was presented to the Mayor of Bristol. This formed the basis of the 1696 Act of Parliament which provided for the unification of all 17 city parishes into a Corporation of the Poor which could collect a poor rate, build a workhouse, and compel the poor to enter it.[15] Such schemes were not new to the city – the City Council had set up two short-lived manufactories for the poor, in 1653 and 1679, which were run by private contractors. What made the 1696 Act appealing to many in the city was its incorporation of parishes, since the abolition of legal battles over settlement among the city's various parishes would result in substantial savings.[16] In addition, the educational emphasis of the new workhouse, which would train the children of the poor, held the promise of structural solutions to urban poverty. It was hoped that the new Corporation would both reduce rapidly increasing expenditure on poor relief and cleanse the city streets of vagabonds and beggars.

The Corporation borrowed a building from the City Council and equipped it for the reception of 100 girls. Subsequently, it purchased a building which had been a mint (hence the workhouse was referred to in

Bristol either as the Mint, or as St. Peter's, a reference to the local church), and installed 100 boys as well as the girls. Soon the Mint came to house the elderly and infirm as well as children, although expenditure on out-relief for such individuals seems to have been greater than that on in-relief for much of the eighteenth century and beyond. The Mint also functioned as a house of correction to which vagabonds, ballad-sellers and beggars could be committed. [17]

At the same time that Cary was organizing the Corporation of the Poor, the Society of Friends was creating its own workhouse in Bristol. The relationship between the two institutions is historically uncertain since few records of either survive. It has been suggested that the Quakers embarked upon their workhouse because of a delay in the inauguration of the city's house. [18] Of course, Quakers had a tradition of looking after their own, and regularly disbursed poor relief through the Men's and Women's Meetings. And Friends were involved in the Corporation of the Poor from its inception. Thomas Callowhill, for instance, served the Friends as meeting clerk and the Corporation as Treasurer. Both the city and Quaker workhouses focused on the cloth trades; both provided children with education – the Quakers' workhouse school was a model followed by other Meetings – and training in weaving and spinning.

Bristolians also had the example of the Quaker John Bellers, who published his *Proposals for Raising a College of Industry* in 1695, which may have served as a model for the Quaker workhouse. On the title-page, Bellers put a motto that John Cary would have seconded:

> The Slugg shall be cloathed with Raggs
> He that will not Work, shall not Eat. [19]

Bellers planned to have 200 different trades represented in his 'college of industry', a utopian community, and to educate children in godliness and industry. Work was the key; as Bellers wrote in a later pamphlet:

> The Poor without Imployment are like rough Diamonds,
> their Worth is Unknown . . . [20]

Just as for John Cary, unemployment decreased the wealth of the nation and diminished its moral worth.

The educational function of the workhouses linked them to the city's charity schools. There were a handful of such schools, like Queen Elizabeth's Hospital, at the turn of the century, but this form of charity became increasingly popular in the early decades of the 1700s. The first parish-based school was sparked by a bequest in 1699 which allowed for the education of seven poor orphans of Temple parish. [21] Arthur Bedford, vicar of Temple, cajoled his patron, Edward Colston, into providing the funds to expand this project and soon there was a small school in operation. Bedford was a correspondent for the SPCK, the London-based organization which served as an intelligence office and pressure group for charity schools nationwide. In a letter to the SPCK about the Bristol Mint, he eagerly described how the workhouse children spent most of their time in weaving and spinning, but were taught reading and their catechism, and prayed publicly morning and night. Only in Bedford's final sentence is the connection made with poor relief, 'such children as are found chargeable to the city are sent thither'.[22] In other words, despite the distinctions historians usually make between poor relief and charity, for Bedford the charity school and workhouse were functionally equivalent, inculcating godly behaviour in the children of the poor.

The founding of the Bristol Infirmary four decades after the city workhouse was also related to anxieties about work and the employment of the poor. The first provincial voluntary infirmary was founded in Winchester by Alured Clarke in 1736, and Bristolians created their hospital on this model in the following year. Although details of the first few meetings of the committee which created the Bristol hospital are scarce, it seems that John Elbridge, the deputy Controller of Customs in the city, had the idea and the initiative to get the hospital underway. What little is known about Elbridge suggests a classic eighteenth-century success story. Before he rose to be the Controller he had already made a fortune at the Customs in Bristol; he subsequently built and endowed a charity school for girls on his estate just outside of the city. Under Elbridge's direction, an Infirmary committee bought a former brewery in St. James' churchyard, outfitted it with blankets and beds, and admitted its first inpatient in December 1737. Outpatients had been seen since the previous June. Subscribers paid 2 guineas a year, for which they might recommend one inpatient and two outpatients at a time. John Elbridge served as the hospital's first treasurer and steered it towards financial stability, often by means of his own pocket.[23]

One of the key features of institutional life was the inculcation of appropriate work habits. Charity schools functioned to educate their charges, not just in reading, but in discipline, and then to find appropriate employment (usually an apprenticeship) for them. In discussions of the adult poor, work was always at the forefront, in hospitals or poorhouses. This emphasis on work derived in part from Interregnum political economists such as William Petty and Samuel Hartlib, who grounded their solutions to the problems of poverty in economic analysis rather than in any conception of charity as a social good or religious necessity. For such thinkers, England's wealth lay in her people; English men and women who were not working were not increasing the wealth of the nation.

Integral to the thought of these Interregnum writers was not only the institution of the workhouse, but also that of the hospital. As Charles Webster has described, many proposals to help the poor included provision for health care.[24] Again and again, hospitals were linked with welfare and workhouses. For example, Henry Robinson's *Certain Proposalls* (1652) discussed the creation of workhouses for training the poor along with schools for their children and hospitals for the poor, where they would receive free medical care.[25] Thus, the hospital and the workhouse were conceived as twins, not identical in function, but mutually reinforcing. Both institutions would transform poverty into wealth through work.

Alured Clarke, founder of Winchester Infirmary, was explicit about the political-arithmetic implications of his institution, saying that 'it is a most certain means of increasing the number of People'.[26] In Bristol, Carew Reynell was more explicit about the link between health and wealth. In an Infirmary sermon, he argued that an entire family would be returned to economic productivity if its head were returned to health, thereby benefitting the city's trade and commerce.[27] At a meeting of the Quarterly Board of Governors of the Infirmary, it was ordered that 'the visitors of the week give preference to the Labourious Industrious Poor'.[28] The hospital, like the workhouse and the charity school, promoted employment for the poor, in this case by ensuring that the labouring head of household was healthy enough to earn a living and contribute to England's wealth.

Underlying this concern with work was a more fundamental anxiety about the behaviour of the English people, particularly the poor. While undoubtedly prompted by the distress of the city's poor, the Bristol initiative to found a workhouse had as much to do with morals as manufacture. Sir John Duddlestone, who drafted the Act which created the Bristol Corporation and served as one of its first governors, wrote to the SPCK about the results of the Bristol Corporation's efforts, noting that:

> the poor in that city are much reform'd for as none Steal or Starve for lack of Bread, so care is now taken that none shall profane the name of God as they us'd to do.[29]

The workhouse had cured starving and swearing simultaneously. It was at Duddlestone's house that the first meeting of a Society for the Reformation of Manners had been held in Bristol in March 1700. Also at the meeting were the vicar of Temple parish, Arthur Bedford, and the city's former Mayor, John Batchelor. The society focused on prosecuting people for swearing and other forms of indecent behaviour. For example, it looked into reports that those who took the waters at the Hotwells on Sundays were also indulging in stronger waters at local alehouses. It usually met in the boardroom at the Mint, making connections between its own regulation of the poor and that of the workhouse explicit. To judge by minutes of its meetings, the initial strong response became somewhat muted; often only half a dozen stalwarts went to meetings. By 1702, the society had moved away from prosecutions, and towards founding and funding charity schools.[30]

Historians place the reformation of manners movement, which started in London in 1690, in the context of a providentialism which grew from perceptions of the Revolution of 1688. It was believed that England had a special relationship with divine providence – and that she must live up to this relationship.[31] As Josiah Woodward, the first historian-cum-publicist for the Societies, wrote, 'National sins deserve national Judgements'. England thus needed to 'endeavour, by a General Reformation, to appease the Wrath of God'.[32] So Societies for the Reformation of Manners sought informers to report on lapses of conduct and attempted to police neighbourhood morals.

For the SRMs, work was morally reforming and idleness sinful. For instance, discussions of prostitutes emphasized the dangers of single people without evident employment who led idle and disorderly lives. Lack of employment rather than sex for sale was central to these women's lack of morality.[33] This emphasis upon the moral quality of work linked SRM campaigners with those interested in workhouses. Sir John Duddlestone, for instance, served as a liaison between the SRM in Bristol and the SPCK, describing the impact of the workhouse on 'the lives and Morals of the Vulgar'.[34] For Duddlestone, the missions of the SRM, the SPCK and the Bristol Corporation of the Poor were all congruent.

Similarly, the ubiquitous Arthur Bedford described Bristol's SRM and charity schools in letters to the SPCK.[35] He wrote in 1699 that he was always ready 'to put a stop to the Growth of Profaneness', and he was pleased to note that in Bristol, 'the magistrates are very zealous, and encourage informers'.[36] Bedford's interest in improving the morals of his countrymen subsequently became focused on the theatre – he wrote several works denouncing plays and actors, and campaigned in Bristol to close the theatre at Jacob's Well. Such attitudes were common amongst charity-school advocates. Robert Nelson, for example, who organized or corresponded with dozens of schools, tried to have a teacher fired because he allowed pupils to act *Timon of Athens*.[37] So too, Josiah Woodward, historian and publicist of the SRMs, condemned the evils of the playhouse.[38] For reformers such as Bedford and Woodward, campaigns to close theatres, to found charity schools and workhouses, and to prosecute blasphemers were all part of the larger design to achieve a reformation of manners.

Efforts to improve the morals of the inmates of the hospital underline its common purpose with charity schools and the workhouse. Not only would the hospital heal the bodies of its patients, it would reform their manners as well. As Alured Clarke said of his Winchester Infirmary, 'It reduces the number of Vagrants by depriving them of one of their most plausible Reasons for begging door to door'.[39] Like the workhouse, the hospital would help rid the streets of the idle and disorderly, and England's special relationship to Providence would thus be apparent to all. Inside the Infirmary, the poor were removed from the bad influences of their friends and neighbours, kept in hospital 'for so long a time as is necessary to beget contrary habits' in the words of Clarke.[40] Bristol patients were exposed to daily prayers, and forbidden to gamble or swear. Other provincial infirmaries' wards were adorned with Biblical texts painted on the walls.

A sermon preached for the Bristol Infirmary by Josiah Tucker in 1746 highlights its disciplinary aspects. Tucker's views on the poor were straightforward:

> Such brutality and insolence, such debauchery and extravagance, such idleness in religion, cursing, swearing and contempt of all rule and authority, Human and Divine, do not reign so triumphantly among the Poor in any other country as ours.[41]

He claimed that the English were so careful of personal liberty that 'our People are drunk with the cup of Liberty'. The Infirmary might serve as a corrective, instilling the poor with appropriate virtues while not robbing them of liberty, since they were only subject to a set of rules to which they had given consent by seeking admission.[42]

Tucker made the link with the earlier reformation of manners campaign explicit in the title of his sermon, 'Hospitals and Infirmaries Considered as Schools of Christian Education for the Adult Poor: and as a Means Conducive Towards a National Reformation in the Common Peoples'. Just as the workhouse had educated children in morals, so the Infirmary would fulfil the same function for adults, complementing the Mint and the city's growing number of charity schools. The hospital provided a remedy for debauchery, extravagance, cursing, swearing and contempt of authority, not to mention bodily ills. By the mid-1740s, Tucker's message was too explicit; he 'could not appear in the streets without being called after and hooted by the boys and rabble'.[43] Nevertheless, the sermon was sufficiently consonant with the views of the hospital governors that they ensured its publication.

The common ground shared by founders of institutions for the poor went beyond the movement to reform manners. At the heart of social reformers' programmes of incarceration was the desire to re-create a primitive Christianity. This return to an earlier, purer, past characterized and linked many of their varied interests, from charity schools to church music. Eamon Duffy has demonstrated how this interest in the primitive church was sparked by William Cave's idealized picture of the early church published in 1673. Anthony Horneck, founder of the religious societies which many understood as the predecessors to those devoted to the reformation of manners, also adopted the return to primitive Christianity as a means of reform.[44] Similarly, Peter King's *Enquiry into . . . the Primitive Church* (1697) combined early church history with a providential interpretation of 1688 and a call for reform. Duffy argues that this impulse was originally Anglican, and fully consonant with developments within the established church. However, primitive Christianity could also imply a critique of the Church's decadence, and by the 1690s was sometimes a rhetoric associated with forms of dissent both within and without the church.

The ambiguity inherent in the appeal to primitive Christianity made it, as we shall see, an ideal vehicle for a number of competing claims. After 1688, it was associated with Non-jurors, and hence with some kinds of high churchmen, Jacobitism and tory politics. But it could also be found in low-church forms, ranging from moderates to those who attacked rite and ceremony and denied power to ecclesiastical hierarchies. Paradoxically, primitive Christianity served as a rallying point for those who wished to augment the authority of the church's representatives, and also for those who sought civil remedies to moral evils.

The interest in primitive Christianity was fostered institutionally through the SPCK. For example, the return to a purer religion was alluded to in a letter to the SPCK from a Swiss correspondent, which described the Society's mission to 'establish the Purity of manners, bring back the antient discipline . . .'.[45] Other reformers held their own more radical views of the return to an older religion. John Bellers, for example, said of his proposed workhouse, 'The Poor . . . will be a Community something like the Example of Primitive Christianity'.[46] Not all reformers shared Bellers' utopian visions of self-sufficient communities of goods, but the appeal to a primitive Christianity was a rhetoric linking a variety of projectors.

For example, the Infirmary in Bristol alluded to this desire to return to a purer Christianity by choosing 'Charity Universal' for its motto. While to a late-twentieth-century reader these words seem tepid, they were an allusion to the return to a primitive church. Matthew Tindal, deist and free-thinker, described his vision of a primitive Christianity. He said, 'Christ and his Apostles inculcated nothing so much as Universal Charity'.[47] Sir Richard Bulkeley, associated with the reformers of manners

and the SPCK, as well as pietistic religion in the form of the French
Prophets, founded a universal charity, a utopian community which
bankrupted his estate.[48] In other words, 'Charity Universal' made reference
to primitive Christianity and to some aspects of the reformation of manners.

'Universal' also had specific meanings in Quaker circles. Friends
rejected Calvinist doctrines of election; although not all would be saved,
there was *universal* access to God's grace and potential salvation. In the
late 1690s, some of the friction between George Keith and the Society of
Friends was due to differences about the possibilities of universal salvation.
Keith maintained that although those who did not know Christ might be
saved, the Scriptures were definite that salvation lay through Jesus, and it
was arrogant of Quakers to claim otherwise.[49] The Keithian controversy
was particularly intense in Bristol, and it seems improbable that the
Friends who founded the Infirmary some decades later were deaf to the
several resonances of the phrase 'Charity Universal'.

Arthur Bedford, the vicar of Temple, provides a good example of the
moderate strand of primitive Christianity which associated itself with
low-church Anglicans and dissenters.[50] He was a correspondent for the
SPCK, although more tolerant than its London members. For example, he
suggested recruiting Bristol's Quakers to the SPCK but the Society
vehemently refused, perhaps fearful of alienating high church support.
Where the SPCK and Bedford found common ground was in moral reform
and the appeal to a primitive Christianity, particularly in issues concerning church music.

William Weber has discussed some aspects of the return to early church
music and the invention of musical 'classics' in the eighteenth century.[51]
He shows how Arthur Bedford, distressed by the rampant commercialism
of the musical establishment, turned to liturgical music by no longer
fashionable composers such as Tallis. Certainly, Bedford's disapproval of
the giddy world of urban entertainment shaped his views on church music,
as they did his campaign to close Bristol's playhouses. For example, he
wrote to the SPCK in 1709, 'complaining of the Abuse of Church Musick,
so that it is become an Introduction to the Playhouse'.[52] He railed against
church organists who raced from one performance to another, overlooking
the sacerdotal aspects to their calling, and hoped that the London SRM
and the SPCK would jointly publish his book on church music.

However, like other critics of the modern commercial world, Bedford's
deepest objections to modern music were grounded in his views on
primitive Christianity. His *Essay on Temple Musick* was advertised thus:

> wherein the Musick of our Cathedrals is Vindicated, and supposed to
> be Conformable, not only to that of the *Primitive Christians*, but also
> to the *Practice* of the *Church* in all preceding Ages.[53]

The SPCK distributed Bedford's book on church music and continued to cast disputes about music in the context of the early church. For instance, the Society wrote to its correspondent in Carlisle in 1716 commending the practice of standing during the singing of the Psalms:

> they cannot but agree with many of the Fathers of the Church who have recommended this laudable custom as not only consonant with ye Primitive Christianity but generally used even to this day in the Church of England . . .[54]

In other words, it was not just the frivolity of church organists or the commercial nature of their employment that bothered Bedford and the SPCK. For both, the issue was the return to a purer past.

The appeal to a primitive Christianity could take a more radical form. It represented a critique of monopoly applied to the Church itself. Such a bold stroke did not suit Bedford or the SPCK; fearful of alienating high-church allies, they did not fault the Church itself for society's lack of morals. But other reformers pointed out that the clergy did not have a monopoly on morality. As the free-thinker Matthew Tindal baldly phrased it, 'As all Monopolys are prejudicial to the state, so most of all are Ecclesiastical'.[55] Such an anti-monopoly argument had two implications. First, and most obvious, it served to justify reformers' meddling in matters of morals and religion. Second, it opened the door to dissenters' participation in reform.

For those reformers interested in institutional treatments of poverty, the anti-monopoly argument had another resonance. Many of the Interregnum proposals for hospitals were related to critiques of the monopolistic stance of the London medical profession. Early dispensaries which provided free medicines and advice for the poor were run by apothecaries in defiance of the authority of the physicians and the Royal Colleges.[56] In other words, institutions providing free health care for the poor were often expressions of protest against the tight hierarchical control of medical practice. In Bristol, of course, control was not exerted by the Royal Colleges but by the city companies – and it is interesting to note that few of the leaders of the Barber-surgeons' Company became involved in the Infirmary.

Reformers were also interested in the anti-monopoly argument as applied to the church because they were defending themselves against high-church critics who alleged that they were usurping church prerogative by prosecuting people for moral offences in secular rather than ecclesiastical courts. Thus Matthew Tindal defended the role of the magistrate: 'none can doubt that he is fully authorized to punish the Evil, the Immoral, the Vicious, and reward the Good, the Moral, the Virtuous'.[57] Of course, plenty did doubt, especially within the high church wing of the Anglican church. As Tina Isaacs has discussed, the Anglican establishment feared any return to Puritan excesses, and wanted to discourage the laity from any involvement in policing morals.[58]

However, the appeal to primitive Christianity had the potential to be double-edged; it was also employed by the arch-spokesman of the high churchmen to denounce the reformation of manners movement. Henry Sacheverell attacked the SRM, writing:

> Instead of this *Ancient, Primitive, Discipline* of the *Church* which for so many Ages has, like a Rampart, secur'd its Religion from *Vice* and *Immorality*, *Schism* and *Heresy*, we must substitute in its Place, a society for the *Reformation* of *Manners*, wherein every *Tradesman* and *Mechanick* is to take upon him the Gift of the Spirit . . .[59]

Sacheverell's slur on the middling sorts who peopled SRMs also illustrates how the reformation of manners could be associated with forms of inner religion and attitudes towards knowledge which tended to diminish the power of ecclesiastical authority.

The power of civil magistrates was defended some years later by Michael Foster, Recorder of Bristol, and one of the founders of the city's Infirmary. Foster, in an historical inquiry into the powers of church courts, argued that crimes subsequently prosecuted in ecclesiastical courts, such as incest and fornication, were originally offences under Anglo-Saxon criminal law. He asked, 'What is there in the Nature of Things, which renders the Suppression of Vice and Profaneness, a work unfit for Lay Hands?'[60] Foster added that if temporal judges did not have the power to judge moral matters, 'That would make the Reverend Judges no better than the Church's Hangmen'.[61] Foster, like other hospital supporters, identified himself with arguments put forward by reformation of manners campaigners and found common ground in the appeal to primitive Christianity.

Matthew Tindal used the return to primitive Christianity and its associated anti-monopoly arguments in relation to the Test Act and the exclusion of dissenters from positions of power. If one were to draw a spectrum of religious beliefs and practices, from pietistic, enthusiastic, revealed religion on one end ranging through middle-of-the-road Anglicans to the high church on the other, it is easy to see why the 'primitive' Christians felt at home with (and sometimes were) dissenters such as Baptists and Quakers, as well as the fringe represented by groups such as the French Prophets. In some measure, such a spectrum represents attitudes to epistemology. In addition, the anti-monopoly flavour of primitive Christianity resonated with opposition to any religious test. As Matthew Tindal put it, 'I can, with submissions, see no necessity for a Religious Test in Civil Imploys' – indeed such a test was 'a badg of servitude'.[62] This was not, of course, idle metaphor, since these reformers were founding and governing institutions which literally badged the poor.

Even within the ranks of those moderates who sought a return to primitive Christianity, rhetoric could be employed for opposite ends. For example, controversy erupted over a sermon preached to the Bristol City Council in 1735 by the Rev. A.S. Catcott.[63] Catcott presented an analysis based upon his friend John Hutchinson's style of Biblical exegesis. Hutchinson wished to return to the pure Scripture, to God's actual pronouncement, by eliminating the points in the Hebrew alphabet which would make the orignal meanings of key words apparent.[64] Bedford disagreed with Catcott's slighting of Arabic sources, and inaugurated a long discussion in pamphlet form.[65] Clearly, both Catcott and Bedford tried to reclaim the authority of antiquity for their own argument. Bedford said, in conclusion to his subsequent pamphlet, 'I bless the Name of God for all the Writing of the Primitive Fathers of the 5 first Centuries'.[66] Catcott, on the contrary, had shown that Christianity was 'contrived and settled . . . before the world was made'.[67] For Bedford, the key problem with a Hutchinsonian analysis was that it denied divine Providence, 'we may as well deny his Providence in all other Particulars, and all the Texts, which speak of it'.[68] Bedford understood God's providence in a literal and day-to-day fashion. Like others involved with reform projects in Bristol, he tended towards an inward style of religion which emphasized a mystical and pietistic form of divine knowledge.[69] Catcott, on the other hand, scoffed at the supernatural. Nevertheless, both employed the appeal to primitive church fathers in support of their arguments.

On a more general level, many of the reform-minded who were attracted to primitive Christianity as a means of purifying the Church looked to a more recent – albeit unspecified – past for an ideal type of social relations. Their model of society was clearly hierarchical; everyone was to know his or her place and stick to it.[70] And, of course, crucial to the well-being of such a society was work, which defined and prescribed social life.

Arthur Bedford's view of social structures was clearly hierarchical, as he noted in a sermon preached for the SRM in London:

Parents are obliged to take care of their Children; Masters of the Families of their Household, Apprentices and Servants; the Clergy of their Parishioners; Magistrates and inferiour officers of those under their Authority; and princes of their Subjects; that Religion may be propagated and Vice discountenanced and suppressed.[71]

Or take this statement of the hierarchical nature of religion, from a sermon preached for the SRM by George Stanhope in London:

> For Religion is a Connection of all Virtues and Graces, a Scheme of Harmony and Order, and the Beauty of it is seen, the Benefit of it is felt, by keeping every one of its Professors employ'd within his own proper Sphere, contented with the lot and business which the good Providence of God hath cut out to him.[72]

This hierarchical understanding of society was so well-known to be characteristic of the reformers of manners that a play which lampooned them made fun of just such a vision of social life. In *The Perjuror*, a character caught accepting bribes pleads:

> Thus every Man is willing to make the best of his Place. We inferiour magistrates can plead both great and antient Examples. Every man must have his share of profit. The Commonwealth is a great Machine, composed of many great and small wheels, and every one must be pleas'd.[73]

In other words, every wheel needs its grease, and the hierarchy is composed, not of men happy with their lot, but of men eager to make the most of their opportunities.

The founders of workhouses and hospitals repeated this theme of reciprocal social relations based upon hierarchy again and again. Indeed, the frequency with which the appeal to hierarchy was made can only lead the reader to suspect that hierarchy was itself under threat. Hospital supporters cast their institution in terms of its paternalistic relationship to the poor, one that would sustain and correct its patients as would a father his children. The letters of Richard Champion III, a Quaker and Infirmary Treasurer, explicate this particular view of the relationship between rich and poor. He discussed the behaviour appropriate to a manufacturer,

> . . . the manufacturer is exercising the Virtues of the Heart by Example. He finds employments for the Poor, he clothes, he feeds, he protects them. He Encourages the Industrious, he rebukes the Slothful, with the spirit of Charity he relieves the distress of His dependents and teaches them by his conduct to look upon him as a Father and their fellow Workman as their Brethren.[74]

This relationship both sanctified the otherwise godless role of the manufacturer, and served to reiterate the natural divisions amongst men. This view of a hierarchical social structure implied mutual obligations, as Richard Champion's wife Julia suggested, 'The common people show by their Actions how much they feel a kind Behaviour to them and more doubly repay it by an affectionate Conduct in return'.[75] Thus, for a hospital governor, a recommendation for admission to the Infirmary was a formal expression of a relationship characterized by obligation on both sides.

The Quaker John Bellers, in his essay on hospitals, stated this reciprocal relationship thus, 'It's as much the Duty of the Poor to Labour when they are able, as it is for the Rich to Help them when they are sick'.[76] He emphasized why the rich should care for the poor, saying that:

> Duty and Interest are Two as great Obligations as can be laid upon Mortals, and they both as Powerful advocates call upon the Rich to take care of the Poor . . .[77]

In a city riven by faction, in which the poor expressed discontent in frequent riot, hospital subscribers could use their power as benefactors to create and reinforce patterns of deferential behaviour while strengthening their own sense of social identity. The structure of the admissions process, in which a prospective patient needed to find a subscriber willing to recommend him or her, emphasized the personal nature of such patronage. It mimicked the politics of the great, and ensured that any petitioner for help could expect to conform to the wishes of his or her patron. For subscribers and supporters, institutions like hospitals and workhouses provided social glue that held together a fragmented society.

And fragmented it was; hospital, charity schools and workhouse represented a tenuous balance between faction and unity. All three were founded as institutions which could overcome the political and religious divisions in the city, and yet all foundered on just such divisions. While primitive Christianity and manners reform could provide moments of civic unity, control over the poor remained a contentious issue in a divided city.

The workhouse was plagued by faction from its outset, in part because the 1696 Corporation of the Poor in Bristol represented a new type of city governance. Parishes, after all, were run by select vestries, self-perpetuating small groups who set the poor rate, chose a churchwarden, and fulfilled a range of other bureaucratic duties. The city itself was run by a sort of select vestry, the City Council, which chose its own replacements for vacancies (which did not include dissenters). Although Bristol had an extremely large electorate (5,000 freemen) even the far-from-universal right to vote did not give one a voice in the real running of the city; it merely entitled one to vote for a member of Parliament. The Corporation of the Poor, on the other hand, consisted of four Guardians elected from each of the city's twelve wards, plus the Mayor and aldermen. Anyone paying more than 1 penny per week towards the poor rate could vote for the Guardians. Cary's plan meant that electors and the Guardians they chose need be neither freemen nor Anglican.

It is impossible to document the real number of dissenters elected to the Corporation, but it seems to have been substantial. In 1696, the Corporation of the Poor included at least six known Quakers.[78] Besides Thomas Callowhill, other well-known Friends, such as Richard Champion, Edward Harford, and Nehemiah Champion, became Treasurers.[79] Political wrangling between the City Council and the Corporation of the Poor reveals the deep differences between the high-church Council and the latitudinarian, dissenting Corporation. Although John Batchelor, the mayor in 1695, helped found the Corporation and his successor was sympathetic, in 1696/7 Mayor John Hine proved to be an 'unexpected Remora' in John Cary's words. Hine stuck fast to the city's funds and refused to grant his warrants for raising monies for the Corporation.[80] The Governors of the Poor dug into their own pockets to provide the means for weaving cloth, and waited out the 'remora'. An amendment to an Act of Parliament finally freed the funds for the Corporation in 1698. No sooner had one political problem been fixed than another erupted. Once the workhouse was established, the parish churchwardens who had formerly distributed poor law monies found that their influence had been greatly diminished by the new body. The churchwardens refused to collect the rate (the tax that provided money for the Corporation to distribute); it took another amendment to an Act of Parliament to ensure that the funds were paid over.[81]

The workhouse remained a fruitful source of discord. In 1706, Matthew Tindal published his polemic *The Rights of the Christian Church*, a defence of low-church practices. He cited squabbles in the governance of the Bristol Corporation to denounce high-church tories, alleging that none of them were 'sober and industrious' enough to manage the workhouse.[82] In 1711, a scandal erupted when an anonymous pamphlet was published accusing the governors of favouritism: 'Charity is commonly confined to those of *their own Perswasion*'. According to the author, all corporations must have been founded due to 'an Itch of *Government* and *Dominion*, in order to carry on their Factitious Designs'.[83] Even institutions founded in moments of ideological unity quickly came asunder in city politics.

Indeed, the moment of accord in Bristol which Arthur Bedford describes in his early letters to the SPCK had broken down by the 1700s. Rather than praising the Mint, Bedford sneered at its efforts to educate children. Of course, Bedford was not without his own interests in the matter – he wrote to the SPCK in 1709 that the development of charity schools in Bristol was hindered by the Mint's pretence to educate the children of the poor. Instead, he sought an ally in Edward Colston, the London merchant who had already supported a charity school in Bedford's parish. Now Bedford sought to entice his patron into becoming a correspondent of the SPCK – to which the busy merchant acquiesced on the condition that he should not have to write very many letters.[84]

The battles between dissenters, latitudinarians, and high-church Anglicans recurred in Colston's subsequent benefactions. In 1710 he founded a new school, providing for 100 boys. It was opened with the blessing of the City Council, which included a procession and special cathedral service. Colston was quite particular about the recipients of his largess; any boy whose parent made the mistake of taking him to a dissenting service was to be expelled forthwith. Similarly, no boy from the school was to be apprenticed to a dissenter. Nor was it solely religion Colston policed. When Arthur Bedford voted for a whig and low churchman, Colston was outraged, evidently considering this act an insult to a patron.[85] Of course, charity schools were caught up in more serious accusations of disloyalty. By 1715, the SPCK was quietly investigating Colston's school, which had been described as 'a nursery of Faction and Rebellion'.[86] In a city known for its Jacobite support, such allegations were easy to believe. On the national level, M.G. Jones has shown how charity schools, as she put it, were the pawns of party politics, captured by high-church and Tory interests after 1710.[87]

Similar stresses continued to pull apart the Bristol Corporation of the Poor. The city's churchwardens remained resentful of the Corporation's usurping of their control of poor relief. In 1714, after the triumph of the tories, the churchwardens benefited from two Acts of Parliament passed with the help of the high-church party. The senior and junior church-wardens now became members of the Corporation of the Poor by right. In addition, potential members had to take a sacramental test in order to become a Guardian of the Poor, barring dissenters from their former roles in the Corporation. However, it was found difficult to run the Corporation without dissenters' experience and skills. When the winds of political fortune shifted in 1718, the sacramental test was repealed and the junior churchwardens removed from the Corporation, despite the protests of the Bishop of Bristol.[88]

In Bristol, conflicts over social policy and the remedies for poverty were characterized by many battles and conflicts of interest. The poor were, in part, political pawns in a city whose governors did not rule without opposition. Given the divided nature of Bristol's civic life, any issue so freighted with questions of public order would have been contentious.

Two factors made charity institutions particularly prone to dispute. First was their nature as voluntary bodies run by founders and funders. Unlike earlier charitable foundations created by bequests, most of these institutions were funded on an ongoing basis by individuals who expected a say in their governance. But the other factor which made care for the poor an especially significant issue at the turn of the century was what David Hayton refers to as the 'moral panic' of the 1690s, that impulse towards reformation resulting from the revolution in 1688. While the Infirmary, founded in 1737, experienced numerous political conflicts in the latter half of the century, its early years were not as controversial as those of the charities of the 1690s. In part, this relative peace was due to its novel form, but it was also because the panic had calmed and the impulse for reform began to take on new extramural forms.

This essay follows a time-honoured historiographic form: it suggests that disparate elements, upon closer examination, make an historical unity. That unity provides an alternate perspective on early eighteenth-century social policy and urban culture. As other authors in this volume have stressed, the politics of religion structured social policy to a very great extent. Workhouses and hospitals were the creations of a loosely-connected group of reformers, linked through national bodies like the SPCK but fundamentally local in character. The poor were incarcerated because they threatened England's moral as well as commercial prosperity. Indeed, when John Cary discovered, to his shock, that his workhouse could not be self-supporting because prices were simply too low, he did not give up on his scheme. The moral benefits of reclaiming the poor outweighed the costs to the ratepayer of maintaining 'uneconomic' institutions. An historiography which emphasizes the 'rational' qualities of eighteenth-century philanthropy fails to account for the powerful appeal of incarceration and other measures which promised returns measured not only in pounds and pence.

But interest as well as virtue structured urban charity; in a paradoxical fashion, charitable institutions derived both from faction and the will to overcome it. As Sandra Cavallo has perceptively noted about Italian cities, charity institutions developed from moments of civic strife, founded as expressions of political power and patronage.[89] In England, these divisions were cross-cut by the curious role of charity institutions in unifying the deeply divided urban polities after 1688. A very local pride in one's own city, coupled with a desire to bury the factional stresses and strains of previous decades – not to mention the wish to control the behaviour of the poor – provided powerful motives to overwrite differences in emblems of civic unity. Where party politics failed or were irrelevant, movements to reform manners and an interest in primitive Christianity served as sites where difference could be overcome in common cause.[90] But the rhetoric of the return to the early church was ambiguous and mutable. Often the political differences embedded in urban life, as well as the ambiguities inherent in primitive Christianity, overcame the moments of optimism and unity in which institutions were founded. While such moments could be re-lived in pageants celebrating the city's common sense of self, they were transitory; parades of clean and tidy charity-school children processing into the cathedral represent only one face of urban charity. The quotidian function of such institutions was the deployment of power and patronage, on both corporate and individual levels.

Certainly, the city elites in Bristol wished to present a picture of civic unity and harmony, but rarely was the wish father to reality. But nor should the quarrels and bickering of political difference blind us to some of the ways in which these men found common cause. Historians have tended to see charity and welfare as separate entities, and to stress the rational natures of their eighteenth-century forms. But a belief in the moral uses of incarceration, of the need to reform the manners of the poor, made charity and poor relief virtually identical. So too, in their intentions to found redemptive communities embodying the ideals of a primitive church, reformers who created workhouses and hospitals owed as much to inward religion as to rational philanthropy.

Notes

My thanks to Sandra Cavallo, Tim Hitchcock and Bob Shoemaker for their valuable comments on earlier drafts of this paper. I am also grateful to the Wellcome Trust for their support of the larger project from which this paper derives.

1   Roy Porter, 'The gift relation: philanthropy and provincial hospitals in eighteenth-century England', in Lindsay Granshaw and Roy Porter (eds.), *The Hospital in History* (1989), pp. 149–178; Gordon Rupp, *Religion in England 1688–1791* (Oxford, 1986), p. 309.
2   Donna Andrew, *Philanthropy and Police: London Charity in the Eighteenth Century* (Princeton, 1989), p. 23.
3   Stephen Macfarlane, 'Social policy and the poor in the later seventeenth century' in A.L. Beier and Roger Finlay (eds.), *London 1500–1700* (1985), p. 253.
4   See, for example, Craig Rose, 'Politics and the London Royal Hospitals, 1683–92', in Granshaw and Porter, *Hospital in History*, pp. 123–148.
5   On Bristol, see Elizabeth Baigent, 'Bristol in 1775', (Oxford Univ. D. Phil. Thesis, 1985); Jonathan Barry, 'The cultural life of Bristol, 1640–1775', (Oxford Univ. D. Phil. Thesis, 1985); *idem*, 'Piety and the patient: medicine and religion in eighteenth century Bristol', in Roy Porter (ed.), *Patients and Practitioners* (Cambridge, 1985), pp. 145–176; John Latimer, *Annals of Bristol in the Eighteenth Century* (Bristol, 1893); Patrick McGrath (ed.), *Bristol in the Eighteenth Century* (Newton Abbot, 1972). On the poor in

Bristol, see E.E. Butcher, *Bristol Corporation of the Poor, 1696–1834* (Bristol: Bristol Record Society Publications 3, 1932); James Johnson, *Transactions of the Corporation of the Poor During 126 Years* (Bristol, 1826).

6 Jonathan Barry, 'The politics of religion in Restoration Bristol', in Tim Harris, Paul Seaward and Mark Goldie (eds.), *The Politics of Religion in Restoration England* (Oxford, 1990), pp. 163–189.

7 Peter Borsay, *The English Urban Renaissance* (Oxford, 1989).

8 On the charitable aspects of hospitals, see Sandra Cavallo, 'Charity, power, and patronage in eighteenth-century Italian hospitals: the case of Turin', in Granshaw and Porter, *Hospital in History*, pp. 93–122.

9 Paul Slack, *Poverty and Policy in Tudor and Stuart England* (1988), pp. 188–204; Macfarlane, 'Social policy'.

10 Julia de L. Mann, *The Cloth Industry in the West of England from 1640–1880* (Oxford, 1971).

11 Butcher, *Bristol Corporation*, p. 2.

12 On the eighteenth-century provincial hospital, John Woodward, *To Do the Sick No Harm* (1972), is still a useful starting point. See also Guenter B. Risse, *Hospital Life in Enlightenment Scotland. Care and Teaching at the Royal Infirmary of Edinburgh* (Cambridge, 1986). On the Bristol Infirmary in particular, G. Munro Smith, *A History of the Bristol Royal Infirmary* (Bristol, 1917); Michael Neve, 'Natural philosophy, medicine and the culture of science in provincial England: the cases of Bristol 1790–1850, and Bath 1750–1820', (University College, London PhD, 1984); Mary E. Fissell, *Patients, Power and the Poor in Eighteenth-Century Bristol* (Cambridge, 1991).

13 Porter, 'The gift relation'; Kathleen Wilson, 'Urban culture and political activism in Hanoverian England: The example of voluntary hospitals', in Eckhart Hellmuth (ed.), *The Transformation of Political Culture: England and Germany in the Late Eighteenth Century* (Oxford, 1990), pp. 165–184.

14 John Cary, *A Proposal Offered to the Committee* [1700].

15 7 & 8 William III c. 32. See also BL 816.m.54 and 55 for Cary's note on a handbill advertising his scheme.

16 Johnson, *Transactions* p. 7.

17 On bridewells and houses of correction, see Joanna Innes, 'Prisons for the poor: English bridewells, 1555–1700', in Francis Snyder and Douglas Hay, *Labour, Law, and Crime: An Historical Perspective* (1987), pp. 42–122.

18 Russell Mortimer (ed.), *Minute Book of the Men's Meeting of the Society of Friends in Bristol 1686–1704*, (Bristol, 1977), pp. xxviii–xxx; Bristol Record Office, (hereafter BRO) 'Minutes of the Women's Meeting', SF/AI–2; Monica M. Tompkins, 'The two workhouses of Bristol 1696–1735', (University of Nottingham, MA thesis, 1962).

19 John Bellers, *Proposals for Raising a College of Industry* (1695), title page.

20 John Bellers, *An Essay Towards the Improvement of Physick* (1714), p. 37.

21 Latimer, *Annals*, p. 12.

22 SPCK Archives, File 1, original letters, Arthur Bedford to John Chamberlayne, 17 Feb. 1700.

23 On the founding of the Infirmary, see BRO, 'Bristol biographical memoirs' vol. 1; *An Account of the Hospitals, Alms Houses and Public Schools in Bristol* (Bristol, 1775); Smith, *Bristol Royal Infirmary*.

24 Charles Webster, *The Great Instauration* (1975), esp. pp. 288–300.

25 Henry Robinson, *Certain Proposalls In order to the Peoples Freedome and Accommodation in some Particulars. With the Advancement of Trade and navigation of this Commonwealth in Generall* (1652).

26 Hampshire Record Office, 'Winchester Infirmary Court of Governors Minutes', p. 55.

27   Carew Reynell, *A Sermon Preached Before Contributors to the Bristol Infirmary* (Bristol, 1738).

28   BRO, 'Bristol Infirmary Board of Governors minutes', 7 March 1739.

29   SPCK Archives, 'Abstract letter book', CR12, letter 2189, 5 Aug. 1709.

30   Bristol Central Library, 'SRM minutes'.

31   Dudley W.R. Bahlman, *The Moral Revolution of 1688* (New Haven, 1957). Historians of the reformation of manners movement are greatly indebted to A.G. Craig's thesis: A.G. Craig, 'The movement for the reformation of manners, 1688–1715', (Edinburgh University PhD Thesis, 1980). See also, T.C. Curtis and W.A. Speck, 'The Societies of the Reformation of Manners: A case study in the theory and practice of moral reform', *Literature and History* 3, 1976, pp. 45–64. For the Restoration origins of the reformation of manners, see John Spurr, '"Virtue, Religion and Government": the Anglican uses of providence' in Harris, *et al* (eds.), *Politics of Religion*, pp. 29–47.

32   Josiah Woodward, *An Account of the Progress of the Reformation of manners* (1706), p. 50. Woodward was quoting from a sermon given by the Dean of Lincoln.

33   Craig, 'Reformation of manners', p. 239; Shoemaker, see ch. 5, above.

34   Rev. Edmund McClure (ed.), *A Chapter in English Church History. SPCK Minutes and Correspondence 1698–1704* (1888), letter 231.

35   SPCK Archive, 'Abstract letter book', CR2/1 Nov. 1699.

36   SPCK Archive, File 1 Original letters, 27 Nov. 1699.

37   M.G. Jones, *The Charity School Movement* (Cambridge, 1938), p. 9.

38   Woodward, *An Account*, p. 30.

39   Hampshire Record Office, 'Court of Governors', p. 55.

40   *Ibid.*, p. 56.

41   Josiah Tucker, *A Sermon Preached in the Parish Church in Bristol* (Bristol, 1746).

42   *Ibid.*, p. 15.

43   BRO, 'Bristol biographical memoirs', vol. 2, p. 768.

44   Eamon Duffy, 'Primitive Christianity revived: religious renewal in Augustan England', in Derek Baker (ed.), *Renaissance and Renewal in Christian History* (Studies in Church History 14) (Oxford, 1977), pp. 287–300. See also, Henry D. Rack, 'Religious societies and the origins of Methodism', *Journal of Ecclesiastical History*, 37 (1982), esp. pp. 582–83.

45   SPCK Archive, 'Abstract letter book', 264, Osterwald to SPCK, 11 March 1701; cited in Eamon Duffy, '*Correspondence fraternelle*; the SPCK, the SPG, and the churches of Switzerland in the war of the Spanish Succession', in Derek Baker (ed.), *Reform and Reformation: England and the Continent c1500–c1750* (Studies in Church History 16) (Oxford, 1979), p. 258.

46   John Bellers, *Proposals for Raising a College of Industry* (1695), p. 13.

47   Matthew Tindal, *The Rights of the Christian Church Asserted* (1706), p. 117.

48   Bahlman, *Moral Revolution*, pp. 19–21; Hillel Schwartz, *The French Prophets* (Berkeley, 1980), pp. 131–32.

49   Melvin Endy, *William Penn and Early Quakerism* (Princeton, 1973), pp. 70–71, 235–236.

50   Bedford, for instance, preached a sermon to the Hanoverian Society in Bristol in 1717, and annoyed his patron in 1710 by voting for a whig.

51   William Weber, 'Mentalité, tradition et origines du canon musical en France et en Angleterre au XVIIIe siècle', *Annales E.S.C.* 44 (1989), pp. 849–873.

52   SPCK Archive, 'Abstract letter book', CR 11, no. 1743, 12 Oct. 1709.

53   Advertisement is in Arthur Bedford, *A Serious Remonstrance in Behalf of the Christian Religion* (1719).

54   SPCK Archives, 'Letterbook' CS 2/5, 18 Sept. 1716.

55   Tindal, *Rights of the Christian Church*, p. 246.

56 Webster, *Great Instauration*; Harold Cook, *The Decline of the Old Medical Regime in Stuart London* (New York, 1986).

57 Tindal, *Rights of the Christian Church*, p. 11.

58 Tina Isaacs, 'The Anglican hierarchy and the reformation of manners 1688–1738', *Journal of Ecclesiastical History* 33, (1982), 391–411.

59 Henry Sacheverell, *The Character of a Low-Churchman* (1702), p. 2, quoted in Isaacs, p. 401.

60 Michael Foster, *An Examination of the Scheme of Church Power Laid Down in the Codex Juris Ecclesiastici* (1735), pp. 17, 76.

61 *Ibid.*, p. 77.

62 Tindal, *Rights of the Christian Church*, p. 287.

63 A.S. Catcott, *On the Supreme and Inferior Elohim, a sermon preached before the corporation of Bristol, August 1735* (1735).

64 See Michael Neve and Roy Porter, 'Alexander Catcott: glory and geology', *British Journal for the History of Science* 10, (1977), pp. 37–60, for a discussion of the careers of the Catcotts, father and son, and mention of this controversy.

65 Arthur Bedford, *Observations of Mr. Catcott's Sermon* (1736); Arthur Bedford, *An Examination of Mr. Hutchinson's Remarks and Mr. Catcott's Answer to the Observations on his Sermon Preached before the Corporation of Bristol* (1738).

66 Bedford, *An Examination*, pp. 106–7.

67 Catcott, *Supreme Elohim*, p. 29.

68 Bedford, *An Examination*, p. 84.

69 For more on 'inner religion' in Bristol, see Barry, 'Piety and the patient'. There were many connections among those interested in primitive Christianity. For example, both Bedford and Matthew Tindal wrote approvingly of the Albigensians and Waldenses, noting that these medieval mystical groups were persecuted by the clergy, drawing a dichotomy between true believers and churchmen applicable to other situations as well. But Catcott also saw himself allied with mystical or pietistic religion: he worried that 'a man who talks as I do is likely to be stil'd a visionary and enthusiast' (p. 6). Like allegiances to primitive Christianity, divisons within adherents of pietistic religion could be as significant as those without.

70 See above, ch. 5.

71 Arthur Bedford, *A Sermon Preached to the Society for the Reformation of Manners* (1734), pp. 8–9.

72 George Stanhope, *The Duty of Rebuking* (1703), p. 24.

73 Quoted in Arthur Bedford, *A Serious Remonstrance in Behalf of the Christian Religion* (1719), p. 226.

74 BRO, 'Champion letterbook', (3) 29 Sept. 1771.

75 BRO, 'Champion letterbook', (1) 7 Sept. 1764.

76 John Bellers, *An Essay Towards the Improvement of Physick* (1714), p. 6.

77 *Ibid.*, p. 44.

78 Tompkins, 'Two workhouses', p. 79.

79 Johnson, *Transactions*, pp. 26–29.

80 John Cary, *An Account of the Proceedings of the Corporation* (1700), p. 3.

81 Butcher, *Bristol Corporation*, pp. 4–5.

82 Tindal, *Rights of the Christian Church*, p. 285.

83 *Some Considerations Offer'd to the Citizens of Bristol Relating to the Corporation for the Poor* (1711), p. 8.

84 SPCK Archive, 'Abstract letter book', CRI 1 no. 1658, 1685.

85 Latimer, *Annals*, pp. 85–86.

86 SPCK Archive, 'Abstract letter book', CS25 14 July 1715.

87 Jones, *Charity School Movement*, pp. 110–113.

88 Latimer, *Annals*, pp. 102–103; Butcher, *Bristol Corporation*, p. 93.
89 Sandra Cavallo, 'The motivations of benefactors: An overview of approaches to the study of charity', in Jonathan Barry and Colin Jones (eds.), *Medicine and Charity Before the Welfare State* (1991) pp. 46–62.
90 David Hayton has recently pointed to the political allegiances structured by an interest in reform. While his Parliamentary actors obviously found common cause in moral reform, much of the reformation of manners movement was local in concept and effect. David Hayton, 'Moral reform and Country politics in the late seventeenth-century House of Commons', *Past and Present*, 128, 1990, 48–91.

7
Paupers and Preachers: The SPCK and the Parochial Workhouse Movement

Tim Hitchcock
Polytechnic of North London

Provide in the house in a regular & comfortable manner for those who by age or infirmities are wholely incapable of work or labour, but those that are able, to be employed therein in such work as they are capable of, for the benefit of the parish, and the children to be bred to labour & industry, virtue & religion & thereby the infinite mischief proceeding from idleness & want of employment (as heretofore) prevented.[1]

The employment of the poor was the favourite panacea of early eighteenth-century reformers. The halt, the lame, the blind and the simply idle were to be exposed to religious education and harnessed to industrial production, pulling the common weal to new heights of prosperity. These groups of people were perceived to be a great under-utilised resource which awaited only the reforming hand of a social-policy projector. One of the means adopted to harness this power was the workhouses, first in the form of the Corporations of the Poor founded in fifteen cities including London between 1696 and 1711 and then, more significantly, through the establishment from the mid-1710s of parochial workhouses in hundreds of communities up and down the country.

By 1777 a parliamentary inquiry could identify 1,916 workhouses in England, the largest proportion of which had been established in the first half of the eighteenth century. These housed and, at least in theory, set on work over ninety thousand paupers.[2] But even the number of people who experienced these institutions directly does not give a fair picture of their true importance. They were used as a deterrent to those contemplating applying to the parish for relief, effectively changing the system of outdoor relief and parish pensions, which had catered sympathetically to the requirements of an economy of makeshift, to one in which applicants were presented with a stark choice between total and institutionalized dependence, and complete reliance on their own and their neighbours' resources. As both threat and resource workhouses came to impinge on the lives of the majority of the inhabitants of the primarily urban parishes in which they were established. Because workhouses were viewed with abhorrence by the labouring poor, their existence affected the behaviour of perhaps forty to sixty per cent of the population, that portion which might expect to find itself dependent on the parish in old age or illness. In parish after parish the existence of these houses drove down the numbers of people dependent on relief by over fifty per cent.[3]

Each of these nearly two thousand foundations represented the success and ambition of eighteenth-century local government – the ability of the smallest and most isolated of government organisations, the parish vestry, to formulate and implement sophisticated social policies with the help of neither central government nor quarter sessions. Moreover, this series of workhouse foundations, which were centred in the 1720s and 30s, falling off rapidly from the early 1740s, was almost entirely the result of a combination of extremely localized initiative and central, but entirely voluntary and non-governmental, direction. Even when the 1723 Workhouse Test Act is taken into account, Parliament and central government must be seen to have played a very minor role in the movement.[4] The Workhouse Test Act itself was backed and probably formulated by the SPCK, and while it did not attract the active opposition of the government, it failed to gain more than Walpole's passive support. Beyond this, there was some interest in the institutionalization of the poor expressed by government at both the beginning of the century and around 1750. First the Board of Trade and then a Parliamentary committee enquired into poor relief expenditure and the success of workhouses in controlling that expenditure. But, between about 1703 when the Board of Trade lost interest in the subject, and 1751 when a Parliamentary enquiry surveyed the number of houses established in England, there was, in effect, no government policy on or interest in workhouses.[5]

Even on a county level, it was found that justices of the peace frequently did more to hamper the movement through their issuance of orders for outdoor relief in contradiction to the requirements of a workhouse test than they ever did to direct or encourage the foundation of these houses. In 1726 Samuel Weller complained that the justices in Kent were against the poor going into a workhouse, advocating instead that they 'be supported by a weekly allowance, because by the power they have over them they can oblige them to buy at their own shops, or compel them to deal with some other person as they shall direct, which he intimates'.[6] In terms, then, of established avenues for the transmission of power and ideas between the parishes and the government in Westminster, the workhouse movement seems to have done without central direction. And yet this movement was one of the most consistent, and best organized social policy reforms to be attempted before the nineteenth century. It was a national movement, but one run not through government but through a voluntary organization – the Society for Promoting Christian Knowledge, the SPCK.

The SPCK ensured that parishes up and down the country had the same intellectual resources available to them, that they used the same accounting techniques and the same set of rules in managing their separate institutions. The Society provided a full range of services to parish government, making possible the establishment of what were extremely complex administrative machines.

This essay will examine the ideology behind the parochial workhouse movement, and the role of the SPCK in both disseminating that ideology and connecting the disparate forces and communities which made up the movement. It will demonstrate one of the ways in which national reform might take place without the help or interest of a strong national government in the early eighteenth century.

The late seventeenth and early eighteenth centuries were periods of rising expectations and economic expansion and as a result the perception of what it was to be poor changed. Parochial poor relief had developed in the sixteenth century as a collateral to vagrancy legislation and wage regulation to deal with the specific problems of the elderly, the sick and the disabled. In the 1660s and 70s, however, the definition of the 'deserving poor', of those whom the rate payers were obliged to support, became wider, while poverty itself became shallower. In other words, while the numbers of those in receipt of parochial relief grew, the standard of living experienced by paupers rose. As the regulation of vagrancy and wages became increasingly difficult the parochial mechanism of the old poor law came to encompass a larger element of the task of relieving distress and ordering the working population. The 'poor' as a category was expanded as a result of rising living standards and a changing definition of poverty to include a larger proportion of the labouring population.[7] In effect the old poor law, which had been created to cope with the demands of those who fell through less formal and voluntary systems of relief, came in the late seventeenth century to affect the lives of an increasing number of people. Every farm hand and journeyman, hawker and servant, however healthy, and regardless of their position within a household economy, came to expect that at some point during their lives they would depend on parish relief.

This put tremendous pressure on the system, raising parish rates and making the face-to-face relationship between parish officer and pauper, which was at the heart of the old poor law, largely untenable.[8] The very expansion of the economy and of the parochial system of relief created a problem which was unprecedented in its extent. A situation resulted in which pressure for the reform of the relief system became ever more urgent – in which rising rates and rising expectations combined to make the system of outdoor relief seem increasingly inadequate.

These pressures and changes were, however, experienced entirely at the level of the local community. And because the parochial system of relief was extremely well established, it was almost necessarily left to local initiative to deal with these problems, ensuring that any seemingly practicable local reform would receive relatively widespread support. What these pressures did not do was determine the nature or direction of that reform. The choice of the workhouse and of institutions more generally was the result of the conflation of an English humanitarian and radical tradition with a European-wide reformation of religious ideology which was centred in pietist Germany, but whose effects can be seen in the activities of the voluntary religious societies of the 1690s and 1700s, and later in the development of Methodism.[9] It was these reform ideologies which were popularised and advocated by the SPCK, and which form the main content of the Society's contribution to English social policy.

In the writings of Richard Vaughan at the beginning of the seventeenth century, in the London workhouse established by Samuel Hartlib during the Interregnum, in Thomas Firmin's flax spinning scheme of the 1670s, and in similar Quaker experiments, as well as numerous provincial initiatives, one can find a consistent strain of thought. From early in the seventeenth century this radical and humanitarian tradition, which itself derived in part from Samuel Hartlib's and others' wide experience with continental reforms, was primarily associated with sectarian religion. It assumed that poverty is for the most part 'curable', that the labour of the poor, once constructively directed, would naturally, and unavoidably, create much more wealth than would be needed to satisfy any reasonable demand from the poor, and that the reform of poor relief would result in the religious reformation of English society.[10] Writing at the end of the seventeenth century John Bellers, the Quaker economist and author of *Proposals for Raising a Colledge of Industry*, expected to achieve three things by employing the poor:

> First, profit for the rich, (which will be life to the rest). Secondly, a plentiful living for the poor, without difficulty. Thirdly, a good education for youth, that may tend to prepare their souls into the nature of the good ground.[11]

The tradition from which these ideas were derived reached a high point with the establishment of fifteen Corporations of the Poor between 1696 and 1711.[12] Under the influence of both John Cary at Bristol and perhaps more tangentially, John Bellers, these large civic projects were based on the idea that in workhouses designed to treat the poor fairly and kindly particular social policy objectives could be reached both through the employment of the poor at a profit, and the exposure of the dissolute among them to the effects of a religious education and a regular, ordered and virtuous life style.[13] In other words, the virtues of Christian piety were to be inculcated in the poor through religious education and labour discipline in workhouses. The Corporations were established by private Acts of Parliament and were intended to unite the small parishes of the larger provincial capitals. In many respects they were similar to the large civic projects common on the continent. They were expected to make an absolute profit from the labour of the poor, and while the founders of these institutions recognised their power over the local labour market, these houses were primarily concerned to discipline and regulate the poor within their walls. Unlike later parochial workhouses, the Corporations did not try to use the poor's own fear of incarceration as a weapon against those applying for relief.[14]

Because of their primarily sectarian origins and also because of their administrative and financial power the Corporations quickly became sites of party political dispute. They were seen by many as a means of attacking established authority. In Exeter the Corporation, founded by Act of Parliament in 1698, was seen 'to cast an envious eye upon the present government by the civil magistrates of the city'.[15] But the failure of the Corporations brought on by these political tensions did not prevent their example demonstrating the possibility of using workhouses for reforming the poor to a powerful if somewhat amorphous Puritan and latitudinarian tradition within the Anglican Church. This tradition achieved an institutional form at the end of the seventeenth century as the SPCK. The Society adopted from the Corporations many ideas which had originated in a sectarian and later dissenting tradition and which had been for-mulated in the more radical environment of the Interregnum. In adopting these ideas the Society brought them more firmly into an established Anglican environment, making them in turn less contentious and providing for the advocates of workhouses and institutional relief an acceptable religious rhetoric which effectively side-stepped the divisions which characterized the debates of Whigs and Tories.

Founded in 1698, the Society, much more than any other reform movement, was a European phenomenon. It was in close contact with numerous continental reformers, and maintained an active correspond-ence, particuarly with the recently revived German pietist movement centred at Halle and by the 1690s under the direction of August Francke.[16] In part because it had these international resources to fall back upon, the SPCK was the only agent of reform able to maintain its vigour and influence over the course of the first half of the eighteenth century. While the Societies for the Reformation of Manners, the first of which was established in 1690 and which dominated initiatives to reform society for much of the next twenty years, gradually restricted their range of activities, and while old dissent was disrupted by internecine arguments following the death of its first generation of leaders, the Society grew in strength and influence.[17]

The SPCK was established as both a reaction to the success of dissenting interests and in an attempt to provide an umbrella organisation for the disparate reforming bodies then in existence. Its original and avowed purpose was to encourage the establishment of charity schools for the eduction of poor children throughout the country and it was organised through a sytem of corresponding and residing members. Within a very few years of its foundation the Society had attracted approximately 450 corresponding and 100 residing members. The corresponding members were located throughout both Britain and Europe, and included a large proportion of the more active and intellectual of parish clergy. Also among the corresponding members were merchants and manufacturers, enlightened gentry and, in a slightly more distant relationship, several members of the aristocracy. The residing members were residents of London who could attend the Society's regular meetings. For the most part they were powerful men holding secular positions; they included MPs, several aristocrats, justices of the peace and members of some of the more important London merchant families.[18] By 1772 the Society could count MPs like Henry Pacey, John Comyns, and Sir John Philipps among its resident members, while its correspondents were typified by men like the Reverend Samuel Johnston the incumbent at Beverley and Maurice Wheeler, a merchant living in Warpenham.[19] While the Society did have an agenda and a point of view, it could welcome members from a broad range of ideological perspectives; it could welcome both men like Francis Fox, a strong Whig, whom contemporaries judged to be sympathetic to dissenters, and Sir Humphrey Mackworth who wrote against occasional conformity and was a Church Tory.[20]

The significant aspect of the Society's organisation is that it provided a sophisticated two-tier system which both facilitated centralised decision making and at the same time allowed for the collection of local information and the dissemination of the products of central discussion. With this system and membership the Society created an effective conduit through which to channel information and ideas to the parishes and from the parishes to London.

That this system worked and survived largely unchanged throughout the eighteenth century was the result of the Society's choice of membership and continuing control over its public image. The SPCK vetted its members extremely thoroughly and maintained a high level of secrecy about its activities. To become either a corresponding or residing member it was necessary for one's name to be put forward by a trusted associate of the Society. Enquiries about the suitability of the nominee would then be made to his friends and various members of the SPCK. Only then, after the process of vetting had been completed and it had been determined that the nominee was suitable, would he be contacted, and the idea of joining presented to him. In the normal course of events he would then begin to receive the Society's annual reports and circular letters, its published material and advice. A correspondence between the new member and the secretary of the Society, Henry Newman from 1708 to his death in 1743, would be undertaken, and the new member would be made responsible for the reforming activities appropriate for his area.[21] The Society strove to maintain a relatively even distribution of members across the country serving the needs of specific neighbourhoods. Each county might contain three to five members, who would in all likelihood be largely unknown to one another, and who would act separately.

This organization and recruiting process helped to maintain a degree of secrecy about the Society's activities which it found extremely useful. In 1709 the Society wrote to the representative of a similar reforming society in Edinburgh:

That ever since they first formed them-selves into a Society they have studiously endeavoured to conceal themselves as far as was consistent with the nature of those designs in which they are engaged and are convinced by experience that the more they do so, the greater success they may reasonably hope for.[22]

The SPCK's publications gave no indication of their origin until late in the century, and although the Society's projects, particularly the charity schools, were the objects of a great deal of controversy, the Society itself was seldom implicated simply because its connections were so little known.[23] The SPCK could not, of course, maintain a complete veil over either its existence or influence. But it was able to maintain a relatively low profile, while in fact becoming increasingly powerful and intrusive in both national and local government.

The SPCK described itself as a religious society, but this description goes only a short way towards indicating why the Society existed and what were its aims. It did produce moralistic pamphlets for the edification of the irreligious, similar in many ways to those now distributed by groups like the Jehovah's Witness, but these sorts of proselytising efforts were only a small part of the Society's programme.[24] Though apparently somewhat high church in its proclivities, it also advocated a peculiarly militant and ecumenical form of Anglicanism, which owed much to the recently revived enthusiasm of German pietism transmitted through the experience and belief of men like Anton Boehme and August Francke, a translation of whose work the Society published in 1706.[25]

The motivating idea behind the Society was not just that religious belief should be encouraged for the sake of the souls of men, but that religion itself, as the glue which held communities and society in one piece, was a means of discouraging aberrant behaviour, which included all forms of able-bodied poverty and indebtedness as well as criminality. The charity schools were established because they encouraged religious belief which it was believed would instil industrial and social discipline. Similarly, the pamphlets were distributed with the expectation that once exposed to the precepts of reformed religion the most obdurate poor would inevitably choose virtue over sin, and in the process virtuous labour over sinful idleness. At the heart of all the Society's activities was the belief that no one could be both devout and lazy; that in the words of the vestry of South Mimms in 1724, 'to preserve . . .' the poor 'from following idle and vagrant courses', they need only be 'instruct[ed] . . . in the knowledge of their duty towards God'.[26] It was in this thought, and the relationship that was perceived to exist between religion and social behaviour, that the active and essential element of eighteenth-century reformed religion lay.

Historians looking back from a period in which the language of political ideology has become the primary and for the most part the only way in which to discuss change, whether revolutionary or gradual, quite naturally tend to give great weight to the party-political dialogue between whig and tory developed in the period after 1685. Few people in the early eighteenth century, however, would have understood the language of party politics in the way we now conceive it. The rhetoric that had formed the context for radical and social change in the recent past, which had formed the ideas and motivated the revolutions which had characterised the previous two hundred years of English history, had all been expressed and thought about in terms of religion. Party politics provided a language in which the succession, warfare and imperial expansion, the liberties of Englishmen, and the sanctity of property could be discussed, but which provided no ideal model of the broader social structure. In other words, party politics provided a language of social stasis, through which class and economic divisions were perceived to be immutable. In the period before Wilkes and the revolutions of the end of the eighteenth century, social levelling, the redistribution of wealth and more subtly, social discipline and the social ideal which lay behind that discipline, could be formulated most easily through the use of religious language and ideas. The rhetoric of religion, the Bible, the Trinity and the Sermon on the Mount, of catholic

charity, primitive Christianity, and the millennium, had, in both established and dissenting traditions, provided and continued to provide the
means of discussing social problems which would only much later be
argued over using party-political terms. While John Locke may be the
person to whom we look back as the seminal figure in the development of a
philosophy of social organisation, most of Locke's contemporaries would
have considered Archbishop Tillotson a more natural advocate of social
change. Even if we look directly at schemes for the reorganisation of poor
relief which might superficially seem to have been formulated in secular
terms, they must likewise be seen to be the products of a religious
paradigm. When George Fox designed an institution for the employment
of poor women in 1669, he was not stepping outside his role as spiritual
leader of Quakerism, but performing a duty integral to that role.[27]

Religion provided the language of social change throughout this period,
and it was only through religious reformation that most eighteenth-
century thinkers could imagine social reformation. The SPCK, as much as
the Quakers, saw religious belief and social organisation as part of a single
whole in which religious reform led inexorably to social change, and in
turn, in which social reform led inexorably to religious reform. Some
attempts have been made to place the Society within the framework of
party politics, to describe it as either whig or tory, but to do this is to
misunderstand the Society's relationship to other reform movements, and
more importantly to misread the Society's goals and aspirations.[28] The
SPCK was certainly in favour of religious reform, in favour of the
reformation of the social system to one in which order and deference were
apparent, but it did not perceive its roles or its goals in terms of either a
narrowly defined Anglicanism, or the success of Jacobitism, the Hanoverian succession or Robert Walpole.

Having said this, it must also be noted that the Society pursued its
essentially religious ends through a series of projects, many of which at first
sight seem largely secular in character, and which required on occasion the
intermeddling of the Society in Parliamentary and party politics. As well
as its commitment to the education of poor children the Society
undertook a range of other projects, several of which required the passage
of Acts of Parliament. It established foreign missions, published moral
tracts for use both at home and abroad, attempted to reform the debtor
prisons of London and was involved in the foundation of the prison colony
at Georgia. The Society translated and reprinted European works on social
policy, and was involved in the establishment of London's Foundling
Hospital in the early 1740s.[29] In some ways it acted as one of the most
extensive and organised pressure groups in English politics. It was
continually advising the ten to twelve MPs amongst its members on what
to think about specific pieces of legislation. And while there was no

organized attempt to place men in Parliament, the Society did ask the occasional favour of those of its members holding seats. Sir Humphrey Mackworth, one of the SPCK's founding members, frequently represented the Society's views in Parliament. He included three amendments giving greater power to the Corporations of the Poor in his 1704 bill at the urging of Thomas Bray and his colleagues, and in the summer of 1705 thanked the Society for its help in seeing the bill through the first stages of what was to be a long and inglorious parliamentary career.[30]

The Society's parliamentary activities, however, were essentially a secondary and adjunctive means of achieving the ends it set itself in the vestries and common councils around the country, where it was a largely silent and surreptitious influence on local government. In the fundamentally local affairs of education and poor relief reform it acted as a strong influence on decision making at the parish level, circumventing the systems of JPs and quarter sessions which for much of the seventeenth century had been used by central government to direct local policy.[31] Because of its membership it could link London and cosmopolitan evangelical interests with supporters in the provinces and as a result was able to take over many charity schools founded long before 1698.[32] By providing books and tracts, trained masters, horn books and primers, all with the peculiar religious slant advocated by the Society, the disparate but substantial local resources available for the education of the young were quickly turned to the use of these religious and London based reformers.[33] The SPCK also helped establish new schools and sources of income. Its correspondents were encouraged to convince wealthy local landowners to endow schools, leaving the Society's local representative and his friends as trustees, or alternatively, to bring together local artisans and shopkeepers in a charitable league in which each member helped support a school with what small amounts they could afford.[34]

The Society also attempted to forge links among the various reforming groups active in England, making connections across the whole range of English religious and political opinion. While one of the Society's best known advocates remained the high churchman Thomas Bray, in 1700 it also tried to interest the Whig dissenter John Cary in its activities, and at this time looked upon the work of the Societies for the Reformation of Manners as simply one facet of the SPCK's own work, rather than as an incompatible competitor for the direction of reform. Moreover, during this early period of the Society's history it attempted to implement the full range of an European-wide agenda for religious and social reform. The reform of Europe's criminal justice systems, of punishment, of manners, and of the poor as well as the revitalization of reformed religion, were all elements of a set of reforms being advocated throughout Northern and Protestant Europe at the end of the seventeenth century.[35] The last of a series of Acts for the foundation of a Corporation of the Poor was passed in 1711, and it was around this date that the Societies for the Reformation of Manners came under sustained attack for their use of paid informers. But while other reform initiatives lost their impetus and importance, the SPCK was able, over the course of the 1710s, to adapt its programme and techniques to new series of reform initiatives more acceptable in the markedly different atmosphere of the new reign. For although it was suspected of Jacobitism at the succession of George I and during the '15, the Society was able to maintain its position of influence and power.

In 1715 the SPCK began to publicise the success of the working charity school at Artleborough in Northamptonshire.[36] This initiative, which was discussed in the Society's periodically published *Account of Charity Schools* and in the yearly circular letter distributed by the Society, freed it from its somewhat over optimistic dependence upon simple religious education. It encouraged at least a partial reliance upon the idea of habituation to labour, an idea at the heart of the establishment of the Corporations of the Poor and an idea advocated by men as disparate in their attitudes and beliefs as John Locke and John Bellers.[37]

The school at Artleborough was also described in the *Account of Several Workhouses*, first published in 1725. The woman who ran it had herself been illiterate up until its foundation, and the sixty or so children employed in the school were so encouraged by the good treatment they received from the mistress and the payment of a small part of the profits of their labour that they 'work about 15. or 16. hours in the day in summer and 13. or 14. in the winter allowing so little time for dinner that some of them earn 5d. or 6d. per day'. The teaching provided in the school was rudimentary and consisted of the daily ministrations of one man for two or three hours to the school's three score students.[38]

Through the school, independent poor relief contractors like Matthew Marryott, the workhouse movement's most influential independent advocate, were brought to the Society's attention, as was the existence of the half dozen parish workhouses founded in the East Midlands and Essex in the mid-1710s.[39] Working charity schools and workhouses came to replace charity schools as the main object of the Society's efforts. By publishing accounts and writing letters the Society encouraged several schools to add work at spinning and carding to their normal curriculum of the three Rs: religion, religion and religion. At Bicester in Oxfordshire, for instance, spinning was added to the curriculum of the by then well-established charity school in 1724 entirely as the result of the encouragement of the Society.[40]

The Society did not reject its earlier reliance upon religious education, nor entirely nor uncritically adopt the philosophy and ideas behind earlier dissenting initiatives. It merely reacted to a situation presented to it, adopting institutions already in operation, most notably the school at Artleborough, while responding favourably to proposals presented to it by its corresponding members. In 1717 for instance, Francis Fox presented the Society with the manuscript of a pamphlet advocating the foundation of parish workhouses. The Society sent it on to Matthew Marryott and on the whole looked upon the ideas expressed in the pamphlet with sympathy and some enthusiasm, although in the end it was not published.[41]

The initiatives of the late 1710s – the working charity schools and parish workhouses – dominated the Society's contribution to English social policy in the 1720s and 30s. Between them they provided a remarkably popular mechanism for the training and moulding of the poor. To a large extent the design of the institutions the Society began to promote was determined by the parish elites who had, independently of the Society, founded the first few examples. The Society simply adopted a type of institution suited to the needs of local vestrymen and then turned it into a platform for its own particular reforming efforts. But, in working charity schools and workhouses the Society had found forms of institutions which fulfilled the requirement of disciplining and reforming the poor better than any previous initiatives had done, and likewise were uniquely suited to the requirements and peculiarities of the English system of parish poor relief. While the Corporations of the Poor had in part failed because they attempted to centralise parish administration, and had been expected to produce profit from the labour of the inmates, while at the same time providing a comfortable and reasonable form of relief,[42] parish workhouses succeeded because they increased the powers of parish officers and relied upon the idea of deterrence, the idea of a workhouse test.

It was in the idea of a workhouse test and this reliance upon parish administration that their influence and effectiveness lay. Parish workhouses were designed to make the poor choose the life of the independent labourer in lieu of that of the parish pensioner. Parochial workhouses were never expected to produce an absolute profit from the labour of the poor.[43] What was expected of them was that they should make parish relief as distasteful to those in need as possible by putting it in a form which demanded a complete loss of independence on the part of the pensioner, and which could be associated in the pensioner's mind with nothing more or less than a house of correction.[44] It was not that conditions in workhouses should be less comfortable than those enjoyed by an independent labourer, that they should be 'less eligible' in the way nineteenth-century workhouses would be, but that the actual necessity of receiving relief in an institution, however eligible, combined with the discipline associated with labour, should discourage the undeserving poor from applying for relief.

As a means of direct control of the daily lives of the poor the schools and workhouses interested the Society only tangentially. The Society saw its role in religious terms and it was the opportunity of exposing the poor to religion and through religion of disciplining them, that attracted it to these new types of institution. The Society saw an ordered and regulated life style as a natural corollary to religious reform, but any forum in which the Society could speak to a pauper audience would probably have suited it just as well as workhouses and working charity schools. When the Society adopted these institutions, however, it found itself supporting two uniquely successful types of parish relief and education, which though designed to instill an external discipline, could likewise be used to promote a religiously based, internal discipline.

The popularity of the schools amongst the tradesmen and labourers who supported and sent their children to them derived from their role as training and production centres. The schools were attractive because they both provided a rudimentary education and at the same time contributed something at least to the household economy. They played on the hopes and aspirations of poor parents, who, in the words of one workhouse master 'are generally very solicitous to give their children learning and spare no cost in their power to make them happy in that respect; it being a common saying with them that learning is all the portion they can give them'.[45] The Society supported the schools because these institutions ensured that the Society's religious message reached an audience drawn from the poorest segments of society – those living in household economies which could ill afford to give up the wages and work of even the smallest and least able of its members. And finally, parish elites supported these institutions because they incorporated the idea of profiting from the labour of the poor, which, while largely discredited in relation to workhouses and the adult poor, was still seen as a possible outcome of training and disciplining the delicate hands of children.[46]

A similar set of justifications lay behind the success of parochial workhouses. Again the Society saw them as an appropriate means of reaching a portion of the poorest members of society; as providing a stage from which to promulgate its own religious views to those whom it found extremely difficult to reach in church or through its printed pamphlets. Alternatively the parish elites who established them, and the local ratepayers who financed them, saw these institutions as a way of reconciling their duty to the poor with their desire to distinguish between the 'deserving' and 'undeserving' – as a way of ensuring that those in real need would receive a kindly and adequate provision, while discouraging the work shy and dissolute from applying for that provision.

Many of the techniques used to support and encourage these two types of institutions, working charity schools and workhouses, were the same as those employed in supporting simple charity schools. The Society published accounts of successful schools and institutions, provided interested parties with educational material for the use of inmates, and tried to make sure that trained staff was available where needed. The Society gave advice to localities on the best way of solving particular problems, and ensured that at least for the first few years of their existence, these institutions had substantial support from London.[47]

The percentage of the SPCK's effort and time taken up with the working charity schools and workhouses grew slowly between 1719 and 1723, but from the beginning its corresponding members were enthusiastic. Reports of workhouses and working charity schools began to filter back in 1718, and the next year Henry Newman, the Society's secretary, was sent on a fact-finding mission to Essex.[48] In 1720 the Society offered a premium to any town setting up either type of institution.[49] And gradually more and more of the corresponding members wrote in to describe and commend local experiments. Pamphlets were submitted for publication and in 1723 it was decided to begin distributing a series of pamphlets designed to satisfy the need for information apparent in the questions and correspondence of the Society's members. But in the mean time the SPCK ensured the success of the new institutions by seeing to the drafting and probably the passage of the Workhouse Test Act in 1722.

John Chamberlayne suggested to the Society 'that it must be a pleasure to you to observe . . . that at so promising a juncture the Parliament are meditating ways to set the poor to work'.[50] And indeed, from the Society's point of view nothing could be better, especially as John Comyns was drafting the legislation and shepherding it through Parliament with Edward Knatchbull.[51] Comyns had earlier defended charity school children against the charge of Jacobitism, and was a longstanding member of the Society; his involvement with the bill ensured that the Society's views on its content would be amply represented in the final Act.[52]

In most respects the 1723 Workhouse Test Act was entirely insignificant, neither exciting active comment at the time, nor receiving a great deal of notice from the founders of later parish workhouses. It was a hodge-podge of poor relief clauses with little obvious direction and few new ideas. It did give legislative expression to a new kind of workhouse, however; a workhouse saved from the fate of the Corporations of the Poor and all earlier experiments by the idea of deterrence. The Act allowed parishes to refuse to relieve any applicant who refused to enter a workhouse and provided a description of the type of institution which the Society had been coming to know and advocate in the previous seven years. More than this, it gave a governmental stamp of approval to the institutions recently set up in the East Midlands and Essex, and with that approval for the Society's newest project, approval of a type the Society could not hope to obtain for its charity schools after the stain of Jacobitism had tarnished their reputation.

With the passage of the Workhouse Test Act and in the same year the publication of de Mandeville's damning *Essay on Charity and Charity Schools*, which argued that the schools encouraged children to aspire above their station and that their attraction lay in the school's ability to satisfy parish elites' lust for power, the Society's conversion to these new institutions was complete, and an extensive publishing campaign followed.[53] The Society published over half the pamphlets dealing with the employment of the poor written in the next ten years and distributed them to the corresponding members, ensuring that information on workhouses and working charity schools was readily available in coffee houses and from provincial booksellers.[54] The most substantial and influential pamphlet it produced was the *Account of Several Workhouses* – a collection of descriptions of workhouses and working charity schools, giving details of their management, examples of sets of rules, diet sheets and lists of clothing for the inmates. The *Account* was in the tradition of the Society's earlier *Account of Charity Schools* but went into more detail, providing models for all practical aspects of the running of workhouses. The sources and types of information contained in the *Account* are important here as they reflect the ways in which the Society encouraged local people to undertake projects which might otherwise have seemed far too complex and expensive for parish government.

The idea of publishing the account came from Caleb Parfect, the incumbent at Strood in Kent. Between 1719 and 1723 the Society had made a great effort to help Parfect in his attempts to set up first a working charity school and then a workhouse. It had ensured that a suitable master was available for the school, and then that the master's wife could be trained at Artleborough in the appropriate techniques for employing children. It had also ensured that the right kind of spinning wheels were available, and later, when the workhouse was in trouble because 'many of the inferior inhabitants have resolved . . . in favour of an unqualified person [for the post of workhouse master] but a poor native of the town against the opinion of the minister and churchwardens and the leading gentlemen of the town', the Society gave Parfect advice on how the situation might be overcome. Parfect considered his institutions to be in a flourishing state by 1722 and proceeded to write a pamphlet about them, which he submitted to the Society for publication.[55] By this time the Society was aware of the existence of perhaps fifty other workhouses and in response decided to put together as many descriptions of them as possible – only later publishing Parfect's pamphlet separately.[56] The result was the *Account of Several Workhouses*. What is perhaps most important about the

Account is that the short articles it contains were a response to specific questions about institutions, and it includes few comments on the usefulness of workhouses, beyond rather bald statements on the lowering of the numbers of people applying for relief.[57] The *Account of Workhouses* was a set of instructions rather than an argument.

The *Account* was finally completed in 1725 and was quickly followed by other publications including two sets of plans for workhouses, descriptions of continental houses, prayers and sermons specifically designed for inmates and calculated to instill a sense of gratitude for what they received, and finally another edition of the *Account.*

By the middle of the eighteenth century there were at least 600 workhouses operating in England, each containing, on average, 47 inmates. Almost thirty thousand people were being housed and set to work – between a half and one per cent of the population. Where less than forty years earlier there had not been three thousand workhouse inmates, now the number could be counted in tens of thousands and would soon approach a hundred thousand inmates.[58]

It has been argued by Catherina Lis and Hugo Soly that workhouses and, by extension, working charity schools were a rather mechanistic response to bottlenecks in woollen manufacture: that they would force up the numbers of people engaged in spinning.[59] Although this was in part true of the Corporations – Bristol's Guardians of the Poor certainly played an active part in the local cloth and wool markets – it is inadequate to explain the spread and popularity of parish institutions.[60] These were founded not primarily as a means of production but of control. The working charity schools were there to inure children to labour, while the workhouses existed to keep the adult poor at that labour. The people in the parishes who established these institutions had a very clear idea of the effects they wished to create, and likewise the preconditions which would allow them to be achieved.

The effect of workhouses and the collateral influence of the working charity schools were extremely potent. While the institutions themselves were for the most part badly run and expensive to maintain, their influence over the poor continued to be strong – familiarity did nothing to dissociate workhouses from correction and imprisonment. As a result, workhouses achieved the desired ends despite the failure of most eighteenth-century parishes to maintain effective long term administrative control over these institutions. It has been frequently noted that early-modern workhouses tended to fall into disuse relatively soon after their foundation; that they failed because they were dependent upon the enthusiasm of their administrators.[61] The effectiveness of the idea of deterrence and of the parochial workhouse movement lay in the fact that as long as a house existed, however badly run it might be, its primary influence upon the poor, its role as a threat, would always remain. Even if only a very small proportion of a parish's pensioners were actually housed in an institution, the rest being given generous outdoor relief, the threat of being sent to the workhouse could still be used to bully prospective applicants.

The successful design of these parish institutions cannot be entirely attributed to the far-sightedness of the Society. The most that can be claimed for it is that the SPCK added energy, influence and a sense of direction to movements which had already taken off and were beginning to gather speed, that it provided central direction to the activities of parish elites. In doing so, however, the Society was promoting institutions only just in keeping with its own views on reformation. The whole thrust of SPCK policy was directed towards the inculcation of an internalised, religious, work ethic. Workhouses played on the fears of the poor to push them into a specific mode of behaviour, rather than, as the Society would have had it, leading them to that behaviour with the carrot of religious belief and enlightenment. In a sense then, what the Society had done was to adopt these institutions in the hopes of using them for the ends earlier expected of the charity schools established in the 1690s: of reforming of the poor through the inculcation of religious virtue.

There is no evidence that the constant and mandatory religious regimen forced on workhouse inmates made much impression, or that the extremely patronizing pamphlets distributed to the poor in these institutions were taken particularly seriously – one member complained that inmates of a Plymouth institution used the pamphlets to light their pipes.[62] But, by the marriage of the two ideas of deterrence and proselytization, and the publishing and parliamentary campaign waged by the Society, workhouses and working charity schools achieved an unprecedented success. They were founded in large numbers and with the lever of the poor's own fear exerted a profound influence on society's least powerful members.

The period of the Society's greatest activity in these spheres ended in the early 1730s. In 1732 the second edition of the *Account of Workhouses* was published, marking a final burst of activity following a period of slow decline in interest. Several workhouse scandals came to light in the early 1730s, and the movement's most professional advocate, Matthew Marryott, died in 1732.[63] These factors combined with the increasing amount of time and money the Society spent on the foundation of Georgia and in its European activities meant that the Society's commitment to the establishment of parish institutions gradually waned.[64] The workhouse and charity school movements did not come to a grinding halt, but with the absence of the Society's influence, the first wave of these movements gradually ended.

The Society had never entirely controlled the workhouse movement, nor any other similar movement. However, it did ensure that the preconditions for these movements, in terms of the distribution of information and trained staff, were met. And moreover, it ensured that the enthusiasm of the parish elites was fostered and directed, allowing the parishes to go down the path of institutional care for the poor, a path that otherwise would have seemed far too daunting for a lone parish to travel.

More than this, the activities of the SPCK provided a centre from which reform could be promoted and through which a European religious agenda could be popularized. Eighteenth-century poor relief was normally an entirely local concern, but while central government largely abrogated its responsibility in this sphere, the SPCK, representing a specific ideological stance, gladly stepped into the breach. And although no more than a minority of parishes felt the direct influence of the Society, it provided the information and opinions which were to shape parochial policy across the country.

In a period which saw little central government interest in the development and control of social policy, the SPCK and its relationship with the workhouse and working charity school movements suggests one of the ways in which national reform was carried out. This relationship is typical of essentially informal, and yet extremely sophisticated sets of interest groups and private organizations, which while they were happy to use the mechanism of Parliament and central government to clarify and change the legal position, had a separate agenda to central government. Moreover, the existence and activities of the SPCK, along with those of the Societies for the Reformation of Manners, the Society for the Propagation of the Gospel in Foreign Parts, and later the Georgia Society and Coram's Foundling Hospital suggest the extent to which domestic social policy was almost entirely within the sphere of the voluntary and the private.

The experience of the SPCK reveals the degree to which our reliance on the categories of Whig and Tory for our understanding of early eighteenth-century politics has blinded us to powerful forces working within society. Religious reform and evangelical Anglicanism was an essential part of the divisions and intellectual traditions which characterized eighteenth-century English society. If we are to understand these divisions we need to place parliamentary politics within the context of a European-wide Protestant reformation.

Notes

1   GLRO, DR05/D4/1, 'Workhouse committee book, 1727–1734, South Mimms, St. Giles, Middlesex', n.p. A letter from Thomas Reynolds dated 3 October 1730.
2   House of Lords Record Office, 'Poor rate returns, 1777', Parchment Collection, Box 162.
3   In 1747 at Tavistock in Devon 31 pensioners were listed in the parish books. When the workhouse was opened 14 people chose to enter, the rest giving up their relief entirely. Devon Record Office, Tavistock, MS 428A/PO15, 6 January 1747.
4   9 George I, c.7.
5   Timothy Hitchcock, 'The English workhouse: A study in institutional poor relief in selected counties, 1696–1750' (Oxford Univ. D.Phil. thesis, 1985), pp. 22–37. The report of the 1751 enquiry has unfortunately been lost, but an abstract of its findings can be found at House of Commons, *Sessional Papers, Poor Law, First Report*, with Appendix, 107, (1818) v, pp. 1–14.
6   SPCK Archive, 'Abstract letter book, 1725–1727', No. 90006.
7   Paul Slack, *Poverty and Policy in Tudor and Stuart England* (1988), pp. 173–182; Tim Wales, 'Poverty, poor relief and life-cycle: some evidence from seventeenth-century Norfolk' in Richard M. Smith (ed.), *Land, Kinship and Life-cycle* (Cambridge, 1984).
8   Slack, *Poverty and Policy*, pp. 173–182.
9   For a discussion of the relationship between the European religious revival and the English experience see W.R. Ward, 'The relations of Enlightenment and religious revival in central Europe and in the English-speaking world' in Derek Baker (ed.), *Reform and Reformation: England and the Continent, c1500–c1750* (Oxford, 1979), pp. 281–305.
10 For a discussion of these experiments see Slack, *Poverty and Policy*, pp. 148–156, 195–200; Valerie Pearl, 'Puritans and poor relief: The London Workhouse, 1649–1660' in D. Pennington and Keith Thomas (eds.), *Puritans and Revolutionaries* (Oxford, 1978), pp. 206–232; H.W. Stephenson, 'Thomas Firmin, 1632–1697' (Oxford Univ. D.Phil. thesis, 1966); *Richard Hutton's Complaints Book, The Notebook of the Steward of the Quaker Workhouse at Clerkenwell*, T. Hitchcock (ed.) (London Record Society, vol. 24, 1987), pp. viii–xviii; William C. Braithwaite, *The Second Period of Quakerism* (2nd edn., York, 1979), pp. 559, 571–594.
11 *The First Workers Co-operators, Proposals for Raising a College of Industry*, by John Bellers (Nottingham, Institute for Workers Control pamphlet no. 68, n.d., c. 1980), p. 12.
12 Corporations were established by Act of Parliament at Bristol, Tiverton, Crediton, Hereford, Exeter, Colchester, Hull, Shaftsbury, Kings Lynn, Gloucester, Sudbury, Worcester, Plymouth and Norwich; and another institution was set up in London on the authority of the 1662 Act of Settlement.
13 For a discussion of the Bristol Corporation of the Poor see chapter 6 above.
14 Slack, *Poverty and Policy*, pp. 195–200; S. MacFarlane, 'Social policy and the poor in the later seventeenth century' in A.L. Beier and R. Finlay (eds.), *London 1500–1700* (1985); Hitchcock, 'The English workhouse', pp. 14–91.
15 Devon Record Office, X1/60f, No. 458.
16 For a discussion of the Society's European connections see Eamon Duffy, '*Correspondence Fraternelle*: The SPCK, the SPG, and the churches of Switzerland in the War of the Spanish Succession' in Baker (ed.), *Reform and Reformation*, pp. 251–280.
17 For discussions of the history of the Societies for the Reformation of Manners see A.G. Craig, 'The Movement for the Reformation of Manners, 1688–1715' (Edinburgh Univ. Ph.D. thesis, 1980); D.W.R. Bahlman, *The Moral Revolution of 1688* (New Haven, 1957); above, chapter 5.

18 Leonard W. Cowie, *Henry Newman, An American in London, 1708–1743* (1956), pp. 35–37.

19 For material relating to these men and their connection with the Society see SPCK Archive, 'Minutes of the Society, 1698–1706' i, pp. 305, 376; 'Minutes, 1706–9' ii, p. 21; 'Minutes, 1724–26' xi, pp. 106, 147, 167, 232, 233; 'Minutes, 1726–28' xii, pp. 4, 5–6, 11; 'Society letters, 1723–4', p. 1; 'Society letters, 18th May 1725 – 23 April 1726', pp. 54–5, 66–7, 67–8, 70; 'Society letters, 4 September 1724 – 15 May 1725', pp. 30, 55; 'Abstract letter book, 1711–12', No.2980; 'Abstract letter book, 1712–13', No.3773; 'Abstract letter book, 1716–17', No.4979; 'Abstract letter book, 1717–18', No.5443; 'Abstract letter book, 1723– 25', No.8028, 8047, 8068, 8122; 'Abstract letter book, 1725–27', No.8644, 8662, 8739, 8759, 8764, 8773, 8789, 8809, 8834, 8849, 8861, 8907; 'Abstract letter book, 1727–29', No.9818; 'Standing committee minute book, 1713–18' ii, p. 262; see also *DNB*, 'Sir John Comyns'.

20 *DNB*, 'Francis Fox', 'Sir Humphrey Mackworth'.

21 For information on Newman see Cowie, *Henry Newman*.

22 SPCK Archive, 'Special letters, 1708–1732', pp. 18–19.

23 The only distinguishing feature about early Society publications was the printer's mark, which for material produced in London was that of Joseph Downing, and for that printed in Dublin, Aaron Rhamees. For example see *An Account of Several Workhouses* (1725) and *Some Few Letters Selected from an Account of Work-Houses and Charity Schools for the Employment of the Poor in England, with a Preface to Excite some such Application of our Charity in Ireland* (Dublin, 1728).

24 For example see the Society's *Kind Caution to Profane Swearers* n.d.; *Dissuasive from Drunkenness* n.d.; and *Rebuke to Uncleanness* n.d.

25 Cowie, *Henry Newman*, p. 35; M.G. Jones, *The Charity School Movement, A Study in Eighteenth-Century Puritanism in Action* (Cambridge, 1938), pp. 37–41; August Francke, *Piettas Hallensis: Or an Abstract of the Marvelous Footsteps of Divine Providence in Building a very Large Hospital . . . at Gloucha near Halle* (1706).

26 GLRO, 'Workhouse proposal, 1724, South Mimms, St. Giles, Middlesex', DRO/62/2a & b, 8 July 1724.

27 William C. Braithwaite, *The Second Period of Quakerism*, 2nd edn. (York, 1979), pp. 570–71.

28 In Linda Colley, *In Defiance of Oligarchy* (Cambridge, 1982), pp. 100, 117 the Society is treated as an unproblematic resource for tory politicians. For a fuller description of the Society's rather uncomfortable and distant relationship to the tories see Cowie, *Henry Newman*, pp. 84–91.

29 Cowie, *Henry Newman*, *passim*.

30 Mary Ransome, 'The parliamentary career of Sir Humphrey Mackworth, 1701–1713', *University of Birmingham Historical Journal*, i (1947– 1948), pp. 239–243, 245.

31 B.W. Quintrell, 'The making of Charles I's Book of Orders', *English Historical Review*, xcv (1980), 553–72; Paul Slack, 'Books of Orders: The making of English social policy, 1577–1631', *Transactions of the Royal Historical Society*, 5 ser., xxx (1980), 1–22.

32 Joan Simon, 'Was there a charity school movement?' in Brian Simon (ed.), *Education in Leicestershire: A Regional Study* (Leicester, 1968). While disagreeing with Ms Simon's overall conclusions about the influence of the Society, she does convincingly suggest that many of the schools which the Society encouraged in Leicestershire had existed in some form for many years before the SPCK was established.

33 For an account of the types of works the Society provided to local schools see SPCK Archive, 'An account of packets sent to the residing and corresponding members, 1719–1726'.

34 Jones, *The Charity School Movement*, pp. 41–56.

35 Ward, 'The Relations of Enlightenment and Religious Revival' in Baker (ed.), *Reform*

and Reformation; W.R. Ward, 'Power and piety: The origins of religious revival in the early eighteenth century' in *Bulletin of the John Rylands University Library of Manchester*, vol. 63, No. 1 Autumn 1980; Jones, *The Charity School Movement*, pp. 37– 41; Cowie, *Henry Newman*, p. 35.

36   Jones, *The Charity School Movement*, pp. 89, 90; SPCK Archive, 'Standing committee minute book, 1713–18', p. 125; 'Abstract letter book, 1717–18', No. 5392, 5646; 'Abstract letter book, 1718–19', No. 5908, 5969, 5981, 6001, 6010; 'Minutes, 1715–16', pp. 18, 23–24.

37   See *The First Workers Co-operative, Proposals for Raising a Colledge of Industry*, by John Bellers; and John Locke, 'Report to the Board of Trade . . . in the year 1697, respecting the relief and employment of the poor' in *An Account of the Origin, Proceedings and Intentions of the Society for the Promotion of Industry in the Southern District of the Parts of Lindsey in the County of Lincoln* (Louth, 1789), pp. 101–126.

38   SPCK Archive, 'Abstract letter book, 1717–18', No.5392.

39   For material on Marryott's career and early workhouse foundations see Joan Simon, 'From charity school to workhouse in the 1720s: The SPCK and Mr Marriott's solution' in *History of Education* (1988), vol. 17, no. 2, 113–129.

40   *An Account of Several Workhouses* (1725), p. 106.

41   SPCK Archive, 'Standing committee minute book, 1713–1718' ii, pp. 125, 209, 232, 263; 'Abstract letter book, 1709–11' No. 2072; 'Abstract letter book, 1715–16' No.4718; 'Abstract letter book, 1716–17' No. 5248; *DNB*, 'Francis Fox'.

42   Parish officers in Bristol, Exeter and Norwich consistently resisted attempts by the Corporations of the Poor in those cities to collect the monies due for the establishment and running of workhouses. More than any other problem it was this lack of co-operation which drained the enthusiasm of the founders of these institutions. See *Bristol Corporation of the Poor, Selected Records, 1696–1834* (ed.) E.E. Butcher (Bristol Record Society, iii, 1932), p. 12; Hitchcock, 'The English workhouse', pp. 50–51, 63, 84–85.

43   *An Account of Several Workhouses* (1725), pp. iii–iv.

44   The term 'workhouse' had, up until the beginning of the eighteenth century, been applied to numerous different types of institution, but most commonly to houses of correction. The Devon Quarter Sessions, for instance, was still calling their bridewell a workhouse in the 1700s, which usage naturally prejudiced the poor against later parochial workhouses. See Devon Record Office, 'Devon quarter sessions records' Q/51/14, *Baptist* 1701, *Epiptic* 1703.

45   *Richard Hutton's Complaints Book*, pp. 7–8.

46   The SPCK corresondent at Artleborough claimed as late as 1725 that the school there earned the town five to six hundred pounds profit each year. *An Account of Several Workhouses* (1732), pp. 151–52.

47   For an example of the types of services and materials available from the Society see SPCK Archive, 'Special letters 1708–32', pp. 183–184; 'Standing committee minute book, 1718–20', pp. 55–56; 'Abstract letter book, 1718–19', No. 5825, 5858, 5885; 'Abstract letter book, 1721–1723', No. 6776.

48   SPCK Archive, 'Standing committee minute book, 1718–20' iii, pp. 83–85.

49   SPCK Archive, 'Standing committee minute book, 1718–20' iii, p. 159.

50   SPCK Archive, 'Standing letter book, 28 February 1721/2 – 8 May 1723', p. 51.

51   *HCJ*, xx, p. 58. For material on Sir Edward Knatchbull and his political associations see *The Parliamentary Diary of Sir Edward Knatchbull, 1722–30*, A.N. Newman (ed.), (Camden Third Series, vol. xciv, 1963), pp. vii–viii.

52   *DNB*, 'Sir John Comyns'; SPCK Archive, 'Minutes, 1724– 26' xi, p. 167.

53   Bernard de Mandeville, *The Fable of the Bees: Or, Private Vices, Public Benefits. The Second Edition, Enlarged with many Additions. As Also An Essay on Charity and Charity-Schools* (1723).

54   The Society's publications in this period included: *An Account of Several Workhouses* (1725); Caleb Parfect, *Proposals made in the Year 1720, to the Parishioners of Stroud . . . for the Building of a Work-House there* (1725); Sir William Fownes, *Methods Proposed for Regulating the Poor, Supporting of some and Employing Others* (Dublin, 1725); Andrea Guevara, *Ways and Means for Suppressing Beggary and Relieving the Poor by Erecting General Hospitals . . . Translated from the Italian* (1726); Samuel Johnston, *The Advantage of Employing the Poor in Useful Labour* (1726); *Regulations which were agreed upon and Established the Twelfth day of July 1726 by the Gentlemen of the Vestry then Present, for the Better Government and Management of the Workhouse Belonging to the Parish of St. Giles in the Fields* (Dublin, 1727); *Some Few Letters Selected from an Account of Workhouses . . . with a Preface to Excite some such Application of our Charity in Ireland* (Dublin, 1728); *Rules and Orders to be Observed by the Officers and Servants in St. Giles's Workhouse and by the Poor Therein* (n.d.); Thomas Trougher, *The Best Way of Making our Charity Truly Beneficial to the Poor; or the Excellency of Workhouses in Country Parishes* (1730); *An Account of Several Workhouses* (1732).

55   SPCK Archive, 'Minutes, 1722–24', pp. 44, 48–49, 205, 213, 216; 'Standing letter book, 9 May 1723 – 21 November 1723' xiii, p. 69; 'Special letters, 1708–32', pp. 183–84; 'Standing committee minute book, 1718–20' iii, pp. 55–56, 58; 'Abstract letter book, 1718–19', No. 5825, 5828, 5885, 5899, 5908, 5911, 5969, 5981, 6001, 6005, 6010; 'Abstract letter book, 1721–23', No. 6776, 7082, 7163; 'Abstract letter book, 1723–25', No. 7848, 7968, 7984, 8123, 8163.

56   Caleb Parfect, *Proposals Made in the Year 1720 to the Parishioners of Stroud . . . for the Building a Work-House There* (1725).

57   For examples of the questions asked see SPCK Archive, 'Special letters, 1723–24', pp. 52–53.

58   Hitchcock, 'The English workhouse', pp. 23n., 218.

59   Catherina Lis and Hugo Soly, *Poverty and Capitalism in Pre-Industrial Europe* (Brighton, 1979), pp. 127–28.

60   For an account of the role of the Corporation at Bristol in the local wool market see Hitchcock, 'The English workhouse', pp. 55–56.

61   For example see Slack, *Poverty and Policy*, pp. 152–53.

62   SPCK Archive, 'Minutes, 1706–9', p. 20.

63   For Marryott's will, proved 26 January 1731/2, see PRO, Probate 11 No. 649, ff. 142–44.

64   Cowie, *Henry Newman*, pp. 223–49.

Index